Home Groups
for Urban Cultures

Other Titles Available in the BGC Monograph Series

Ed. Daniel Rickett & Dotsey Welliver
Supporting Indigenous Ministries

Lonna Dickerson & Dianne Dow
Handbook for Christian EFL Teachers

Mark Shaw
The Kingdom of God in Africa

David Filbeck
Yes, God of the Gentiles, Too

Stewart G. Snook
*Developing Leaders Through
Theological Education by Extension*

Ed. James H. Kraakevik & Dotsey Welliver
Partners in the Gospel

Paul Goring
The Effective Missionary Communicator

Robert W. Ferris
Renewal in Theological Education

Daniel E. Fountain
Health, the Bible, and the Church

Home Groups for Urban Cultures

Biblical Small Group Ministry On Five Continents

Mikel Neumann

◆　　　◆　　　◆

A · B G C · M O N O G R A P H

William Carey Library

Pasadena, California

© 1999 by the Billy Graham Center

Published by William Carey Library
Publishers and Distributors
P. O. Box 40129
Pasadena, California 91114 U.S.A.

and

The Billy Graham Center
Wheaton College
Wheaton, IL 60187-5593 U.S.A.

Printed in the United States of America

Library of Congress Cataloging-in-Publication Data

Neumann, Mikel, 1939-
    Home groups for urban cultures : biblical small group ministry on five continents / Mikel Neumann.
      p.   cm.
    Includes bibliographical references.
    ISBN 0-87808-281-6 (alk. paper)
    1. Small groups--Religious aspects--Christianity. 2. Church growth.
    3. Church work with groups. 4. Evangelistic work. I. Title.
BV652.2.N48 1999
253'.7--DC21   98-12297
                                          CIP

For information about releases available from William Carey Library, 1-800-MISSION, Email - orders@wclbooks.com

William Carey Library ISBN 0-87808-281-6

For information about other publications or the resources of the Billy Graham Center, E-mail BGCADM@wheaton.edu or visit their web site: http://www.wheaton.edu.

Billy Graham Center ISBN 1-879089-29-7

Printed in the United States of America

Contents

14.95

98030

Contents

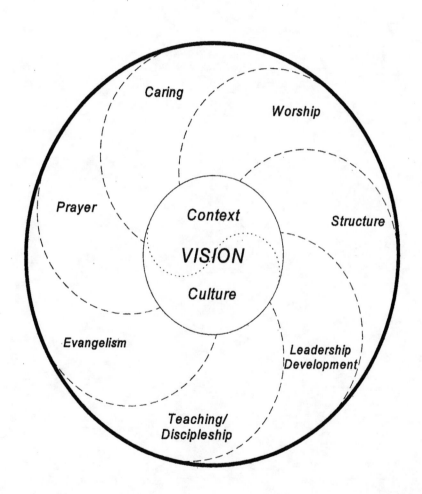

Acknowledgments

Many people played a significant role in making this book possible. Many more people, too numerous to name, on five continents gave input that made this book viable.

The first acknowledgment goes to my wife, Karen, who was co-researcher, reader, and encourager in the project. She took care of many of the logistics of travel and journeyed with me to gather data. She, too, took copious notes, which later became part of the field notes. She was present at the interviews and home groups. Some notes are uniquely hers as she attended women's and children's groups while I went to men's groups. She read and re-read the text helping me express my ideas. Her participation and insight gave the project greater depth and wider dimensions.

The Billy Graham Center gave me the fellowship and grant that supported the project. Personnel from the Wheaton College Graduate School and the Billy Graham Center gave valuable help and advice. These included Dr. James Kraakevik, at that time Billy Graham Center Director, who encouraged and guided the project's overall progress; Dotsey Welliver, who edited the manuscript; Dr. C. Douglas McConnell whose helpful insight, enthusiasm for the project, and interest in rows of analytical numbers is outdone by few; Dr. A. Scott Moreau, who helped with much of the anthropological analysis and whose skill in graphic representation is evident in the graphics; Dr. Carla Waterman whose understanding of research and whose kindness helped me at the point of need; and Dr. Ken Gill who kept me apprised of strategic publications and continually encouraged me in the project. All were generous with their time and insights that guided the project.

CBInternational, the mission with which I am associated, and Western Seminary in Portland, Oregon, where I teach, allowed me to take a leave and move to Wheaton, Illinois, for a year to do the project. Rev. Richard Jacobs actually put me in touch with the Billy Graham Center and has given wise counsel and encouragement not only during the project but for the many years we worked in Madagascar under his supervision. Rev. David Wedin, my current supervisor at CBInternational, gave wise advice at points of need, and his insightful questions often pushed me past my comfort zone.

Dr. Donald D. Smith, my divisional chair at Western Seminary, was supportive and often gave valuable insight benefiting the direction of research and conclusions of the book. He is the source of some of the theoretical framework on which this research rests. He has been my friend and mentor for most of my missionary career.

In each locale key people welcomed Karen and me as we researched data for the book. We are indebted to them because of their sacrifice of love. God worked through them to teach us. In almost every church and home group, people laid hands on us to pray for this project. The prayers of a multitude of saints in these five cities are a part of God's blessing on the work.

In Accra, Rev. Philemon Quaye, a senior Christian statesman, and one whom many see as their mentor, organized our time, leading us to three dynamic cell group churches. Rev. Jide Oladimeji, National Overseer for the Deeper Christian Life Ministry, gave us time and access to many key people in the church. The Rt. Rev. (CDR) F. H. Gbewonyo, Moderator of the Evangelical Presbyterian Church of Ghana, and the Rev. S. Y. Kwami, Pastor, warmly welcomed us, gave us insight and godly wisdom relevant to home group ministry, and guided the questionnaire distribution in their church. The Rev. Fred Deegbe, Senior Pastor, Calvary Baptist Church, spent time with us even though he was leaving on a prolonged international trip later the day we visited with him. One of his associates, the Rev. Dr. Osei-Bonsu, also helped us in understanding the Baptist ministry. Finally, Mr. Martin Obeng, of the Ghanaian Fellowship of Evangelical Students, whom we met at Wheaton College Graduate School before he returned to Ghana, spent time helping with logistics and cultural understanding even though he had a busy teaching schedule, both in Accra and other cities. Many people in the churches in Accra welcomed us warmly.

In Bombay, Pastor Willie Soans of the New Life Fellowship put us in contact with a wide range of people throughout Bombay so that we might sense the diversity and spirit of the work of God in that huge city.

Pastor Willie took valuable hours at an extraordinarily busy time to help and to oversee the questionnaire distribution. The Rev. S. Joseph, Senior Pastor, gave his approval and prayers to the project and shared valuable information about the history and current direction of New Life Fellowship. Jerry D'Souza from the senior leadership arranged for us to visit different types of churches and home groups.

In Caracas, Jeffrey Denlinger and David Dawson, missionaries with CBInternational, gave logistical support, carried out several interviews, and took oversight of the questionnaire administration. Pastors Sam Olson, Senior Pastor of the Las Acacias Church, and Francisco Liévano, Senior Pastor of the Dios Admirable Church, gave much help and time as they opened doors for us to research the home groups in their churches and interview leaders and home group members. Rev. Jose Pablo Sanchez, a student at the Wheaton College Graduate School, translated the questionnaire.

In Chicago, Rev. Mark Jobe and Rev. David Garratt were especially helpful in leading us to fruitful areas of research. The church opened its heart to us. We attended it often over the course of this project and have seen God at work. The continued prayers of the home groups have kept us focused and energized to complete the book.

In Moscow, Ms. Beverly Nickles, missionary, gave us housing and led us all over the city. She supervised the translation and administration of the questionnaire. Pastor Pavel Saveliev, Senior Pastor of the Rosa Church, and his wife Marina warmly welcomed us and opened doors of contact with home groups and leaders in their church. Their prayers, enthusiasm, and input greatly encouraged us.

Ms. Leanne Winters, a student at the Wheaton College Graduate School, did much of the data analysis and questionnaire answer layout for the appendices. Dr. Galen Currah also gave helpful input in the questionnaire analysis.

Drs. Rex and Jeanne Blumhagen furnished us with lodging, many trips to the airport, and excellent wisdom concerning the project. Their kind support and good humor helped keep us functioning throughout the work.

Scripture quotations are taken from the Holy Bible, the New International Version, copyright © 1973, 1978, 1984 by International Bible Society. Used by permission Zondervan Bible Publishers.

We also express our thanks for permission to use the chart on leadership roles in Figure 1 of Chapter 3. Source: *Visionary Leadership:*

Creating a Compelling Sense of Direction for Your Organization by Burt Nanus. San Francisco: Jossey-Bass, 1992.

Introduction

We were spending a rather astonishing amount of time in the Frankfurt airport. That thought struck me with force when, after another particularly wearing experience through the terminal, Karen said, "Remind me again why we are doing this." This introduction is my attempt to explain why we did this.

We were making overseas trips with extremely short turn-around times. One breathtaking turn-around consisted of only one day between returning from India and charging off to West Africa. It became increasingly difficult to make ourselves drag out the suitcases again and pack the necessary stuff. However, in less than one year, our journeys allowed us to experience and learn exhilarating new things.

Praise must be given to God who kept us going spiritually, physically, emotionally, and logistically. We experienced no illness. The necessary visas arrived on time—though some did come in at the last hair-raising moment. All flights arrived close enough to schedule that we were never seriously delayed, and no baggage was lost. These few items represented an enormous logistical effort, one that we feel God in his grace arranged for us.

Personal Pilgrimage

In his heart a man plans his course, but the Lord determines his steps (Proverbs 16:9)

This story begins in Madagascar where my wife, Karen, and I served as urban church planters following our appointment in 1966 with CBInternational (formerly the Conservative Baptist Foreign Mission Society). Consequently, our home group ministry pilgrimage began there as well. Humanly speaking, the home group ministry developed quite by accident. However, it is clear to us now that God led us to that ministry and that He alone has given the fruit from it.

The home ministry developed out of need in our lives. By 1984 we had been in Madagascar for 16 years as missionaries working in church planting and leadership training. We had been involved in a wide variety of ministries including literature, TEE, Bible School teaching, and evangelism. Karen had a ministry with women and helped train Sunday School teachers to develop biblically based teaching aids from local materials. We were busy. We had seen fruit. God had blessed.

But something was wrong. Life in Madagascar involved the stress of living under Marxism while our children were away in boarding school for three-month periods. We sensed a lack in our lives. Even though we were actively ministering, we felt a need for more spiritual nurture. Some dimension of our spiritual life was missing.

Driven by our need we invited two Malagasy Christian couples to meet with us weekly for Bible study and prayer. We informally shared the Scripture each week, applying it to our lives, while also spending large parts of each meeting in prayer. Because we knew almost nothing about small group theory or methodology at that time, we followed no specific program. We knew few of the principles we subsequently discovered. We were simply searching for spiritual renewal. In some meetings we would spend one or two hours in prayer after working through a Bible study and sharing personal needs. We all sensed that God was at work in our lives, and our spiritual needs began to be met. It was indeed God who met our needs by working through his people and his Word, but it was the structure of the home group that facilitated the process.

Some eight to ten months later one of the other men in the group suggested inviting a neighbor. Soon another couple was added. We were not really seeking numerical growth, but it came. Within a year, two more home groups started in other areas of the city. But up to that point in 1985, the home group ministry was still something we did in our spare time.

A real joy in the Lord returned to our lives. We began to sense the Spirit's presence working in and through our little group. The truth of that came home to me one day about a year after we started our meetings. Roger, a university professor who attended our church, approached me and said, "I hear God is really at work in your neighborhood."

"Is He?" I queried, a bit astounded. I thought, "This is great if God is doing something in our part of the city," but I did not understand what he was talking about.

"Yes," he said, "we have heard how He is answering prayer."

Then he began to list several answers to prayer that he had heard about. As the conversation continued I realized that he was talking about our home group! These were answers to petitions made by our members. I was astonished.

He then asked us to come and start a group in his home like the one we were conducting in our neighborhood. We were having such a good time in the first group that we agreed, but it did not occur to us at the time that these activities might be ministry. The experience had ministered so profoundly in our lives as we sensed personal spiritual revival that we thought of it as building up our own lives. Ministry, as we considered it at the time, was giving out in the lives of others.

A third group eventually started with a group of professionals on another evening. We experienced God's work in these people over the following weeks and months. Some came to Christ and grew in grace. Others shedded addictions. Still others worked through painful problems. A group member's child died suddenly. Another member's husband abandoned her and their two small sons. We wept through the hurts and became part of a family as we learned how to minister in a deeper way in Madagascar.

We also rejoiced together over victories and answered prayer. A child passed an all-important exam. Some home group members obtained good jobs. A university professor was asked to give a lecture to the national Academy of Science. His entire home group went to that meeting, encouraging him with their quiet presence and silent prayers.

We spent most of 1985 in the United States and during that time learned more about home group ministries. God has used small groups in powerful ways in many nations of the world. People such as Yonggi Cho, Eddie Gibbs, Carl George, Ralph Neighbour, Jr., and others taught and instructed us through their writings and seminars. We returned to Madagascar with a vision to make the expansion of home groups our major ministry emphasis.

Between 1986 and 1991 we focused on home group ministry. We began slowly, seeking to obtain the approval of various local church pastors and elders before launching a concentrated effort to develop a structure that would multiply home groups. A certain amount of suspicion prevailed. The church leadership felt it might create ministries that would not be under local church control. They also feared the onslaught of heresy when laypeople were given too much responsibility.

Working slowly and modeling good home groups appeased most fears, and the ministry grew. From the original three groups, the number of home groups in Antananarivo grew to more than 80. In the same period of time five new churches were planted, with home groups playing a major role. One of the best evidences of acceptance of the home ministry came when a pastor told me that over 80 percent of the baptismal candidates came to Christ through home groups.

In the previous 17 years, two churches had been added to the one existing Baptist Church in Antananarivo. These three churches also grew significantly during the time the new churches were started. Although home groups were not the only reason for the growth of those churches, it is not without significance that the explosive growth arrived with the home group ministry.

Home groups also caused attitude changes. Before these ministries became common, Christians and church leaders did not feel they could minister without the presence of a local church with a trained pastor. When church members moved elsewhere, they would look for a church like the one they left. If they did not find one, they would sometimes cease attending church and become spiritually apathetic. However, when people in home groups moved they were far more likely to initiate a home group with their new network relationships. Christians who moved to another part of the city felt qualified to begin a ministry by launching a new group. They had found a structure and methodology they could replicate.

Within our context in Madagascar, the concept of home groups also became more closely associated with evangelism. Christians who had never been highly active in church ministry started small groups with their families, friends, neighbors, and other network associations. They felt empowered to do evangelism and other ministries because of the home groups.

While still in Madagascar, Karen and I were invited to Kampala, Uganda, to share with a church planting team what we had learned about home ministry in Madagascar. I was also invited to speak at an international conference in Ndola, Zambia, about the biblical basis and use of home groups in ministry.

Since our return to the USA in late 1991 due to health concerns, we have served as international resource consultants for missionaries and national leaders in other nations while I teach in the Intercultural Studies Division of Western Seminary in Portland, Oregon. Much of our work now deals with small group ministry in the world's urban areas as we consult with Christians who are trying to implement these types of ministries.

The Reason for This Study

Good understanding wins favor (Proverbs 13:15)

The specific events that led to this study came about in Portland in 1994. By that time Karen and I had visited some 12 urban areas in South America, Europe, and Africa, as well as several in the United States to consult and give seminars related to home group ministry. We had concluded that different cultures require different approaches. People who had sought to import models of small group ministry "made in the USA" or elsewhere had mixed results. Often they failed, or at best had limited results. So some leaders had decided home groups were not a valid ministry model.

In November, 1994, several events came together dramatically. First, I was invited to apply for the Billy Graham Center Missionary Scholar fellowship in Wheaton, Illinois. Shortly after that invitation two missionaries came by my office at different times, from different contexts, but both asked similar questions. "How are home group ministries going to vary between Brussels and Nairobi?" And, "What is the difference in home group ministries between your experience in Madagascar and Portland?"

They wanted to know not only the variations that applied but also the commonalities. While I had some preliminary ideas and many anecdotes to illustrate my opinions, I lacked the necessary structured research to make conclusions. I had been thinking about ways to search out answers even before the Billy Graham Center fellowship invitation appeared.

The chief purpose of this book is to give a preliminary answer to those questions. What are the commonalities and differences of small group ministry across cultures? How can we ascertain what those differences are? Thus, the churches chosen for this study were selected because of their cultural and contextual differences and because they had a serious small group ministry—not necessarily because they were the most "typical" evangelical group in their area.

Culture does affect how small group ministry is done. I hope that many studies will be done in the area of small groups and how they can effectively and appropriately be used in different cultures to build the church. The New Testament gives us the basis for all ministry, including that of small groups, but the way this is applied will include cultural considerations. This book deals primarily with cultural applications for home group ministries.

Methods Used in the Study

Consider what God has done (Ecclesiastes 6:13a)

I used three basic methods to obtain the data on which this book is based. The first, and probably the most important, was participant observation. Karen and I traveled to the urban sites and visited the churches and home groups there. We each took notes. Usually, a translator was present who could relate the happenings to us. When no translator was there we observed more of the nonverbal clues, which proved instructive. After each meeting, we combined our notes into one large body of field research.

A second method was the personal interview. We interviewed at length the senior leadership in each church. We also questioned middle-level leaders, home group leaders, and home group members. The interviews consisted entirely of open-ended questions. We sought to know how the home group ministry operated, what place it played in the larger church life, and how it had changed over time.

The third method was a questionnaire we administered to people in the home groups (see Appendix A). I sought cultural and social structure data through this instrument. The questionnaire was not a random sample, but selective. It had the advantage of applying a uniform test to each site, corroborating data gained from participant observation and interview. Our aim was to administer it to members of the home groups, although in some cases a high percentage of home group leaders filled it out. In Moscow and Caracas it was translated into the local language. To assure accuracy it was checked. Afterwards it was translated back into English. In the other sites it was used in English. Questionnaire results are tabulated in Appendix B.

Perhaps this is the place to also mention terminology. Nuances of meaning can be a problem for the researcher in any language. Here I have chosen to use the term "home group" rather than "cell group" for several reasons. I agree with Ralph Neighbour, Jr., that the name you give to this ministry and these small groups is important and says something about the vision.[1] Normally, I would use cell group because of the biological model. The cell is an organic and integral part of the body and made of the same material.

But few of the churches in this study used the term cell group. Chicago, Moscow, Bombay, and the Deeper Christian Life Ministry in Accra all used the term home group or house group or house church in their ministry. The Baptists in Accra used the word "sheepfold" for the home groups and "family" or "tribe" for the aggregation of home groups. The Las Acacias Church in Caracas used the word family for the small groups while the regional groups were tribes. In the Dios Admirable Church in Caracas, the word popularly used was "basic" group. These churches have considered the implications of the names and have chosen names that communicate their vision within their contexts.

I have also chosen not to use cell group because some who took part in this study find the word offensive. One of our contacts in Moscow told me that they do not like the term "cell" because of the communist implications. "It hurts our ears," he explained. So they call their meetings home groups. Thus, I have decided to follow the lead of the groups researched and speak of home groups. But I use the term as many of us in other places would use the term cell group.

Research Explanations

Make plans by seeking advice (Proverbs 20:18)

This book is a study of eight churches in five cities on five continents, all in different contexts. The Russian situation looked different from the American or the African. Yet in these churches I discovered eight underlying factors for home group ministry. Each factor is affected by its unique culture. The question has been asked, "Are all eight factors necessary for a successful home group ministry?" All I am saying here is that they were evident in all the churches we studied.

I am also aware that the conclusions are my interpretation of the data. I have sought to discover the basic factors of home group ministries that apply in different cultures rather than to investigate home group methods. My wife and I have visited more than 20 different countries during the past few years. We have worked with many Christians who tried to import methodologies that failed. Those observations led us to seek the underlying factors of successful home group churches. Another researcher might have come to different conclusions in some areas or organized the conclusions differently.

While our conclusions derive from these five sites, we trust that the reader will find applications for his or her local situation. Normally, home group ministries in geographical contiguous areas are more similar than home group ministries in the same denomination in different areas. However, variation is sufficient in the world's great urban centers that an idea discovered in one urban site might better apply in a distant urban setting than in another part of the same urban area. For example, we field-tested our questionnaire in the Chicago suburbs. When we used it in the Chicago city church we received different results. Some qualities of the Chicago church are more like other Chicago city churches of different denominations than the nearby suburban churches of the same denomination.

The eight basic factors of home group ministries we discovered will certainly have different outworkings in diverse urban settings. For that reason the chapters are intentionally descriptive. Cases can be studied as legitimate examples of how a particular factor works in a given setting.

How to Read This Book

All hard work brings a profit (Proverbs 14:23)

This book is not about method. I sought to discover the basis behind the various methods.

I start the book with an introduction to the five sites where the research was carried out. That first chapter gives a brief overview of the context and character of the church(es) studied in each area. Because this study is an urban, church based study, I sought in the site introduction to give my impressions of these areas rather than demographical studies.

To provide a theoretical framework, in the next chapter I have reviewed three missiological areas that form the basis of my research. The chapter begins with a brief review of biblical data concerning small groups and how the small group relates to a larger group. The biblical data is the overarching basis for the book. The next section in this chapter deals with cultural issues. I briefly review the work of three scholars who have influenced my thinking: Geert Hofstede, Edward T. Hall, and Donald K. Smith. The third section, with the most narrow focus, deals with network analysis and its importance for urban studies. The chapter ends with a brief review of the implications of this data for home groups in particular and the church in general.

Those not interested in theory may proceed directly to the eight chapters (3–10) forming the core of the book. These chapters present the direct results of our research. They represent a series of factors important for home group ministries. The core chapters can stand alone, so if the reader has particular interest in one factor more than another it can be read out of order.

I discuss the five sites in each core chapter but usually highlight one or two by beginning the chapter with those locations. We discovered that each site has an underlying factor that seems to drive the entire home group ministry. For the five sites the strong underlying basis around which these ministries are focused are: Accra—structure, Bombay—evangelism, Caracas—teaching, Chicago—caring, and

Moscow—prayer. By identifying one underlying factor for each place, I am not indicating that the site is stronger in that factor than the other urban locations were. Nor am I saying that the churches at that site are weak concerning the other factors. I am simply pointing out that of the eight core factors, one seems to drive the others at each place.

Toward the end of almost every core chapter is a section entitled "Questionnaire Evaluation." That section analyzes appropriate questionnaire data. The chapter is complete without that section, which can be skipped if the reader desires content without analytical details. In the concluding chapter I speak of areas for further research as well as giving some overall implications of this study for home group ministries.

As stated earlier, this study was a quite a journey for Karen and me. The project was far more vast and complicated than we at first understood. In less than one year we researched urban sites on five continents, evaluated the data, and wrote up the most important conclusions.

We sat at the feet of people of God who shared their hearts and experiences. We heard many testimonies of God at work, freeing individuals from addictions and dysfunctional lifestyles. We learned more about God and his people while we sat under a mango tree in Accra and on the floor of a small house in Asia's largest slum in Bombay. We felt God's presence as we sat on a bed in one room of a communal apartment in Moscow. We sensed his love as we waited for keys to pass us through many locked doors to reach a home group in a Caracas high-rise. We walked out of a home group on a winter day on Chicago's South Side to see several young men with their hands against a patrol car as police interrogated them. But at all locations, we saw home groups making a difference in large cities.

Our focus was on home group based churches, not theological differences, but the churches we studied represent a theological range. Some were traditional evangelical churches. Others were charismatic. All the churches studied were Bible based, with a love for the Lord and a desire to follow Him. The similarities and differences we discovered in the home groups had little to do with theology. Churches of different theological persuasions in similar cultures had far more in common than churches from the same theological stripe in different cultures. The three churches we researched in Accra had much in common, though they were from different denominations.

We have been challenged and blessed by God's people in all the places we traveled. Sometimes we found it difficult to focus on research. We became so engrossed in the prayer, worship, and teaching in the home groups that our "research glasses" would get tucked away for a time. So this book is a result of our research but, far more than research, it represents our genuine experience of fellowship and worship with the Body of Christ that God so generously provided for us in these places.

Endnote

[1].   Ralph Neighbour, Jr., *Where Do We Go From Here?* (Houston: Touch Publications, 1990). See 209–210 and 254 ff. for a discussion about the importance of giving this ministry the right name.

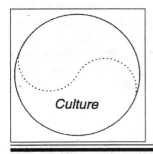

CHAPTER 1

Culture

Churches Where God Is Making a Difference

Chicago: An Urban Church in the Postmodern Era

New Life Community Church
Mark Jobe, Senior Pastor

Context of the Church

On Chicago's South Side, the industrial core of the city, is a church making a difference for the Kingdom of God. In the midst of an area known as much for crime as for industrial production, one finds an assortment of drug dealers, gangs, and people whose lives are being destroyed. While the skyscrapers of downtown are within easy view, the scene at hand is much less picturesque.

A generation ago, the region was populated by Polish and Lithuanian people who came to find jobs in the booming local industries. While many of the place names reflect that heritage, the people have a different look today. Store windows have signs in Spanish as well as English. English is still the language of commerce and education, but Spanish is common along with a smattering of other languages. Rows of brick homes reflect a bygone industrial era. I drove by factories, warehouses, storage yards, trucking centers, and fast food cafes. It is not affluent. And not hard core inner-city. Just city.

Tough. Rugged. Street-smart survivors. Those are some thoughts that came to my mind the first time I drove to the church offices to meet with the pastoral staff. When I parked my car on the street bordering the church, I found I had locked the door at some point while driving through this area. Interesting reaction. I put all security devices in place and walked toward the church.

The 85-year-old church building reflects the area. A security system is in place so I buzzed to be let in. It was a good feeling to be in the relative safety of a church office. A young woman was doing a Bible study in one corner of the room where I was sent to wait. These offices are not downtown, high-rise, corporate style offices. These are more like bunkers on a battlefield. Everyone at New Life feels the sense of spiritual battle. They operate in the power of God's Spirit for they know they are in a spiritual war zone. Let's take a look.

Brief History of New Life Community Church

The church began as a ministry to Hispanic children in the 1940s. This ministry, the Berean Mission, was spearheaded by middle-class Anglos who came from outside the immediate area to minister. The work grew and in 1970 the work organized itself into a church then called the Berean Memorial Baptist Church. The church joined the Conservative Baptist Association and built the building that holds the present-day offices.

Berean Memorial Baptist Church fell on hard times in the 1980s. By the time Pastor Mark Jobe arrived, only about 20 adults were left in the congregation. The church had a program appropriate for the white middle class of earlier decades. They met in a sanctuary and sang from a hymnbook to the accompaniment of an organ. However, today the neighborhood reflects a different era and a different culture.

Few in this postmodern generation are wealthy. They are scrambling for the lower-level factory jobs that their parents had managed to find. The area appears to be a difficult one to reach with the gospel. Many of the youth see little hope of a good future. Such was the context that Pastor Mark Jobe entered when he arrived in December 1985 to work in this traditional church fallen on hard times.

New Life Community Church Today

I knew nothing of this background as I sat waiting to meet with the pastoral staff. New Life was becoming known as a home group church reaching many in the area, as well as beyond Chicago's South Side. I was eager to learn more.

When I first met with the church staff, my initial impression was that of youth. They seem to be in their 20s and 30s. For a moment I felt conspicuous because I was two decades older than most of those present. Some of them are younger than my children. However, as I listened and sought to understand I was impressed with the level of dedication, understanding, and wisdom that existed in the group. Their youth was only chronological. At the Sunday morning celebration service I saw some gray hair, but the impression there is also of a young church. According to my questionnaires, the average age of the church is in the mid-30s.

While I took the time to tell my story (our personal pilgrimage), I also described the project on which I was embarking. They seemed more than willing to cooperate if it would make a difference for the Kingdom and help facilitate understanding of the "home group based" church. They opened their hearts and lives to Karen and me. At the end of our time together, they laid hands on me and committed me and the project to the Lord. I came away feeling that I had been in the presence of some special people.

By the end of 1995, the church had an average of 730 people attending the Sunday celebration service. Some 45 home groups were operating with several others about to begin in the new year. The church had set a prayer goal of 150 baptisms for 1995 and had actually baptized 154 people. Their goal is to double the number of home groups and baptisms in 1996. By early spring 1996, the number of home groups had grown to more than 50 and celebration attendance reached 1,000.

For some time, the small 85-year-old church building has been inadequate as a place for this growing church to meet. They have rented a high school auditorium for the Sunday services, but as their numbers grow the auditorium is becoming too small as well. The church leadership struggles as to whether or not they should seek some type of permanent building or look for other solutions as the church grows.

The Pastors

Senior Pastor Mark Jobe grew up in Latin America and Spain as the son of missionary parents. He has always had a burden for Europe, especially Spain, and expected to serve as a missionary there. After he completed Bible school in 1985 Pastor Mark committed to help the struggling church in Chicago for three years. In 1995, he celebrated his tenth year at New Life.

Besides Pastor Mark, the church supports two pastors full-time: Dave Garratt and Mike Berry. Asa App, a son of missionaries from Latin America, is part-time. Each of these three men has oversight of an aggregation of home groups they call a zone.

While Pastor Mark is the visionary, motivator, and evangelist, the other pastors complement his leadership gifts. Asa is gifted in music and worship and has a burden for youth. He oversees the youth zone.

Dave is a gifted teacher and works on the details of administration. Mike has a teaching and encouraging gift which he uses in the overseeing of his zone. None of these men is particularly focused on his gift, but the focus is on the task and using the spiritual gift to complement the overall ministry of New Life Community Church for the Lord.

Bombay (Mumbai): An Urban Church in the Hindu World

New Life Fellowship
S. Joseph, Senior Pastor

Context of the Church

All the furniture had been removed and mats placed on the floor. Walls were covered with Bible verse posters, mostly in English, but a few in Hindi. As we entered this modest home, someone placed a couple of straight-backed chairs along one wall, motioning us to sit there. We indicated we would be happy to sit on the floor, and 27 men and 15 women soon joined us on the mats for a 2½ hour area meeting for home group leaders.

Bombay, recently renamed Mumbai, is the largest of the cities where we did research. I will use the name Bombay because of its worldwide familiarity. The city's immense size defies description. New Life has divided the city into 15 areas of one million population units (MPUs). Within the city limits live some 400 different people groups who speak most of the languages of the land. Besides the nearly 15 million who live in the city, another six million make the daily commute into the city to work.

Highly industrialized and home of India's stock market, Bombay's economic engine propels the Indian economy. At the same time it houses the largest slum in Asia, containing more than one million people. To add to the contrast Bombay is home to the world's largest movie industry, locally called Bollywood. Bombay has it all, from the India stock exchange and Bollywood to multiple slums and leper colonies.

We experienced Bombay traffic from the seat of a motorized rickshaw. Bustling streets reveal a great variety of traffic: smaller vehicles such as automobiles, vans, motorcycles, and small trucks, huge lorries, buses, the ubiquitous motorized rickshaws, and pedestrians. The rickshaws, too numerous to count, keep the roads clogged, but they are also an efficient and affordable way to travel. Someone always came to escort us to each appointment, whether a house group meeting, a leader's training session, a celebration service, or an interview.

Because Bombay is highly industrialized, it has pollution to match. Property costs continue to rise. Originally, Bombay consisted of seven islands with villages on each. Over time the space between has been filled in as the city has grown to become one of the great ports of the world. Into all of this variety of peoples, places, lifestyles, and social groups, New Life Fellowship ministers with a goal of reaching this great city with the gospel.

A contextual description cannot be complete without a word about the spiritual life of the city. We read in *India, a Travel Survival Kit*,

> India is one of the few countries in the world today in which the social and religious structures which define its identity remain intact and have continued to do so for at least 4000 years despite invasions, famines, religious persecutions, political upheavals and many other cataclysms.[1]

I saw shrines on all sides, on street corners, in neighborhoods both wealthy and poor, along streets and footpaths. While most of these shrines are Hindu, some are Roman Catholic. Public buildings, such as restaurants and shops, also display gods or shrines with incense burning. Many non-Christian homes have a god shelf with the family's deities. I felt I was never out of sight of at least one and often more religious shrines.

As the writer of *India, a Travel Survival Kit*, observed,

> There is possibly no other country where religion is so inextricably intertwined with every aspect of life.[2]

Brief History of the Church

New Life Fellowship was born in 1968 in Bombay. The church had been aiming to become one megachurch for the city, but until July 1980, it had grown to less than a hundred people. Then the Lord gave them a different vision. Pastor S. Joseph and a few young people spent time in prayer and fasting, seeking the Lord. The Lord spoke to them as a church and told them "to stop circling the mountain and go forward." Going forward meant to put aside the vision of a megachurch and begin planting house groups in different areas. Later their vision grew to include 10 percent of the city's population.

They began a systematic combing of the city's slums, bungalows, and low- and high-rise buildings so that every home might have an opportunity to hear the gospel. They had been given millions of rupees worth of literature that they used in this massive door-to-door effort. As people came to Christ and were formed into house groups the church grew rapidly. Although the growth was fast, people were able to build family relationships in the loving atmosphere of home groups.

In the 1990s explosive growth came to New Life Fellowship in Bombay and throughout India. In May 1992 a special outreach effort called "Love Bombay '92" brought 1,200 workers from other parts of India into Bombay to work with local Christians. They targeted 15 areas of the city and conducted direct evangelism throughout that month. The results, according to their own publications, were 5,500 conversions and another 6,500 responsive people. They had prayed for 10,000 conversions. After the campaign they began a strategic follow-up effort that added people daily to the church. The "Love Bombay" effort brought the Christians of New Life Fellowship together in a special way to focus on one short-term goal with a long-term mission. People gave sacrificially of their time as many took vacation days to evangelize Bombay. Others gave of their material resources, and not a few gave both.

In December of 1993 New Life Fellowship began what they call house churches. House churches in Bombay are groups that meet during the week. They take communion and an offering. They are churches in the sense that they care for the flock. However, they continue as part of a larger celebration center.

New Life Fellowship Today

Our flight arrived in Bombay in the middle of the night. Emerging from the various formalities necessary for entry into the nation, we were greeted by three men holding a sign, "Welcome Brother Mikel Neumann." I felt joy and a certain relief. It was a good beginning.

Four levels of meetings are mentioned in New Life's vision document.

1) Celebration Centers and Sunday Services
2) House Churches
3) Outreach Centers
4) Prayer Groups, some of which are functioning daily

A house church averages at least 10 committed people and includes communion and the taking of offerings. All the groups participate in praise and worship, teaching of Scripture, and the manifestation of the gifts of the Spirit. Actually, the lines between a house church, a house group (a type of pre-house church), and an outreach center are not always evident. For the purposes of this study I will use the term house group to refer to any of the three types of meetings. They all work together, bringing amazing growth to New Life Fellowship.

Some 1,200 house churches and house groups are clustered into approximately 250 worship or celebration centers. House groups meet during the week, and the celebration centers meet on Sundays. They have divided the city into 25 zones, each with a pastor. The zone pastor is not usually a full-time minister but has a job to support himself. That pastor is the shepherd for the leaders of the celebration centers in his area.

The offerings taken at the home group level, as well as those at the celebration centers, are collected and put into one of a number of church bank accounts in the city. The leadership practices diligent accounting procedures. This is necessary since groups exist who desire to find that the church has made a careless mistake or committed even a minor infraction that could lead to a cessation of church activities.

The church has few people on its payroll, given its immense size. In addition to the central pastoral staff, 250 full-time evangelists minister on the streets of the city every day. Hundreds of additional Christians are engaged in volunteer evangelism. We saw some of this work firsthand when we spent two days with area pastor Bonny Serrao, who took us to the Dhararai area (reputedly Asia's largest slum) on an evangelistic trip. I will write of this trip later in the chapter on evangelism. Contacts from these outreach efforts are followed up by the house groups in the area.

Pastor Jacob Serrao, who oversees a district in northern Bombay, began seven house Bible studies in 1993. His story is significant because it reflects the kind of growth we saw. By the end of 1993 the work grew to 11 house churches. As 1994 ended, the 11 had become 85 and at the end of 1995 the groups numbered 700. Sixty-three full-time evangelists work in that area, along with 240 unpaid evangelists who work almost full-time.

While this section deals only with the church in Bombay, the New Life Fellowship is a nationwide movement with work in most major cities, all 26 states, and several foreign countries.

The church owns little in the way of property. All the worship centers use rented quarters or houses. The house groups meet mostly in homes. Even the church offices occupy a rented house. This concept is strategic. Given the antagonistic and pluralistic context, there is little to be destroyed in case of a violent persecution. And given the cultural diversity, the necessary mobility exists to move quickly about the city.

The Pastors

Pastor S. Joseph is the senior pastor and leader of the church, the visionary who guides the overall direction of the work. Pastor Willie, who has been a part of this ministry since 1973, is one of four pastors who work with Pastor Joseph in leading New Life Fellowship. Shelton Davidson started in 1977, Jerry D'Souza in 1980, and Shekar Kallianpur in 1981. Each of these pastors has been responsible for a region of Bombay.

The four associates have different and complementary gifts. Pastor Willie is a gifted teacher and discipler. He creates and develops training programs for the house group leaders. Pastor Shelton's gift is in the area of prayer, insight, and prophecy. Pastor Jerry has pastoral gifts and pastors a large celebration center. He also gives help to other celebration center leaders. Pastor Shekar is an evangelist. I attended a meeting where people reported on a recent evangelistic campaign he led. Whenever he preaches, people are saved. My time with these men was limited, but the above insights come also from those who work with them.

While each pastor is gifted for ministry, my greatest impression of these men was their commitment to God. They are seeking to know God better whether in their families, personally, or as they serve together. It is not uncommon for them to spend a day, or even a day and a night, together in prayer and fasting. They are moving their ministries to areas of giftedness rather than areas of geography. I will write more about that later.

Accra: Urban Churches in the Animist-Nominal Context

Context of the Churches

"You have studied the home group ministries in Accra. Now tell us what you have learned that might be helpful to us." This statement by Rev. Philemon Quaye in a final debriefing helped me realize that my time in Accra had been special, significant, and with its own unique twist. Rev. Quaye worked with me to organize my time with maximum efficiency. He initiated contact with the churches, had a preliminary meeting with church leaders prior to my arrival, faxed me a schedule organizing my time in Accra, and wanted to know precisely what information I would need for the research. He brought together the leaders of three churches and one parachurch organization to work together. We left with a sense that God is certainly at work in this place.

People in Accra respect spiritual leaders. When we went to the various home meetings we, along with the person who accompanied us, were often put in a special place, usually on the best chairs, and given a soda to drink. Ghanaian Christians showed us warm and gracious hospitality as they brought us into their homes for meals and took us to meetings.

Accra, the fast growing capital of the West African nation of Ghana, spreads out along the coastal plain. Only 5 degrees north of the equator, it remains hot and muggy most of the time. Like many large African cities Accra has a mix of the new and the traditional. We visited home groups in a variety of social settings. Christians were studying the Word of God and reaching out to people at the university and among professionals in other contexts. At the same time the dynamic outreach touched every level of society from the wealthy to the poor, from the educated to the less educated.

Home groups in Accra were often a part of the larger community. It was not uncommon to visit a home group that met outside in a courtyard. We would sit on chairs lined up under a tree in earshot of several homes. While the people involved in the home group sat in a circle close together and near the light, other people in the community listened from the distance of their courtyards or from the paths that passed by the group of believers.

Background of the Churches

In Accra we were able to visit and study in some depth churches from three major evangelical movements: The Deeper Christian Life Ministry, Calvary Baptist Church of Accra, and two Evangelical Presbyterian Churches of Ghana (at Madina and Kotobabi).

The Deeper Christian Life Ministry
Rev. Jide Oladimeji, National Supervisor

The Deeper Christian Life Ministry originated in Nigeria and grew out of the personal ministry of W. F. Kumuyi, a university lecturer of mathematics. This home group based movement is one of the fastest growing movements in Ghana. And Nigerian missionaries are working in most of the nations in sub-Saharan Africa, the Middle East, India, the UK, and the USA.

Pastor Jide Oladimeji, the Nigerian leader of the Deeper Christian Life Ministry, and his family moved to Ghana in October 1980 to begin the work. He started ministry in Kumasi but moved to Accra in 1990. Today they have branch works in 105 of the 110 counties in Ghana. He began the home groups in 1982. Alan Isaacson's work, *Deeper Life*,[3] chronicles the history of this dynamic movement from its inception in Nigeria. When Pastor Oladimeji arrived in Ghana, he supported himself and started the ministry and that has been their pattern. People who have jobs are expected to seek transfers into areas where new works can be started. If that is not possible, then the person might start a small business. The national organization will sometimes help with the initial funding needs for such local initiatives.

Of all the groups we studied, this one is the most structured. They have followed quite closely the system brought from Nigeria. Their churches are called Deeper Life Bible Churches while the home groups are referred to as "Home Caring Fellowships (HCF)." Purpose and vision is clear. Every HCF follows the same curriculum, has the same order of events, and the same time schedule. Leaders know what is expected of them, whom they report to, and who reports to them. Each HCF is expected to reproduce within certain time limits. Supervisors assist HCFs that are having difficulty in any aspect of small group life.

With these home groups this ministry is aggressively reaching the city. The ministry has divided Accra into 12 districts, each with an overseer called a district coordinator. Within the 12 districts are 31 local churches pastored by either coordinators or the zone leaders who serve under the coordinators. Most of their leaders work full-time at an outside job. Pastor Oladimeji asserted that everything they do depends on their Home Caring Fellowships.

Calvary Baptist Church
Rev. Fred Deegbe, Senior Pastor

Calvary Baptist Church comes out of the Southern Baptist ministry and is one of the large, prestigious, downtown churches today. The church staff numbers 32, of which six serve as full-time pastors. Rev. Fred Deegbe, the senior pastor, and Rev. Dr. Osei-Bonsu were our two main contacts. This large church has closed circuit television so those in the back one-third of the church can better see what is happening at the front. The Sunday morning attendance numbers about 2,500 in two morning services. Calvary Baptist also currently has four satellite churches.

This somewhat traditional church has 200 home groups called "Sheepfolds." These are distributed among seven areas, each with its own pastor. Each zone has a name such as Judah or Israel and is referred to as a family. In the last three years Calvary Baptist Church has baptized between 350 and 500 people each year. The church is seeking to place more emphasis on the sheepfolds and less on some of the traditional programs. While the church would still exist without home groups, Pastor Fred believes that the future is in the sheepfolds.

I will speak more of worship in the appropriate section, but we were impressed with the worship in these churches. It was an excellent combination of a biblical basis, an African worship style, and Western influences. Because this is a city church where many of the worshipers have been educated in the West, the mix of cultural influences seemed appropriate.

The Evangelical Presbyterian Church of Ghana
Rt. Rev. (CDR) F. H. Gbewonyo, Moderator

This group began through the ministry of German missionaries from Bremen in 1847. In 1991 the denomination split. Today two denominations have almost identical names: The Evangelical Presbyterian Church of Ghana and The Evangelical Presbyterian Church, Ghana. The "of Ghana" church, as they call it there, is the one we researched. The Rev. Philemon Quaye was the man who organized our entire trip to Ghana. While he works with this denomination, he is known and appreciated as a Christian senior statesman across denominational lines.

The Evangelical Presbyterian Church of Ghana has grown rapidly since the split in 1991. The two churches we researched (Madina and Kotobabi) have grown to 1,500 and 2,500 people respectively since their beginning in 1991. Both have important home group ministries. However, what differentiates the home group ministries in these churches from the other Accra churches is that people go from the central church to the home groups. They normally enter the larger church through the Sunday worship service and are later assigned to a home group. This normal method of assimilation is not always followed, however, because we met some who came directly to the home group through personal witness.

In Accra, the Evangelical Presbyterian Church of Ghana has 40 churches of more than 150 people each. We attended Sunday services in the Kotobabi church, an all-day leader's training course in the Madina church, and several home groups associated with both churches. A former engineer, Pastor S. Y. Kwami, now leads the Kotobabi church, the largest church in the denomination. He has authored several books dealing with discipleship, spiritual warfare, and other aspects of the Christian life. His help was invaluable in gathering information.

Rev. Quaye, who has been a denominational leader, is a senior leader at the Madina church. That church has no full-time worker but many capable lay leaders. Among them is Dr. Seth Gbewonyo who teaches microbiology at the university and leads the home group ministry for his church. He led the all-day training seminar we attended.

All the churches we researched in Accra evidenced many of the same qualities. They are growing fast, with home groups an important part of that growth. They are extraordinarily well organized, and they have excellent leaders.

Caracas: Urban Churches in the Latin World

Context of the Churches

Five million people live in the small geographical area of Caracas, a beautiful modern city of high rises nestled among the mountains. The elevation in this tropical area gives the city its pleasant year-round climate. Some of the hills are covered with squatters and slum areas.

Local Christians told us that the rural areas were more responsive to the gospel than Caracas. Caracas has been called the "missionaries' graveyard" because so few missionaries have stayed beyond a second term. It is a city physically pleasant but spiritually difficult.

My first and last impressions of Caracas focus on keys. As we drove into the driveway of the high-rise building complex going to one of the homes (true both of missionaries and Venezuelans we visited), the first key came out. That opened the gate to get into the compound. Then the second key let us into the downstairs hallway. A third and different key took us into the elevator. When we reached the appropriate floor, we needed a fourth key to get into the little entryway of the apartment. Finally, a fifth key let us into the apartment. I have not counted the triple security system for the automobile, which can add three more keys. Persons may enter and exit their apartment several times a day, and all those locks must be dealt with on each trip: going to work, taking the kids to and from school, grocery shopping, attending various meetings, and so on.

Most of the home groups, leader's meetings, and interviews took place in the high-rise complexes. Much of Caracas lives in these high-rises—locked away and inaccessible. The evangelical population of Caracas is estimated at 0.5%.

Background of the Churches

I researched two Caracas churches that are effectively using home groups. The first church, Dios Admirable, is the largest Evangelical

Free Church in Caracas, with some 400 people participating in Sunday worship. I also spent significant time with church leaders and visited the church and home groups of the Las Acacias Evangelical Pentecostal Church. With some 4,000 people, it is the largest church in the nation.

Dios Admirable Church
Rev. Francisco Liévano, Pastor

Rev. Francisco Liévano is the third pastor of the Dios Admirable Church, which began in 1965 as an evangelistic Bible study targeting college students. The first two pastors were Free Church missionaries who had an evangelistic vision and were highly respected by the Venezuelans.

Rev. Liévano has served there for five years. Before that he taught in the seminary. He says, "I came with the idea of planting churches. What was I going to do? Just preach and run programs for the church? Yes, I preach and run the programs but I also plant churches!" He brings to this church great pastoral and teaching experience gained in other areas of Venezuela, as well as being a gifted evangelist with a heart for church planting.

While planting five new congregations in five years, he has also seen the Dios Admirable church grow from 200 to 400 people. They are outgrowing the theater they use for their services. The original church building is used for offices and some meetings but is too small for the church services. At the special thirtieth anniversary service, which I attended, there was a standing-room-only crowd.

Dios Admirable has 25 home groups presently because other home groups were used to plant the five new churches in Caracas. They call the home groups "Grupos Basicos Discipulado Cristiano" (Basic Christian Discipleship Groups). Each word has significance. "Group" indicates a gathering of limited size. "Basic" refers to the concept that the groups are foundational to the aims and function of the church. "Discipleship" indicates that the groups are not just Bible studies but full-fledged discipleship groups. The word "Christian" defines who they are. They seek to be like Christ in all they do. While the church has always had some Bible study groups, it has moved seriously into a home group program since Pastor Liévano arrived.

Las Acacias Church
Rev. Samuel Olson, Senior Pastor

Sam Olson's father, the first Assembly of God missionary to Venezuela, planted this megachurch in Caracas in 1954. He became an independent missionary when this work started. Although the work struggled for years, today it is a rapidly growing church with some 4,000 people involved. Sam came to the church in 1972 and copastored with his father until 1979. Since then he has been the pastor of the church. By the end of 1985 the church leadership had defined the church's mission, taken some intense training in management, written goals, and defined procedures for evaluating goals. In 1988 the church accepted the master plan.

Olson's ministry goals revolve around social concerns: economic, health and medical, counseling, drug and alcohol rehabilitation, and so forth. While it has not been his goal to plant churches, he now counts about 10 churches that have spun off the Las Acacias church and associate together in an organization they call the "Fellowship of Churches and Ministries." Ten full-time associate pastors serve the Las Acacias Church, one of whom heads up this organization of churches.

The church has divided the city into 14 geographical sectors. They are planning to increase the sectors to 25. Each sector has an overseer called a shepherd or coordinator. Shepherds are full-time paid staff, while coordinators are volunteer lay ministers. In the 14 sectors they have eight shepherds and six coordinators.

Las Acacias Church has various departments staffed by full-time professionals. These people minister in the church by exercising their professional training and giftedness. Some of the areas of specialization are social work, Christian education, psychology/counseling, worship/music, evangelism, missions, prayer, administration/accounting, and maintenance. Each professional is to take the work he or she does in the central church and reproduce it in the other sectors. The leadership recognizes this will take time, but the mission is clearly stated.

Home groups in the sector are encouraged to have their own Sunday afternoon worship services. These services are not to replace the central Sunday morning service but are in addition to it. At the time of the interview about seven sectors had such worship services varying in size from 30 to 120 people.

Currently the church has about 400 home groups with about 150 being added each year. Olson stated,

> What cell groups have done is allow us to focus on the city rather than on the church. Cell groups are not a program but are the church's thrust into the future. The church runs and supervises some excellent programs and fine organizations. The cell group ministry really does not fit into any of this. It is a different kind of thing. Cell groups are the strategy and not

the organizations of the church. Cell groups are the local beachheads where people come into the church and into ministry.[4]

Moscow: An Urban Church with New Freedoms and Challenges

Moscow Christian Charismatic Church or ROSA Church
Pavel Saveliev, Senior Pastor

Context of the Church

My first and last impressions of Moscow are of whizzing along in a minivan on the outer ring road, a road that skirts the city. We were 20 to 35 kilometers from the city center but even there we saw unending rows of huge apartment buildings. I can only guess how many thousands of people live in each of the 15- to 25-story buildings, which seem to go on in an endless progression, marching from the city's center to the outskirts.

While the buildings are huge, the space each person occupies is not. Apartments and rooms are small. In some cases more than one family shares an apartment. We visited one home group in a communal apartment. Each of the three renters has a room, while they share the kitchen and bath.

The roads are broad, and traffic is heavy at times. Public transportation is extensive and takes people to most points in the city. We traveled by bus and metro. The metro is a marvel. It runs on time and to all major areas in the city. The stations are often showcases for works of art. While the metro is impressive, some of its riders are not. Alcoholism is a huge problem. In the kiosks throughout the city one finds vodka for sale in small plastic containers. It is not uncommon to see men who have had too much alcohol, both on the metro and in the streets.

People often travel an hour on public transportation to reach a home group and many travel two hours to attend the Sunday celebration service. The reliable and efficient transportation system makes this possible. While the leadership encourages people to participate in home groups near their homes, that is not always possible. Personal contacts through network relationships in Moscow are not always with the nearby neighbors.

The great tradition of Russian art, culture, and history is embodied in the capital, Moscow. When we arrived at the apartment where we stayed as house guests, a new group that focuses on artists, writers, musicians, and other creative people was finishing tea after a meeting. Because of the important part culture and art play in people's lives, this group has been created to reach artists and intellectuals with the gospel—a creative way to reach creative people.

The current changes in Moscow can hardly be overstated. The social, political, and religious situations, after decades of communism, are undergoing profound changes. There is a sense of transition and uncertainty in the midst of the new freedom. The West has arrived with products ranging from Mars Bars to the multitude of Christian agencies. But one cannot ignore the effects of earlier decades. Red Square, the Kremlin, and Lenin's tomb are reminders of the history of Moscow. The restored churches are also a reminder of the past, as well as the changes now in progress.

Brief History of the Church

Because of the new freedoms in Russia, many churches have short histories. The Rosa Church, one of the fastest growing churches in Moscow, had its beginnings in 1989 though it was not officially registered until 1991 when Pavel became the full-time pastor. It is the newest of all the churches in this study and practically the only one in Moscow with a serious small group ministry. The church's official name is the Moscow Christian Charismatic Church but it is known as the "Rosa" church. Rosa means dew and comes from the many references to that word in the Psalms such as Psalm 110:3.[5] Pavel told me of the church's roots.

> Marina and I grew up in the Pentecostal Church. When freedom came we began to preach in hospitals, schools, on the streets, in drug centers, everywhere. I was in the underground church and starting another church was a crime. After some time our (Pentecostal) church would not care for all the new converts. So on the other hand it was a crime not to start a new church. In 1990 Marina and I and three people organized meetings and met each Sunday. In the former Pentecostal Church we had house meetings so we were familiar with the home group ministry. Those were started in the Pentecostal Church in 1975.[6]

Pavel and his wife Marina were among the first to begin preaching in public places when freedom was declared. Many people responded to their ministry. However, when the church reached 200 members, it stopped growing because of a lack of leaders. As they located leaders, the church grew again. But they have had a similar problem at various stages in the church's growth; when the church reached 700, then again at 1,000, and even now. Lack of leaders continues to slow their growth.

When the church reached around 200 people, Pavel and Marina began work on a system of home groups that continues to the present. It was only through their system of home groups that they could even begin to keep up with developing leaders and caring for the church members.

The Church Today

Karen and I, along with Beverly Nickles, our missionary guide, traveled by bus and metro, and then finished the hour-and-a-half trip with a rather convoluted walk to a third-floor apartment to attend a meeting of home group leaders. Though Sergei, the zone leader, and his wife are young, they impressed me with their commitment and spiritual maturity. Freedom is new and many converts are students, so it is not surprising that many of the more mature leaders are young in years. But youth in no way reflects negatively on their ability to serve with wisdom and humility. Many of these young leaders have recently married and some are becoming parents, adding to their responsibilities.

Rosa Church has about 1,000 official members. They have 65 home groups divided into 10 zones. On Sunday between 1,200 and 1,400 attend the celebration service, depending on the season and the weather. The church meets in a rented theater seating 1,500 people. The worship team, complete with dancers and flag wavers, leads from the stage. The various speakers and the preacher stand on the floor level in front of the stage. Each week on Thursday evening, in the same theater, they have a second celebration service directed more to believers. It is less well attended because of work schedules.

As one of the largest Protestant churches in Moscow they would like to have a church building and are saving money toward this goal. They needed office space so recently purchased an apartment with building fund money. Inflation is high and most churches are discouraged about trying to find land and build.

One interesting aspect of this church's ministry is the Jewish outreach. Marina's background is Jewish, and Pavel has always had a heart for reaching the Jews. He prays in the services for the nation of Israel and the Jewish people. People with Jewish backgrounds heard about that, and some began coming to the church. They now have more than 100 people with Jewish heritage in the congregation. They also have a Jewish home group meeting on Saturday. Many of these people are older, in their 50s to 70s, and come out of atheism.

The Pastor

Pavel is the pastor of Rosa Church. In addition, two full-time administrators and a half-time zone leader serve with him. His wife, Marina, is full-time without salary. She directs much of the home group ministry. He is seeking three more full-time staff but indicated that they must come through the ranks. They should first be home group leaders, then zone leaders, and then staff. The worship leader, home group leaders, and zone leaders are almost all volunteers. Pavel and Marina both feel the need to develop good leaders who will stay in the ministry.

That their young leadership is effective is seen at the macro level by the extraordinary growth of the church over its six-year life and at the micro level in what is happening in the growing and maturing home groups. This young church is experiencing change, yet is still affected by its history and its context.

General Information

In the chart below, the figures for city population are intended only to give the reader a sense of the relative sizes of the cities. Often it is difficult to find a recent census with precise data. While the church information may be more accurate, it changes rapidly and will soon be outdated. The purpose is to give an idea of the diversity of size and type of church.[7]

CITY: Approx. Pop. Listed from Largest	Name of Church	Av. Sun. Celebration Attendance	No. Home Groups
Bombay: 15 mill.	New Life Fellowship	250 Celebration Centers*	1,200
Moscow: 11 mill.	Rosa Church	1,300	65
Caracas: 5 mill.	Dios Admirable	400	25
	Las Acacias	4,000	400
Chicago: 3.3 mill.	New Life Comm.	900	50
Accra: 2.5 mill.	Deeper Christian Life Min.	3,300 adults in 31 Celebration Centers**	600
Evang. Pres. Ch. Ghana: Kotobabi		2,500	52
Evang. Pres. Ch. Ghana: Madina		1,500	31
Calvary Baptist Church		2,500***	200

*I do not have any numbers for the New Life Fellowship, Bombay church beyond the approximate number of celebration centers and home groups.

**These figures consider all of Accra for The Deeper Christian Life Ministry since it is one ministry divided into districts, much like New Life Fellowship, Bombay.

***These figures do not include the four satellite churches that are part of the Calvary Baptist Church family.

Key Points

• All the churches in this study were fast growing churches before becoming home group based churches.

• Home groups accelerated church growth by involving a greater percentage of people in ministry.

• The churches studied are in diverse urban cultures.

Endnotes

[1].   Geoff Crowther, et al, *India, a Travel Survival Kit*, 5th ed. (Hawthorn, Australia: Lonely Planet Publications, 1993), 22.

[2].   Ibid.

[3].   Alan Isaacson, *Deeper Life* (London: Hodder and Stoughton, 1990).

[4].   Sam Olson, interview by author, Caracas, Venezuela, 19 March 1996.

[5].   Beverly Nickles, "Russians Spread Joy in a Time of Crisis," *Charisma*, January, 1994.

[6].   Pavel Saveliev, interview by author, Moscow, Russia, 2 May 1996.

[7].   The data in this chart comes from the interviews with the Christian leaders.

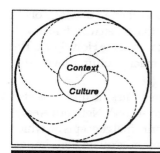

CHAPTER 2

Framework for Insight

...Call out for insight and cry aloud for understanding (Proverbs 2:3)

Many social sciences such as anthropology, sociology, and communication and educational theory can be brought to bear on the study of small groups. I do not intend here to relate directly to them all, but they have influenced me. What I hope to do is arrange the most obvious levels of a theoretical framework so the reader can understand my theoretical base and study further for more insight. Readers not desiring such theoretical background may wish to proceed to Chapter 3.

I have arranged this chapter in order, beginning with the most universal concepts to those more specific to urban aspects of small group theory. The subject is vast and a huge body of secular literature exists. Although Christians have used the principles and applied the knowledge, little has been actually researched from a Christian perspective.[1] For that reason I begin with a brief overview of the biblical basis for small groups ministry. Although it is not comprehensive, I have referred to a number of works that give an excellent biblical undergirding.

Because the Bible is the guide for all we as Christians are and do, at the most macro level the Bible is the final authority. Research implications must be measured according to biblical norms. Interpretations are always subject to human error, but we must still attempt to align our theories and applications with biblical truth. That is my aim in the Biblical Framework section.

God created us as humans and since Babel (Genesis 11) we have been subject to different cultures and their languages. Scholars have done us a great service by studying these cultures. People involved in urban ministry recognize cultural diversity within the urban context as well as among more geographically distant cultures. But the work of the Holy Spirit in Acts 2 saw the people of God understanding one another in a new and miraculous way. Whatever one's theology of the Holy Spirit may be, we can perhaps all agree that when we interact with culture, we must do so in the power and wisdom of the Holy Spirit. The second division of this chapter is at the macro cultural level—the Cultural Framework section.

Within the larger cultures are subcultures. These in turn consist of interlocking networks of people. In the third section, Network Analysis, I look briefly at network theory and the principal concepts on which this study is based. I will define basic terms and explain their importance for home group ministry.

In the final section, Missiological Implications, I present some missiological implications for home groups based on this framework. These summary statements are the theoretical assumptions on which this book is based. The anthropological and sociological discussions below only touch the surface, but they explain the basis of conclusions I reach in subsequent chapters.

Factors Underlying Home Group Ministry Research

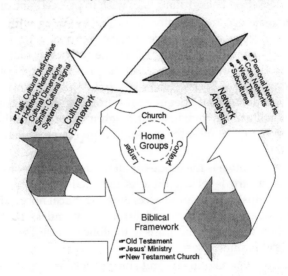

Figure 1

Biblical Framework
Your word is truth (John 17:17b)

Edmond and his wife were a part of our original home group in Madagascar where we learned much about ministry. Now they lead their own groups, and both are active in their church. After we had developed new home groups, Edmond and I would meet and talk. One day he said, "I know you have the same training as a pastor. However, even though you know theology, that did not prevent you from teaching us how to lead people to the Lord and disciple them." Scriptural truth was modeled for him in the context of a biblical home group.

Few will deny that home group ministries have caused both qualitative and quantitative growth in the church. However, early in my home group pilgrimage I received criticism of the home group ministry from quite a different aspect. Some critics stated that meeting together in small groups had no biblical basis. According to the Bible, they told me, people gathered only as the complete body of believers called the church. The church may have been few or many. They may have met in homes or in larger quarters. But the point was, the groups were not divided into some kind of subset like a home group. Because these people felt that home group ministry had no scriptural basis, they thought it was doing more harm than good.

In our ministries, we must seek to be scriptural in all that we do. A self-perceived success in numbers or other attributes is really no success at all if the programs, their goals, implementation, and results are not thoroughly biblical. Those believers who critiqued the home group ministry did us a good service by calling us back to biblical roots.

The following paragraphs attempt to answer the above criticism. Data in both the Old and New Testaments support dividing the larger group into smaller groups. In the New Testament the larger group is usually called the church or the assembly. In the Old Testament the larger group is called God's chosen people. The smaller groups which the Bible refers to as meeting in homes, I call home groups. Neither small group nor large group exists in isolation. The evidence presented below should demonstrate the small group-large group relationship.

Home Groups and the Old Testament

Carl George,[2] Gareth Icenogle,[3] and Jim & Carol Plueddemann[4] relate pertinent Old Testament data to small group ministries. These authors point out that God worked through the family group to accomplish his purpose in Israel, the children of God. This reference to Israel as the children of God demonstrates the importance of family relationships. The family is the primary small group in the Old Testament and serves as a model for people who meet together in a covenant relationship.

When Nehemiah rebuilt Jerusalem's walls, he divided the work among family groups, placing families close to their own homes. In so doing, Nehemiah decentralized the power and responsibility while keeping the groups networked together. Icenogle states,

> The detailed description of the craftsmanship of every family group is a trophy to Nehemiah's wisdom in being small-group-oriented and sensitive...Nehemiah was a networker of people groups. He was a macro group strategist. He, along with the family group leaders, developed a plan of shared building. His was a strategy of intergroup partnership with a common mission and a mutual ministry.[5]

Nehemiah's ministry was not through a massive hierarchical structure, but through a series of interconnected networks. He used existing family networks to accomplish God's purpose and empower the family leadership.

A second Old Testament small group model comes from Exodus 18 where Jethro advised Moses in judging the people. Jethro's model of leaders of 10s, 50s, 100s, and 1000s (Exodus 18:25) was not simply another hierarchical structure. These leaders came from within the group and were appointed out of the group. Jethro encouraged Moses to empower the people and to transfer his power as a judge to capable people within those groups.

The Old Testament models speak not only of small groups but of large. Plueddemanns point this out in the story of Ezra reading the Law to the people.

Nehemiah 8 describes one such occasion when Ezra read the Book of the Law while the Levites helped him explain the meaning to the people, so they could understand what was being read. This seems to have been a combination of large group and small group teaching.[6]

Home Groups and the New Testament

The relationship of small group to large group is a theme that carries into the New Testament. In this I focus primarily on biblical history, the Gospels, and Acts, beginning with the ministry of Jesus in small groups.

The Ministry of Jesus and Home Groups

Although much of Jesus' ministry was in the synagogue as well as the open air, a significant part of his work and teaching occurred in homes and with smaller groups of people.

Jesus' explanation of the Kingdom parables was given to the smaller group of his disciples (Matthew 13:36). He was in Peter's home when He healed Peter's mother-in-law (Matthew 8:14). Jesus was in a home teaching when the paralytic whom He healed was lowered through the roof (Mark 2:1). He visited homes to heal the sick (Matthew 8:14), raise the dead (Mark 5:38–42), and converse over a meal (Luke 7:36). He entered homes to teach salvation (Zacchaeus, Luke 19) and to disciple those who believed (Mary and Martha, Luke 10:38–42).

When Jesus sent out the twelve (Matthew 10, Mark 6) and later sent out the seventy-two (Luke 10), He sent them to homes. They went out in pairs to minister in the context of the home group.

When you enter a house, first say, 'Peace to this house.' If a man of peace is there, your peace will rest on him; if not, it will return to you. Stay in that house, eating and drinking whatever they give you, for the worker deserves his wages. Do not move around from house to house (Luke 10:5–7).

During the last part of his ministry, Jesus focused on the small band of disciples. His teachings, the final Passover, and his prayer in Gethsemane were all done in the presence of this small group (Mark 14). After his resurrection, Jesus appeared to the small band of disciples who were gathered in a home (John 20:19).

Although Jesus ministered to the multitudes and in the synagogues, much of his ministry concerned a small group of disciples. Even within the twelve He had the special group of three (Peter, James, and John) who were part of an inner group (cf. Matthew 17:1 and 26:37). He gave his teachings in a much more complete form to this smaller group.

Home Groups in the Early Church

From the earliest days, the church met in homes. All the activities associated with the community of the redeemed took place in homes. They broke bread together, ate together, and praised God in home worship (Acts 2:46–47). These believers had the favor of all people, and many unbelievers were saved. Evangelism took place as a result of the believers meeting in their homes.

Besides worshiping and breaking bread together, we see that both teaching and preaching took place in homes as well as in the temple courtyard (Acts 5:42). Prayer was an important element in the early church home meetings. A group was meeting in Mary's home praying for Peter's release when God answered in a miraculous way (Acts 12:12–17).

The early disciples reported on God's work in these home groups. After Peter and John's release from prison they returned and shared with their companions what God had done (Acts 4:23). In Acts 12:17 not only does Peter report to the home group, but he tells the Christians to report the happenings to James and the brothers as well.

The early church was a home based movement. Although teaching and preaching were done publicly, in the temple courtyard, the synagogues, and open fields, the real life of the church was in homes. The home of Aquila and Priscilla was the base for a church in Ephesus and later in Rome (1 Corinthians 16:19 and Romans 16:3–5). The church in Laodicea met in Nympha's home (Colossians 4:15), while the church in Colosse met in Philemon's home (Philemon 2).

Howard Snyder states, "Large group worship and small group fellowship are basic, complementary structures."[7] Several of the above verses emphasize this small group-large group aspect of church life. "And day by day continuing with one mind in the temple and breaking bread from house to house" (Acts 2:46, also cf. Acts 5:42; 20:20). This pattern of large group-small group was effective, and an important result was the astonishing growth of the early church.

The Cultural Framework
Say among the nations, 'The Lord reigns' (Psalm 96:10a)

A three-day conference was beginning at a conference center on the shores of Lake Victoria in Uganda. The 4:00 P.M. tea time would launch these meetings. However, the milk truck did not come. Rains were heavy and the road into the center was almost impassable. We waited.

Finally, about 7:00 P.M. the leader decided to begin the meetings without tea. We sang for several minutes and Karen and I had just started our presentation when we were politely interrupted. "The milk truck has come." That meant tea would be served and the presentation put on hold. We had no trouble with that since we had spent most of our adult lives in a similar culture where events are more important than a time schedule.

The original premise of this study is that home group ministries differ according to culture. That premise perhaps seems obvious to the cross-cultural worker, but when we look at ministries around the world and especially at models of home group ministries applied indiscriminately, the conclusion may not be so obvious.

The works of three scholars guided my research in this area: Edward T. Hall,[8] Geert Hofstede,[9] and Donald K. Smith.[10] Hall gives some overall cultural parameters that can be applied across cultures to discover significant differences. Hofstede has researched many cultures and compared them through four cultural paradigms. Smith, especially through his study of signal systems which I use extensively in the chapter on worship, gives tools to discover the differences that Hall and Hofstede delineate.

Cultural Distinctives according to Edward T. Hall

Hall has helped me enormously in his writing about cultural distinctives. He analyzes several aspects of culture by placing each on a continuum that contrasts two extremes. I make only brief mention of a few. I define the four distinctives below because of their acknowledged importance, and because they played a key role in the participant observational aspect of this study.

Temporal Conceptions

One of Hall's contributions to cultural understanding concerns temporal orientations. He writes about monochronic and polychronic cultures.[11] Monochronic cultures see time as more tangible and linear. They characterize time by tight schedules, dealing with one event at a time. These cultures place a higher importance on promptness. "Time is money" is a popular proverb of a monochronic culture.

Polychronic cultures, in their extreme form, have opposite characteristics. Schedules are loose. Multiple simultaneous activities are commonplace. Time is less tangible and last-minute changes of schedule are more likely. "Whatever will be, will be" might be a proverb for this culture. While cultures tend toward one of these two extremes, most will be on a continuum somewhere between.

Temporal factors play a role in how a home group is organized. In polychronic cultures, beginning and ending on time will be less important. The meeting may also be less structured. In a monochronic culture, these tendencies will be less likely as promptness and orderliness are valued.

Contextual Differences

The differences between high context and low context cultures is a key concept Hall develops.[12] In high context cultures, communication tends to be more cryptic as people pay closer attention to their surroundings (their context). They are more attuned to tone of voice, spatial, and kinesic dimensions of communication than to the words. Procedures are 'understood' by the local people. Bureaucracies are elaborate and rigid. Human relationships (who you know) are important and the procedures are secondary, so institutional procedures can be bypassed through insider personal contacts. Social class distinctions are maintained.

Low context cultures tend to rely more on verbal and written explanations while paying less attention to the context. People discuss abstract ideas that are often remembered, although the person who stated them may not be. Procedures are important and more difficult to bypass. Society seeks to minimize distinctions in social class.

While we tend to see these variations as macro cultural differences (such as between Asian and Western cultures), they also exist within Western cultures.[13] European and American cultures, both Western, maintain significant cultural differences. Centralization is often a fact of European life. Procedures are important. Oral agreements are considered binding. Organizations through bosses are responsible for the people within that organization. American culture tends to have decentralized power. Policies and law are important. Written, not oral, agreements are binding.

Home group leadership styles will vary between high and low context cultures. Home groups in high context societies will be closely linked to a larger structure, the local church. Senior church leadership will play a more directive role in the home group administration. Another difference may be a greater need for written lessons in the low context culture. Leadership in the low context group, in part, comes from the written lesson because the leader is seen in a more egalitarian light.

Space and Tempo Differences

Hall studied how humans relate in terms of non-verbal communication, particularly body movement which he called synchrony.[14] Synchrony is the degree to which people move in harmony with others. He classified cultures as low-sync and high-sync. He discovered that people move in harmony with others as they speak or listen within a group. However, the way they move and the relative importance of harmony is a function of culture. In high-sync cultures social structure is tighter. Behavior is more predictable as people are expected to conform to societal expectations. In low-sync societies behavior is less predictable and conformity less valued. But in either case, when everything is "in sync" one has a sense of well-being.

Skilled home group leaders in all cultures take advantage of synchrony to sense a group's well-being. He or she inherently knows if something is wrong through the way the group interacts. A home group leader contributes to maintaining healthy relationships by being in touch with home group members and encouraging them to intensify relationships among themselves. The appropriate relationship contacts will vary according to culture, tending to a higher number in high sync cultures and fewer in low sync ones.

Reasoning Styles

Linear logic speaks of knowledge gained through analytical reasoning. Words are important in this process. Logic and the ability to reason linearly are often equated with intelligence. Comprehensive reasoning contrasts to the linear. Knowledge is gained through intuition, spiral logic, and contemplation. Feelings are important and are part of the process of reasoning and gaining knowledge. Preferences for these different reasoning styles are culturally conditioned.

Understanding reasoning styles is important for effective home group ministry. Teaching styles will look considerably different in differing cultures. Some home groups will be quite methodological while others, reflecting their cultures, will have a higher emotional content. In some, one person speaks at a time while in others, several speak at once.

Dimensions of National Cultures according to Geert Hofstede

In Hofstede's book, *Culture's Consequences*, his massive research project which includes the works of others doing similar kinds of research, he has created a model by which cultures can be compared at the macro level. In seeking to study the cultural differences of home group ministries, it was critical that I locate cultures as dissimilar as possible in order to identify those differences and how they might affect the ministry. Hofstede[15] aligns 50 national cultures along four continua. I assumed the accuracy of the four dimensions in his writing and used that data to help select my research sites.

Power Distance[16]

Hofstede states that power distance deals with the issue of human inequality. The tendencies to increase, maintain, or reduce power distance are societally determined. Unequal distribution of power within an institution is the essence of organization. It is this inequality of power that keeps organizations from becoming disorderly to the point of being unable to function. The power distance index (PDI) measures the interpersonal power or influence between a boss and a subordinate as perceived by the subordinate.

Hofstede defines power distance as *"the extent to which the less powerful members of institutions and organizations within a country expect and accept that power is distributed unequally"* (italics his).[17]

The differences are seen primarily between egalitarian societies and hierarchical societies. High PDI cultures have social institutions, including religions, that stress stratification with elite leadership. Leaders are expected to exercise power and to protect that power. Power is demonstrated by outward appearances such as clothing or special buildings. Home groups can be considered threatening and dangerous in high PDI contexts because they often stress egalitarian values.

Low PDI cultures have social institutions that stress ideologies of power equalization. Society is considered pluralistic and the different societies have equal value. Leadership is 'of the people' and more decentralized. Although home groups may be viewed as a logical ministry mode in these cultures, leadership will have high qualification expectations, making leadership more difficult to find.

Leadership style will also be different. In low PDI countries leadership seeks trust, and there is a latent harmony between leaders and followers. Change comes through the majority, and power can be redistributed. Leaders in high PDI countries tend to seek power and lead through inducing fear and respect.

While the extremes of these cultures are modified in Christian experience, tendencies in these directions will continue to exist. But home groups help mitigate these cultural extremes.

According to Hofstede, the highest PDI nation in my study was Venezuela and the lowest was the United States. Both India and West Africa were high, but not extremely so. Because Hofstede did his study before the Iron Curtain came down, Russia was not in his study. Russia, at this writing, is still a nation in major cultural transition, and no attempt is made to place it on any of the Hofstede scales. My hope is that people in ministry in Russia will recognize the appropriate cultural attributes in the charts and comments and make suitable applications.

The range of the four nations in this study with their values on Hofstede's scale are as follows:

Venezuela (81)   *India (76)*   *West Africa (75)*   *USA (40)*[18]

To give a little perspective here, in Hofstede's fifty-nation study the highest score was 104 (Malaysia) and the lowest was Austria (11).

Uncertainty Avoidance[19]

How humans deal with uncertainty about the future is what Hofstede calls "uncertainty avoidance." All humans live with uncertainty but not all persons deal with it in the same way. Predictability is the opposite of uncertainty. A society that needs a higher predictability level (low uncertainty avoidance) will give up freedoms in order to maintain high predictability. Totalitarian ideologies are an attempt to avoid future uncertainties.

Hofstede's definition of the Uncertainty Avoidance Index (UAI): *"the extent to which the members of a culture feel threatened by uncertain or unknown situations"* (italics his).[20]

Human societies deal with uncertainty in three different ways: by rules (law), technology, or rituals (religion). Rules are used to make behavior predictable. Hofstede makes a distinction between the authority of *rules*, which deals with uncertainty avoidance, and authority of *persons*, which deals with power distance. Technology is another way people deal with uncertainty. Automation of a process creates short-term predictability. Rituals, a third way people cope with uncertainty, support traditional values in a society, maintaining adherence and cohesion.

The major differences in this category can be summarized in the difference between loose (low uncertainty avoidance) and tight (high uncertainty avoidance) cultures. Loose cultures have less structure, less bureaucracy, less time orientation. Future uncertainties inherent in life are more easily accepted. People in these cultures are more apt to take risks. They see disagreements between leaders and followers as opportunities for creative solutions.

Tight cultures (high UAI) will have more organization with specialists in key roles in every sector of the society. People do not solve their own problems but look to professionals who solve problems.

Authority is accepted, not criticized. Higher anxiety levels exist in the culture with overt aggressive behavior and showing of emotions. Hard work is valued highly for its own sake. Younger people are seen as suspect. There is a search for ultimate truth, whereas low UAI nations tend to be more pragmatic and less concerned with the ideological.

None of the countries in this study were high UAI. Venezuela is the highest of the four countries in the study. However, it is in the middle range, while the others were all fairly low.

Venezuela (76)   West Africa (54)   USA (46)   India (40)[21]

The highest UAI country in Hofstede's list is Greece (112) and the lowest is Singapore (8). In any culture one will find elements of both high and low UAI. In fact, even within any urban area one finds high and low UAI cultures. Variances will be found across age groups, gender, and educational level. The person working in a local area should study his or her own context and analyze it.

Younger home group leaders will be more easily accepted in a low UAI culture. There is a strong belief in common sense, and the generalist will be acknowledged. The high UAI cultures may have older leaders and feel the need for specialists to lead.

Any of the above characteristics can be problematic when carried to the extreme. However, home groups often moderate cultural extremes, helping people deal with them in a positive manner.

Individualism[22]

Individualism is defined in comparison to collectivism. A society where individual interests prevail over the group is called individualist. By contrast a society where group interest prevails over the individual is called collectivist. Most of the world's societies are collectivist. People relationships denoting these traits are in terms of the larger group, but not the government. The larger group may be the family, the workplace, friendship groups, or the church.

Hofstede defines the individualistic index (IDV) and contrasts it with collectivism as follows:

> *Individualism* pertains to *societies in which the ties between individuals are loose; everyone is expected to look after himself or herself and his or her immediate family. Collectivism* as its opposite pertains to *societies in which people from birth onwards are integrated into strong, cohesive ingroups, which throughout people's*

lifetime continue to protect them in exchange for unquestioning loyalty (italics his).[23]

Factors indicating a more collective culture are elements such as training, physical conditions, and use of skills. People desire good training opportunities to improve or learn new skills. Good physical working conditions such as lighting, atmosphere, and space are important. Because collectivist societies have a more developed 'we' consciousness, the group is the center for one's life. Belonging to an organization carries significance. Friendships are predetermined by social relationships within a stable society. People desire to be honored and admired by their groups. Certain value standards are applied only with the ingroup, while different standards would be applied to the outgroup.

Factors indicating a more individualist culture are items such as personal time, freedom, and challenge. People want free time outside their job and normal social responsibilities. They have considerable freedom in choice of career and job options. They prefer a job that will be a challenge and give them a personal sense of accomplishment, which may be reflected in a search for wealth or position. They have individual friendships where they seek trust. They feel that value standards are universal and should apply to all people.

Differences in the collective and individual cultural patterns have implications for Christian work and for home groups. Collective societies emphasize traditional ethics and their roots. Conversions tend to be collective or greatly influenced by the group. Individualist societies stress individual conversions and one-on-one discipleship. Worship and religion are personal and individual matters.

In individualist cultures one hears phrases such as, "If it works for you, fine." In collectivist cultures individuals consult the group before making a major decision, such as converting to another religion. But of course, individuals do sometimes convert to other religions. When this happens either the individual has had a need met that is greater than his or her desire to be a part of the group, or else she or he decides to become a secret believer. Converts who are able to maintain ties to their group face huge obstacles, but they also have many opportunities to share their new faith.

When a person from a collectivist society converts to Christianity, the process will be helped along if the convert can see the collective side. Home groups aid in this area because of the new relationships formed in the small group, which are helpful toward bringing people into the larger church group relationship. One-on-one discipleship can seem too individualistic for collectivist cultures where learning is a group process.

The highest individualist nation in Hofstede's study, both in the overall study and in the four nations of this study, is the USA. The four nations researched in terms of Hofstede's scale are as follows:

USA (91)   India (48)   West Africa (20)   Venezuela (12)[24]

The scale is general but does not apply in every instance. In an urban area in Venezuela or Ghana one might find people who are highly individualistic, even as there are North Americans with a collective mentality.

Gender Role Separation[25]

Hofstede's fourth index refers to a masculinity-femininity continuum as a dimension of societal norm. Some characteristics are more associated with masculinity and others, femininity. Of course, that does not mean that all men or all women feel that way, but it presents a scale to measure differences.

Predominant socialization patterns around the world tend to encourage men to be more assertive and competitive while women are encouraged to be more nurturing, with a concern for relationships. Hofstede defines masculinity and femininity as follows:

> *Masculinity* pertains to societies in which social gender roles are clearly distinct (i.e., men are supposed to be assertive, tough, and focused on material success whereas women are supposed to be more modest, tender, and concerned with quality of life). *Femininity* pertains to societies in which social gender roles overlap (i.e., both men and women are supposed to be modest, tender, and concerned with the quality of life (italics his).[26]

When gender roles are societally distinct, the society leans toward the masculine side and when these roles overlap, it leans toward the feminine. The items deemed important in masculine oriented societies are opportunities for high earnings and advancement, recognition for good work, and challenging work leading to a personal sense of accomplishment. Assertiveness and recognition are basic elements.

The importance attached to the feminine side includes having a good working relationship with one's direct superior, working with people who cooperate well with one another, and job security. Environment and relationships are key elements.

Hofstede comments that in feminine countries both boys and girls learn to be nonambitious and modest. Assertiveness and excelling, both masculine ideals, are ridiculed in feminine countries. In masculine countries children learn to admire the strong, and both boys and girls learn to be ambitious and competitive. In some countries, girl's ambitions may be oriented toward their brothers and later their husbands and sons.[27]

Where there is a difference between men and women in any aspect of society, such as education, job possibilities, or relationships, that society is more masculine. When women and men have the same general possibilities in such matters, the society is more feminine. Interestingly, masculine cultures foster more aggressive women's liberation movements since the genders are more separate, and assertiveness and aggressiveness are seen as ideals.

All of this affects the church and ministry. In feminine cultures equality, relationships, and moderation will be emphasized. In masculine societies, appeal will be made to inequality of the sexes, 'tough' religious currents, and stronger male leadership.

In the four countries of this study one ranks high on the masculinity scale and one ranks in the low middle range. The others fall somewhere between.

Venezuela (73)   USA (62)   India (56)   West Africa (46)[28]

The highest masculine is Japan (95) and the lowest is Sweden (5).

Putting the four countries together reveals that the four have significant differences across the four comparisons.

Comparison of National Characteristic Ranks on Four Continua

High - *Low*

Power Distance
Venezuela (81)	*India (76)*	*West Africa (75)*	*USA (40)*

Uncertainty Avoidance
Venezuela (76)	*West Africa (54)*	*USA (46)*	*India (40)*

Individualism
USA (91)	*India (48)*	*West Africa (20)*	*Venezuela (12)*

Masculinity
Venezuela (73)	*USA (62)*	*India (56)*	*West Africa (46)*

Figure 2

In addition to the four countries listed in the chart, this study includes Russia, a country in the midst of great social upheaval. The research sites include one large city from each of the five national areas mentioned and touch five continents. Because of urban heterogeneity the societal characteristics for one area may actually be found in another. For instance, the Chicago church could be found quite collectivist, even though it is located in North America which is rated highly individualist. However, sufficient cultural variety exists within the five selected sites to give us viable samples of how culture affects home group ministries.

Culture does matter. When Karen and I were in the United States on a home assignment, we attended a popular seminar. I talked with a pastor friend about it later. He thought there was a lot of good material in the seminar that would help me in my ministry in Madagascar. While I agreed that the material was good and I was edified, I replied that there was little, if anything, I could use in Madagascar. He was astonished. I explained that the material, dealing with self-worth, self-fulfillment, family relationships, and personal difficulties, did not address the primary areas of struggle for Malagasy. Family relationships can be a struggle, but the relationships are dealt with in a totally different way. The other issues were far too individualistically packaged to have much use in a collective society.

Signal Systems according to Donald K. Smith[29]

While Hofstede helped in distinguishing broad cultural differences necessary in site selection, Smith furnished tools for examining cultures at the micro level. In his book on intercultural communication, he states that all human communication occurs through 12 signal systems that vary with culture. Participant observation was one important part of this research. One part of that observation included how people used the different signal systems. They are stated below with a brief explanation of each one.

1. Verbal. Verbal is simply communication through speech or language. Each site I visited had one or more languages different from my native English.
2. Written. Symbols that represent speech comprise the written signal system. Although thousands of verbal languages exist, they are represented by far fewer written systems. The Latin alphabet, for instance, is used to represent many languages.
3. Numeric. Numbers and number systems carry meaning. Some numbers have religious significance. We hear of 'lucky' and 'un-

lucky or evil' numbers. Mathematical systems furnish the vocabulary and syntax of the numeric system.

4. Pictorial. Two-dimensional representations, such as pictures, photos, and drawings vary in different cultures. They can be part of a communication system to the degree that the symbolism becomes a part of the culture.

5. Artifactual. Three-dimensional representations and the objects of daily living can be included in this signal system. At one level, architecture, sculpture, and the way cities are planned can be a signal system. At the more personal level, hair styles, jewelry, clothing, and room furnishings also communicate.

6. Audio. Silence and non-verbal sounds, such as laughing, crying, whistling, and instrumental music are strong communication vehicles. They vary considerably in different cultures. Christians are often divided on how this signal system should be used.

7. Kinesic. Body language has been studied in different cultures. Various body movements can have different meanings in dissimilar cultures, as many foreign tourists have learned to their embarrassment. Even a smile can vary in its meaning in different societies.

8. Optical. Use of light and color can carry meaning. Light is a metaphor with a strong positive message. Yellow tracts have negative meaning in many places, contradicting their written message.

9. Tactile. Some cultures are 'touch' cultures. People shake hands, hold hands while speaking, reach out and touch people to communicate. Touch can be pleasant, offensive, or profound, depending on the type of touch and the society. The use of appropriate tactile gestures in a greeting helps communicate sincerity.

10. Temporal. Clock time, while the most obvious, is not the only sort of temporal system. Time is also used to convey meaning. People communicate by coming early, late, or on schedule. Societies, too, tend to look forward (future orientation) or back (historical orientation).

11. Spatial. Space communicates. We speak of personal space, work space, and living space. We stand a culturally appropriate distance away to speak with people. Public places are built with a certain amount of space. The use of space can make a church building seem foreign if copied from another culture.

12. Olfactory. Taste and smell can be powerful communication media. Perfume, incense, and food smells can send subtle messages. Eating together is a clear example of communication.[30]

Two or more signal systems occur together in most communication situations. When they are used together in culturally appropriate ways, communication will be clear and understandable. When two of the systems contradict each other, communication may be fuzzy. When two signal systems contradict, the one lower on the list will usually be believed because it is a less conscious medium.

Network Analysis
...A neighbor nearby... (Proverbs 27:10)

Liva, a young woman from the country, arrived in the capital looking for a way to better herself through education or employment. She was one of thousands who migrate to the city. A home group met near her and as she became acquainted with the people, she started attending. In the weeks that followed she came to Christ and began to grow in her faith. She was baptized and joined a Baptist church. Eventually, she had to return to the village because she had none of the skills needed in the city, nor did she have the qualifications or funds for further education.

She returned to her village with little status but a desire to make Christ known. She began to teach Bible stories and songs to the children. Soon parents saw a difference in the children and asked Liva about it, so she shared her testimony. The village mayor sent for the pastor and a missionary to visit. Over the next several months many in that village came to faith. A lay pastor visited on weekends and more than 60 people were baptized in the next six months. Through that process a church was born.

Then a former village school teacher returned for a visit. He came to Christ and was baptized. When he returned to his new village school, he began a witness that became a small village church. People from the capital also came to Liva's village to visit their relatives. They heard the gospel and took the Good News back to the city with them. They started a home group in their part of the city, which later became a church.

The story continues but enough is given to show the importance of networks in bringing the gospel to those who do not know it. Network analysis is a key factor in the study of home group ministries.

Personal Networks

The urban areas of the world, with their teeming populations, are not simply masses of individuals suffering in greater degree from "man's inhumanity to man" than those people living in rural areas. The urban way of life has often included negative stereotypes, such as relationships that are impersonal, superficial, transitory, and indifferent.[31] But that view does not truly reflect urban reality. It is too simplistic and negative.

People in the cities are linked together in face-to-face connections called social networks. Each individual is normally a part of several social networks including family, friendship, professional, special interest, religious, and many others. Clusters of these social networks are themselves loosely connected to larger entities which have been called subcultures. A generic definition is given by Knoke and Kuklinski.

A *network* is generally defined as a specific type of relation linking a defined set of persons, objects, or events. Different types of relations identify different networks, even when imposed on an identical set of elements (italics theirs).[32]

The authors continue to explain that people are the actors or nodes in these networks and the way they relate to each other within a network and to other networks will reveal important aspects of human behavior, especially in cities.

A premise of network analysis is the structure of relations among actors, and the locations of individual actors in the network have important behavioral, perceptual, and attitudinal consequences both of the individual units and for the systems as a whole (italics theirs).[33]

Our goal as Christian workers is to reach urban people with the gospel. A prerequisite to that effort is to understand how people are 'connected' to each other, which makes the study of networks important. The process quickly becomes complex. Everett Rogers states that people have far more acquaintances than we usually realize.

The average individual has over 1,000 acquaintances (someone whom you would recognize and could address by name if you met him/her). Thus friends of friends would number over one million except for overlap.[34]

Of course, there is overlap so a person's secondary connections normally do not number a million. However, if an idea or innovation such as the gospel begins to flow along network lines, we see that many people can be reached quickly. Rogers again states, "The most fundamental principle of human communication is that *the exchange of ideas most frequently occurs between transceivers who are homophilous*" (italics his).[35] People in the same network have similar characteristics, common meanings, and mutual values and are considered homophilous. Claude Fischer emphasizes this point in his work, *To Dwell Among Friends*:

People tend to build networks composed of others very similar to themselves. The dominant factors which produce this homogeneity are: personal preference and structural constraint.[36]

Core Networks

Relationship density within a network is a measure of the actual number of relationships as a percentage of the potential number of relationships. When the actual number of relationships is high, the network is considered dense. Dense networks usually result in many personal contacts in short periods of time. These networks, not always family, are called core networks. McCallister and Fischer give the following definition of a core network:

The set of people who are most likely to be sources of a variety of rewarding interactions, such as discussing a personal problem, borrowing money, or social recreation.[37]

Most people have a core network, and it is within that network where felt needs will be expressed and met. One result of urbanism is that network relationships are both intensified and expanded. People develop more intense relationships with the people in their core networks, while at the same time being exposed to other networks which may have values and ideas radically different from their own. The gospel and its implications may be one such new and radical concept.

If people only relate to others within their narrowly defined core networks, new ideas never enter those networks. New concepts come from outside the homophilous network. People have links to other core networks but those links are weak. Mark Granovetter who has developed this concept in depth states:

The argument asserts that our acquaintances ("weak ties") are less likely to be socially involved with one another than are our close friends ("strong ties"). Thus, the set of people made up of any individual and his or her acquaintances will constitute a low-density network (one in which many of the possible relational lines are absent), whereas the set consisting of the same individual and his or her *close* friends will be densely knit (many of the possible lines present).[38]

In a network of strong ties, the people one knows are much more likely to know each other. In the case of weak ties, that is not usually the case. It is, however, the weak ties that serve as communication bridges between core networks. New information often flows through the weak tie into the strong or core network. When the new information crosses the weak tie bridge, it is not necessarily accepted. The decision power comes from within the core network.

McConnell rightly points out that the advantage of weak ties can be negated by action that is non-purposeful. If we have the weak ties and do nothing toward communicating along those lines, then the bridge is ineffective. Another way the weak tie can fail is when people in a core network are so focused on maintaining the core, they have few weak ties.[39] This concept has tremendous implications for home groups multiplication.

Subcultures

Subcultures are essential in understanding urban networks. Every individual is part of a core network. Each member within that network is also part of a core network that differs slightly. A network is not static but continues to change, expand, or contract. Overlapping networks create a subculture.

The subculture has a high degree of homogeneity depending on the level of contact outside. In the urban context an individual has more opportunity to expand his or her core network within the subculture. Also, as people from different subcultures interact, they bring new ideas to the complete network and eventually to each individual in the network. As McConnell notes, "In this way, networking is a means of connecting people beyond the realm of known contacts."[40]

Subcultures are important because they provide the large-scale connections in city life. Interaction between the subcultures and networks gives the city its heterogeneity. "Universal subcultures are those to which virtually everyone belongs: ethnic (sometimes also racial), social class, gender, and life-cycle."[41] These subcultures, consisting of many core and loose networks, overlap and create a myriad of social structures.

Fischer also speaks of the subculture in seeking to ascertain how urban life affects social life. He states:

> Urbanism does shape social life—not, however, by destroying social groups as determinism suggests, but instead by strengthening them. The most significant social effect of community size is to promote diverse subcultures (culturally distinctive groups, such as musicians, college students, or Chinese-Americans). Like the compositional theory, subcul-

tural theory maintains that intimate social circles persist in the urban environment. But, like determinism, it maintains that ecology significantly changes communities, precisely by supporting the emergence and vitality of distinctive subcultures.[42]

When we look at cities as simply masses of people, the task of communicating the gospel can be overwhelming and discouraging. However, when we see cities as consisting of overlapping subcultures made up of various networks, and within those networks are core relationships, then the task becomes a potentially rewarding challenge. We do not have to preach the gospel to every person, but we need to find the networks and begin circulating the "gospel and its implications" within the network. Once a network receives the gospel, the people in that network can carry the gospel to others along the network bridges.

Universal Missiological Implications for Home Groups
...from every nation, tribe, people, and language (Revelation 7:9)

Home groups work through personal relationships. Because a home group is informal with little in the way of member boundaries, it must take advantage of the natural social links within networks in order to grow. Home groups can bridge into other networks through weak links. While a given individual may actually become a part of another network, it is more likely that the gospel will be brought into his or her group, which will help develop ownership and leadership from within. Therefore a new home group is created in a different network.

Home group members should be sensitive to network links as the means for effective communication. Most Christians who spend time following their own networks, strong and weak, will use their resources more efficiently and effectively.

The cross-cultural worker will want to become part of a series of networks. Through these he or she can begin to follow the natural relationships. The worker brings new data (such as the gospel), but it is the people within the network who have the power of decision.

One implication is the necessity of a prayer focus in the evangelism process. Christians need to pray that they will become a part of networks bearing spiritual fruit. They must pray that the gospel and its implications for that society will be clearly understood. Finally, they should pray that people in the network will decide to follow Jesus and influence those in their networks to join them.

Missiological Implications for the Church
...I will build my church (Matthew 16:18)

In terms of networks, I would like to show how the home group and the church relate to each other and to the larger community. While this relationship will vary with one's ecclesiology, I suggest a pattern which I feel is honest to Scripture and to current social theory.

I spoke earlier of the scriptural pattern of large group-small group relationship. The large group is a formal structure. Rules for members (boundaries), designated leaders, and purposeful action are features of formal structures. Our society has many such structures, the local church being one. While people may be present who are not really a part of the church, they nonetheless recognize the formal relationships within the structure and they are viewed as visitors.

The small, home group is an informal association of people. Rules for membership are casual, if they exist, influenced by national cultural characteristics. Leadership does exist, but it is not usually highly formal. As the group grows, it overlaps with other social networks. And people in the groups are all a part of many overlapping networks. But people in the home group attend the same church, some are in the same family, and all are a part of the same subculture.

These overlapping relationships have both positive and negative aspects. Positively, they serve to strengthen the network. Negatively, they can lead to an ingrown network which, if sustained, may lead to a dormant home group and an ineffective network. Most home groups have a degree of heterogeneity which will furnish the weak ties to other networks and bring new dynamic relationships into the group.

As home groups grow and give birth to new groups, a home group subculture is created. As this subculture grows through ever-expanding network associations, a church is born. That local church will have a higher degree of heterogeneity than the home group.

The church, in obedience to Scripture, will reach out to subcultures considerably different than itself. The urban area offers an excellent milieu for this expansion since subgroups are likely to connect with each other in a city. Workers trained in intercultural studies, missiology, and biblical and theological studies should be prepared to analyze the networks. The "weak ties" that link core networks will play a key role in the mission endeavor.

So reaching the lost means locating them within their networks. Combining networks will give birth to churches. As people within core networks follow their weaker ties to other networks, different subcultures will be reached with the gospel and the process will repeat itself. As the process accelerates, a people movement may well be established.

Endnotes

1.   See Doug McConnell, *Maps, Masses, and Mission: Effective Networks for Urban Ministry*, Leonard Buck Lecture in Missiology (Victoria, Australia: Bible College of Victoria, 1990), 3.

2.   Carl F. George, *Prepare Your Church for the Future* (Grand Rapids: Fleming H. Revell, 1991).

3.   Gareth Weldon Icenogle, *Biblical Foundations For Small Group Ministry: An Integrational Approach* (Downers Grove, IL: InterVarsity Press, 1994).

4.   Jim and Carol Plueddemann, *Pilgrims in Progress: Growing Through Groups* (Wheaton, IL: Harold Shaw Publishers, 1990).

5.   Icenogle, *Biblical Foundations*, 106–107.

6.   Plueddemann, *Pilgrims*, 2.

7.   Howard Snyder, *The Community of the King* (Downers Grove, IL: InterVarsity Press, 1977), 146.

8.   Edward T. Hall, *The Dance of Life* (New York: Anchor Books, Doubleday, 1983), and *Beyond Culture* (New York: Anchor Books, Doubleday, 1976).

9.   Geert Hofstede, *Cultures and Organizations: Software of the Mind* (London: McGraw-Hill Book Company, 1991) and *Culture's Consequences: International Differences in Work-Related Values*, abridged ed. (Beverly Hills, CA: Sage Publications, 1984).

10.   Donald K. Smith, *Creating Understanding* (Grand Rapids, MI: Zondervan, 1992)

11.   See Hall, *Dance of Life*, 46ff., and *Beyond Culture*, 77ff., for a discussion on monochronic and polychronic cultural differences.

12.   See Hall, *Dance of Life*, 61ff., for further discussion.

13.   Ibid., 110ff.

14.   Ibid.

15.   Hofstede, *Culture's Consequences*, 1984.

16.   See Hofstede, *Culture's Consequences*, 65ff., and *Cultures and Organizations*, 23ff., for a complete discussion.

17.   Hofstede, *Cultures and Organizations*, 28.

18.   Ibid., 26.

19.   See Hofstede, *Culture's Consequences*, 110ff., and *Cultures and Organizations*, 109ff., for a complete discussion.

[20]. Hofstede, *Cultures and Organizations*, 113.

[21]. Ibid.

[22]. See Hofstede, *Culture's Consequences*, 148, and *Cultures and Organizations*, 50, for a complete discussion.

[23]. Hofstede, *Cultures and Organizations*, 51.

[24]. Ibid., 53.

[25]. See Hofstede, *Culture's Consequences*, 176ff., and *Cultures and Organizations*, 79ff., for a complete discussion.

[26]. Hofstede, *Cultures and Organizations*, 82.

[27]. Ibid., 88–89.

[28]. Ibid., 84.

[29]. See Smith, *Creating Understanding*, chapters 11 and 12.

[30]. Ibid., 146ff.

[31]. John Gulick, *The Humanity of Cities* (New York: Bergin & Garvey, 1989), 2.

[32]. David Knoke and James H. Kuklinski, *Network Analysis*, Quantitative Application in Social Science, Paper 28 (Beverly Hills: Sage University, 1982), 13.

[33]. Ibid.

[34]. Everett M. Rogers and D. Lawrence Kincaid, *Communication Networks* (New York: Free Press, 1981), 127.

[35]. Ibid.

[36]. Claude S. Fischer, *To Dwell Among Friends* (Chicago: University of Chicago Press, 1982), 6, 179.

[37]. Lynne McCallister and Claude S. Fischer, "A Procedure for Studying Personal Networks," in *Applied NetWork Analysis*, eds., Ronald S. Burt and Michael J. Minor (Beverly Hills: Sage Publications, 1983), 78.

[38]. Mark Granovetter, "The Strength of Weak Ties," in *Social Structure and Network Analysis*, eds., Peter V. Marsden and Nan Lin (Beverly Hills: Sage Publications, 1982), 105.

[39]. See McConnell, *Maps, Masses and Mission*, 21.

[40]. Ibid.

[41]. Gulick, *Humanity of Cities*, xviii.

[42]. Claude S. Fischer, *The Urban Experience*, 2d ed. (San Diego: Harcourt Brace Jovanovich, 1984), 35–36.

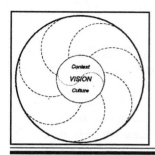

CHAPTER 3

Vision
A Necessity for Ministry

Vision emerged as one of the outstanding characteristics of the senior leadership in all the churches studied. All leaders have articulated a clear and simple vision, including home groups as an integral part of what the church is. To the degree that the vision is accepted by the members of the church, it becomes reality. Looking at their vision, I was impressed at how much context plays a part. Vision, though God-given, is birthed in a human context and profoundly affects all other factors. For that reason I have put it in the center of the graphic circles used in this book.

Of all the aspects of home group ministry, the concept of vision is most affected by culture. However, although vision derives from culture and is influenced by it, it also transcends culture. Vision must be more than copying a method developed in a different context. I was impressed by the insight of some Spaniard Christians as to what they perceived as an American method.

> They noted that 'cell groups' as we think of them are very American. That to a Spaniard he already has a cell group in terms of family and close friends. One of the elders wisely commented, "You Americans don't stay close to your family. Therefore, in ministry in the U.S. you have to have cell groups for the communion, counsel, encouragement, etc…In Spain, what we need is more emphasis on how to utilize the cell groups that already naturally exist." Maybe we are pushing too much method. Maybe we should step back and consider the philosophy of cell groups, guard these ideas and priorities, but find a more culturally appropriate means of applying it to local ministry.[1]

Vision changes. In all the churches researched, the vision has grown. Since vision involves the future, once it is reached it is no longer vision. Before the vision becomes reality, it is altered to include new factors, such as growth and changed context.

Vision Defined
The preferable future

In his introduction to *Visionary Leadership,* Burt Nanus reinforces this idea of vision being rooted in the context while looking beyond it.

> Vision also entails looking at your personal values and life purposes. In fact, for many great leaders, personal and organizational vision are one. Such leaders have an innate sense that their life is part of a larger purpose, which is tied to the organization or social movement they lead.[2]

His definition of vision is simple, succinct, and clear. "Quite simply," he says, *"a vision is a realistic, credible, attractive future for your organization"* [italics his].[3] Vision is an idea of what the future holds. But the right vision can so captivate and motivate people that they will strive to see it happen.

In his book, *The Power of Vision,* George Barna also defines vision: "Vision for ministry is a clear mental image of a preferable future imparted by God to his chosen servants and is based upon an accurate understanding of God, self and circumstances."[4] Barna's definition has an advantage for the Christian in that it takes a God-centered approach, while not forgetting the context which he calls "self and circumstances."

According to Nanus the visionary leader must skillfully balance four critical roles along two continua. The first is a present-to-future continuum and the second is the internal to external environment.

Leadership Roles[5]

External Environment

Spokesperson | Direction Setter

Present ——————————— Future

Coach | Change Agent

Internal Environment

Figure 1

The visionary leader will encompass the four attributes listed here. The senior leader sets the direction because of a clear vision of how the future should look. A successful direction setter will establish such a compelling vision that others in the organization will recognize its value and want to help make it happen. The senior leaders in the churches we researched have all motivated their followers to take ownership of the vision God has given.

The role of change agent is almost like a prophetic gift. The visionary leader must be able to anticipate developments in the outside world, understand their implications for the organization, and create a sense of priority in the members of the organization so they will act on the leader's vision.

The leader is also a skilled speaker who can communicate the vision to those outside the organization. As spokesperson, the leader will relate to other organizations with whom his or her group might partner to further the goals and aspirations of both parties.

Finally, the visionary leader is a person who can empower individuals inside the organization and build teamwork. The coach comes alongside the people through explanation, caring, and modeling to impart his or her vision. Coaches are committed to the success of their people.

The church leadership studied demonstrates the fourfold leadership roles. The vision of all the churches comes out of prayer. Each church senses it has discovered God's vision for its ministry in the local context. As the vision has grown, so has the church's ministry.

New Life Fellowship, Bombay
A vision for outreach in the multicultural context

Bombay is a multicultural and antagonistic context for the gospel. This setting could affect the church in a variety of ways, one of which would be to hunker down and defend what they have gained until the Lord returns. But vision is lost where fear takes over. The New Life Fellowship of Bombay has seen the multicultural context as God's gift to them. Through the multitude of social levels, people groups, and languages ("every nation, tribe, people, and language," Rev. 7:9), the church has an evangelistic vision to reach into every part of Bombay and also beyond. First, they want to plant a church in every unreached village in India by the end of the decade. Secondly, in Bombay they plan to establish 200,000 house churches averaging 10 members each, bringing the church membership to two million people by the year 2000.

These numbers were not arrived at in a vacuum. They spent time together asking the Lord for guidance. They also searched Scripture. One verse written on their vision statement is Psalm 2:8, "Ask of Me, and I will surely give the nations as thine inheritance, and the very ends of the earth as thy possession." So the vision does not cease with numbers for India alone. Their vision has changed over the years, and today they articulate a clear vision motivating many people to participate.

Pastor Willie Soans, one member of the four-man team that leads the church under Pastor Joseph, spoke of the important role of their senior pastor.

> Pastor Joseph is the visionary. He sees things we would never imagine. He is our father and we highly respect him. I have known him for 23 years. His character, doctrine, growth, humility, and zeal are all amazing.

Home groups are their key to reaching the city. They recognize that their greatest resource is people. In February 1995 when they wrote the first draft of their current vision statement, the people were distributed in 1,500 house groups and celebration centers in Bombay and 3,000 groups throughout India.

The vision is verbalized in a simple way to communicate to all people. The following, quoted from some of their unpublished material, summarizes their three-pronged vision:

1) Evangelizing the nations (ethnic groups) of India and beyond her borders

2) Establishing local, Spirit-filled, indigenous, self-supporting churches in cities, towns, villages, and tribal colonies in all States and Union Territories

3) Equipping saints to be disciples to do the work of the Lord Jesus Christ

Senior leadership, as well as many people in the home groups, can articulate this threefold vision. We met with several house group leaders and asked specifically about their vision for their ministry. More often than not they answered, "Evangelize, equip, and establish."

The senior leadership realizes that their vision of the "preferable future" must be communicated and understood by increasing numbers of people if it is to be fulfilled. While their office in Bombay serves the city and the nation, it is only a rented house. Their focus is on people, not buildings. Each state, while related to the home base, is independent. As Pastor Willie said, "We can develop a model in

Bombay but because it works in Bombay does not mean it will work in other contexts."

Vision has become lay driven. Many of the grass-roots-level leaders serve in more than one capacity. One person I talked with leads seven house groups. Sometimes a person will lead several house groups and also be responsible for a celebration center. These workers are usually volunteers and have another job with which they support themselves. One concern the senior leadership expressed is to protect families by limiting the number of groups a person may lead.

Christianity has purportedly existed in India since the days of the Apostle Thomas. Yet less than three percent of the population, according to Pastor S. Joseph, is Christian today. He did not in any way try to explain why that is the case. He simply sees those numbers as a challenge.

The vision at New Life Fellowship, Bombay, affected as it is by the antagonistic context and the diverse cultures, is focused on evangelism. Their choice of a small group strategy has several advantages. The house group concept keeps them mobile and flexible. New groups can start or people can be redistributed into other groups. Groups can form along language and cultural lines. The high level of commonality inside each house group helps the church reach a maximum number of the 400 people groups there.

New Life Community Church, Chicago
A vision for generation X—reaching through caring[6]

"This conference is not about home groups, it is not about methods, it is not about small groups or curriculum or programs," were the first words out of the mouth of Pastor Mark Jobe when he opened the October home group leader's conference for New Life Community Church, Chicago. He followed up by saying that the conference was about spiritual renewal of God's people, about bringing people to Christ and making them fully devoted followers of Christ. He reminded us that home groups without the moving of the Spirit of God are simply empty containers. The primary emphasis throughout the church is purpose, not method.

About 80 people met together for the all-day Saturday conference at a hotel near Chicago's O'Hare airport. All the home group leaders (shepherds), their assistant leaders (undershepherds), and potential group leaders joined the church staff for a day of practical training and spiritual encouragement with Pastor Mark leading most of the sessions.

The care element in their vision was obvious to us. Since we were researchers seeking to learn about this home group based church, Karen and I were invited to the conference. People received us warmly, showed interest in what we were doing, and invited us to attend their groups. As missionaries who visit many churches, we were impressed that an unusually high number of people greeted us with genuine love and interest, even before they knew we were missionaries.

The people of New Life Community Church, Chicago, often recite their purpose statement in the celebration service as well as in the home groups: "To be a family of love that cooperates with God in making fully devoted fruitful followers of Christ."

This purpose statement derives from their vision and mission statements, which I received in pre-published form from church leadership.

> The vision of New Life Community Church is to become a city-wide church that impacts Chicagoland at large by the equipping and mobilization of multitudes of disciples to ministry through an unleashed priesthood, unceasing prayer, and unlimited power resulting in the discipleship of urban masses.

> The mission is, "To glorify God by cooperating with his love in making disciples of all nations baptizing them in the name of the Father, Son, and Holy Spirit and teaching them to obey all things that Christ commanded."[7]

Pastor Mark and the senior leadership are asking God for one percent of the Chicago metropolitan population within the next 10 years. That would be about 33,000 people. Their vision is for a multi-ethnic church reflecting the diverse cultures of the city. Their vision also encompasses the need to cooperate with other churches in order to impact metropolitan Chicago. Within the next four years they expect their current attendance of 1,000 people to double to 2,000. Pastor Mark told me that vision is like a movie. It continually changes as the Lord gives greater faith and understanding.

In terms of the Nanus model discussed earlier, Pastor Mark is an excellent spokesperson and direction setter. His gifts of preaching and motivating people are clearly seen each Sunday morning when he gives the message. He is a dynamic speaker who keeps the congregation listening attentively for an hour. At the invitation people come forward to make life-changing decisions. Always other Christians come alongside to kneel and pray with them.

While the vision is one of growth (and that growth is through evangelism), I am impressed at how this actually works out in the day-to-day life of the church. This rugged inner city church is reaching people in the city, many who have been involved in lifestyles leading to self-destruction. They have lovingly and with great care challenged the loyalties of people involved in gangs, alcohol, or drug abuse. Genuine caring is shown to saved and unsaved alike.

The church population centers around the generation X or postmoderns, who respond positively to focused care and loving relationships. This generation grew up with MTV, AIDS, the national debt, abortion, and rampant divorce. They are said to be seeking heroes, a sense of community, and significance beyond material wealth. They desire involvement but have difficulty with long-term commitment.[8] They have grown up in a pluralistic context where all worldviews and religions are equally valid. Brokenness has been a significant part of their experience, and relationships are important for them.[9]

Evangelism, teaching, prayer, and worship are all a vital part of this church, but it is primarily through caring that the church manifests its vision.

Accra Churches
Accomplishing vision through structure

A woman in Accra told a story about what happened to her a few days previously in answer to prayer. She had enough fare to get to her destination, but she was not sure she had enough money to return home. She paid her fare to her destination. Then, having no other choice but to get as close as possible to home, she boarded a vehicle for her return. After some distance the vehicle broke down. Everyone got off and no one had to pay. The next vehicle went almost to her stop, then it halted. The conductor said the bus would go no farther, and everyone had to get off. The first half of the people who got off paid their fares. But then the conductor announced no one else would have to pay. The women was in the last half departing the bus, so she walked the remaining distance home with her return fare still in her pocket.

As seen in the woman's story, life in Accra can be uncertain, but the churches are growing rapidly. The Accra churches of all denominations studied are well organized and highly structured. Pastor Oladimeji has articulated a clear goal, "Our goal for Accra by the end of 1996 is 50 churches and 15 districts with 700 Home Caring Fellowship (HCF) locations." He only sets goals year by year. He has not articulated an over-arching vision statement but told me his philosophy. "We look at the city as if no other church is working there. Otherwise the problem is that everybody's job is nobody's job and the work will not be accomplished."

At the time he stated the goal, Deeper Life had 31 churches, 13 districts, and 600 HCFs in the city. Only one of the 31 churches has its own building. All others rent quarters, which is a significant challenge to the stated goals. Land is expensive to buy, and finding places to meet is becoming a problem.

The home group system (HCF) is essential to the accomplishment of their vision. They have had few mass campaigns or rallies in the past 10 years. They rely on the home groups for evangelistic contacts, spiritual growth, and care. To emphasize the importance of the small group ministry Pastor Oladimeji made this statement.

Leadership must throw its weight behind this kind of ministry for it to succeed. Don't give it to young people. We have to train adults as leaders to show we are serious. The leaders are mature adults.

Adults lead when a work is serious. This is significant throughout Africa. Another twist on that truth came from the Rev. Kwame's Kotobabi Church in Accra. In all their home groups they have a home group leader and a home group supervisor. The supervisor is older and acts as an advisor or counselor to the home group leader and to the entire group as needed. The home group leader may have more education and small group leader skills, but the supervisor has age and the wisdom that accompanies it.

Location is an especially important aspect of home group ministry in Accra. Because of financial constraints and transportation difficulties, people must meet near where they live. While logistics is a stated reason for their emphasis on locally based home groups, another reason surfaced with further questioning. The home groups are seen as an outpost of the Kingdom of God, reclaiming territory from Satan. They are like little guerrilla units reaching the lost, training them, and sending them back to the battle.

All the Accra churches appear to be highly organized. Military metaphors abound. However, the home groups are not as rigid as such a metaphor might imply. They acknowledge the warfare but also realize it is won with weapons of love and care. I asked people in several groups why they attended. Many said they attended a particular group because it met close to their home. But others answered concerning spiritual need. "I couldn't pray or read or write on my own. But since I came to this group I have learned to pray and I can read the Bible." "Sometimes I need explanations and I come here where others help me. If I don't turn up, others check on me and encourage me."

The Rt. Rev. Gbewonyo, a retired military man, pushed the military metaphor further as he talked about the unit, which is divided into platoons, each with a commander. "Every member," he stated, "should be equipped and have the confidence to go out and spread the word. When that is done by many people the enemy is at more of a disadvantage than if only the officers went out." He ended with a quote, "Hard training, easy battle."

The vision of the church here seems to manifest itself in organizational structure. But they are reaching the unreached. Why does organizational structure play such a large role? Two reasons come to mind. First is the hierarchical structure of the society at large (in Hofstede's terminology, a high power distance). A second reason might be a context that is unstable. Stability within the church and cell structure as seen through a tight organization may add a sense of outward stability to the inward stability people develop in Christ as they grow spiritually.

Moscow Churches
Prayer is central to the vision

I asked Pastor Pavel if he had written down his vision or if he had some kind of purpose statement or goals. His response was informative in terms of culture affecting vision. "No," he stated, "I was raised in communism and we avoid documents. I repeat the vision to leaders every Saturday at the leaders' meeting but I do it verbally. People are tired of slogans and they mistrust them."

That is not to say that he and his wife, Marina, have no vision. They have an inherent grasp of what vision is—that "preferable future." The aftereffects of communist culture impact the home group ministry in Moscow. While it has not thwarted vision, it has certainly affected the way it is communicated. But the Rosa Church is young and has a sense of being guided by the Holy Spirit as vision develops.

Pavel and Marina's vision for home group ministry came out of the church's rapid growth. They preferred a smaller church, but they also recognized their responsibility to minister to the many new people coming to Christ and to their church. In the home groups people receive the necessary pastoral care and develop spiritual gifts.

Prayer and worship are key elements of their vision for small groups as well as the celebration service. Pastor Pavel emphasized, "People want to come together to worship and praise God. They don't want to go home." In the home groups we visited, large blocks of time were spent in prayer, sometimes as much as two hours.

Sergei, a zone leader, told me that he receives his vision for the zone from the pastor. He meditates on the vision, and then he communicates it to the home group leaders in his zone. He asserted that the goal in the home group is to meet the Lord. In the large celebration services that they have twice a week, in the Saturday leaders' meeting, and in the home group, the goal is always to meet God.

That may help explain their somewhat unstructured program that is more free-flowing than others we studied. At every level of church life, the focus was less on what the program should be and more on waiting upon God. Years of communism taught these people the importance of waiting and being sensitive to God's leading. Teaching, caring, and evangelizing all take place, but these activities come out of a center where prayer is the focus.

When I asked what the leaders were doing differently now, one remarked, "I felt God wanted less of me and more of Himself in the meeting." When they started they had a more formal, programmed approach. The leader prepared a lesson, and the time was allotted to specified activities. But now they bring less human preparation and seek to come prepared by the Spirit of God.

The near vision is to serve people in the zone. They are concerned for the poor and have worked through government agencies to locate needy populations in their area. They have gathered needed goods and distributed them, as well as sharing the gospel with these people. While none of the people who benefited from their gifts of mercy have yet come to the home groups, the groups in the zone have grown more since those efforts took place.

Pastor Pavel's greater vision is for each zone to have its own celebration service, with all the zones coming together once a month. Development of the zones requires leaders. The pastor is spending much of his time working with zone leaders who will one day be pastors of those areas. Pastor Pavel sees the home groups at the core of the expansion process.

> Home groups are organisms. They will always exist. The
> large service will never replace home groups. We need to be a
> large church in a large city. Why? First, we are called a sect.
> That is how society sees us—large or small. But because we are
> large, people listen to us. Also, because we are large we have
> some influence with the government.

Both Pastor Pavel and Marina spoke of hindrances to fulfillment of the vision. They feel that years of communism and the pervasive influence of the Russian Orthodox Church have given people an incomplete view of the Bible and biblical Christianity. Another diffi- culty is that many people do not stay long. They feel that one reason for this is an inadequate communication of their vision. This is a young church and they are still learning.

However, as their vision develops, they are making a difference in Moscow. People are seeing others who know God, and they are drawn to them and to their God. I asked Masha, a zone leader and also a home group leader, what the most important elements were in home group ministry. She responded, "That everyone should know God. That requires evangelism and unity in the home group."

In every meeting large and small, the longest single block of time was devoted to prayer. The current prayer emphasis seems to reflect new freedoms and old tradition. New freedoms have resulted in the desire for more openness in their prayer and witness. But prayer was also important in past traditions and now has taken on new life.

Caracas Churches
A vision for teaching brings God's Word to increasing numbers

Pastor Liévano talked about his vision and in so doing articulated the struggles of a midsized church in the megacity. The church he pastors is not new, with traditions and programs that people are used to and expect. The city of Caracas is the least responsive of the cities in this study. He stated:

> We only have one property. We are going to tear down the current structure and build a hall to seat 500 people. We want to plant many churches. We already have seven. Our goal is to have ten churches. This is all with only one pastor. If we had more full-time pastors we could have more churches. Of course, the ten churches should plant new ones.

The current congregation is already close to 400 people but they meet in a rented hall. The church building is small and the largest they can build on the existing property would be a hall for 500 people. Land is expensive, beyond the reach of this church. Only one of the new churches has land, and that church is outside the city.

Currently the church's home group ministry has grown to 25 groups. Pastor Liévano envisions it growing to a hundred with 1,000 people in the groups. Further growth he sees coming through new churches that will be planted. His concept of new churches is similar to that of Rev. Deegbe's satellite churches in Accra. In both cases the churches planted are integrally related to the mother church. The people all belong to the same church, and the leadership has responsibility for all the congregations.

His vision is for growth and it is helpful to see how he envisions that growth and what factors are driving it. He has studied the megacity and has become intimately acquainted with Caracas. In a document he wrote, *Grupos Basico De Discipulado Cristiano (Basic Groups of Christian Discipleship)*, Liévano begins with a statement of the problems of the megacities. A summary of these are:

1) The church does not go, it says come.
2) Believers must travel long distances to get to church.
3) Transportation is complicated and difficult.
4) Parking is a problem.
5) Evangelism time is wasted traveling to the church.
6) Church buildings are small.
7) The believer does not know where to start evangelizing[10]

Liévano proposes the home group (they call them "Basic Groups") as the solution to reaching the city and discipling the believers. The core of his vision came to light as he carefully defined each part of the *Basic Groups of Christian Discipleship* (GBDC). He pointed out that a disciple is one who receives the teaching of his Master and follows Him. Jesus chose 12 men to constitute a GBDC. This organization, established by the Lord Himself for his earthly ministry, transformed the world. The GBDC is not only social, not only for prayer, although both are indispensable, but also for Bible study, which is one of the main characteristics of the GBDC.[11] With Jesus and the 12 as the prototype home group, the focus is on discipleship, which he defines as teaching.[12] Although their home groups include caring, evangelizing, prayer, and worship, teaching is at the center.

While Dios Admirable church is a good example of an older midsized church, it is worth looking at the vision of another church in the city, Las Acacias church. This church is older but is also the largest and fastest growing evangelical church in the city. Pastor Sam Olson made a succinct statement of vision and focus that embodies the basic idea of all the senior pastors in this study. He said, "The city became our focus, not the church."

Sam Olson sees home groups as the major factor in turning the focus of his church from being self-directed or inward, to being other-directed, or outward. "Home groups began in our church as one program among many. Today they are the beachhead for the whole church." Their church is adding about 150 home groups annually.

His vision for the next five years is to see the central service grow to 10,000–12,000 people requiring five to eight worship services on Sunday. They expect to have 20–25 additional city churches that will be related to the mother church. This growth is primarily driven by the home groups. He believes that violence, revolution, and catastrophes might impact the ministry of the church. Because of that they are developing a plan whereby the church can function entirely in the home groups.

The groups I attended in this church were similar to those in the Dios Admirable church. Both churches emphasized teaching, and most of their time was taken up with Bible study. Evangelism was an outgrowth of teaching ministry here.

Why do the churches in Caracas have such a focus on Bible study? Two possible reasons come to mind. First, the educational level is high. The questionnaires bear this out. Of all the populations studied, the amount of graduate degrees and higher education was highest in Caracas. Many of these people have spent their lives in some form of study and research. They understand how to study and how it should yield positive results in their lives. A second reason was suggested to me by a colleague. The Roman Catholic openness to Bible study in the vernacular is a relatively new phenomenon. The effects of Vatican II have only recently come to Venezuela. Openness to the Bible and understanding its contents leads to more evangelistic contacts. Therefore, teaching is the key component even of the evangelistic home groups.

Key Points

• Vision must derive from the leadership's clear biblical understanding of the church (ecclesiology), with home groups seen as an integral part of church.

• When leadership has a sense that the vision comes from God, they are aware that his supernatural power will bring the vision to fruition.

• Vision functions in the local context with its roots in reality.

• Vision must be communicated effectively and repeatedly from the senior leadership to everyone who has a part in the home group ministry.

• Vision focus must be outward—beyond the church's membership and building.

• The vision core may vary—evangelism, caring, prayer, teaching, organization, worship.

• Vision is long-term but grows and changes over time, especially in its implementation.

Endnotes

1.   From an unpublished E-mail forum for Christian workers in Spain, 47D, 22 April 1996.

2.   Burt Nanus, *Visionary Leadership* (San Francisco: Jossey-Bass, 1992), xxv.

3.   Ibid., 8.

4.   George Barna, *The Power of Vision* (Ventura, CA: Regal Books, 1992), 28.

5.   Burt Nanus, *Visionary Leadership*, 1992, 11–15.

6.   Generation X, those born between 1961 and 1981, is defined by Kim Macalister in *HRMagazine* 35, no. 5 (May 1994): 66.

7.   New Life Community Church, unpublished document, (Chicago: n.d.).

8.   See Kim Macalister, "The X Generation," *HRMagazine* 35, no. 5 (May 1994): 66–71.

9.   See Andres Tapis, "Reaching the First Post-Christian Generation," *Christianity Today* 38, no. 10 (September 12, 1994). Tapis analyzes Generation X from the Christian perspective with a view to ministry.

10.   Francisco R. Liévano, *Grupos Basicos De Discipulado Christiano* [*Basic Groups of Christian Discipleship*], (Caracas: Dios Admirable Church, n.d.).

11.   Ibid., 5–6.

12.   Ibid., 7.

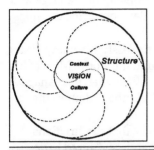

CHAPTER 4

Structure
Implementing the Vision

"We are children of God and we should be involved in the expansion of the Kingdom of Heaven," asserted one small group administrator. Another quickly echoed, "We are fulfilling the Great Commission." I was in Accra, Ghana, attending a meeting of district coordinators and zone leaders, and I had asked them why they became involved in such ministry. Their vision was compelling. But it was their structure that provided the means to accomplish the vision.

One Minute Manager coauthor and management specialist Ken Blanchard once responded to the question, "Is vision overrated?"

I don't think it is. But vision alone can't get it done. Too often we spend all our time on vision and none on implementation. At some point you've got to move.[1]

The way vision works out in the world is largely a function of what I call structure, or the way a group is organized. While goals come from vision, structure or organization shows how the goals can be reached. Structure deals with home group ministry on three levels:

   (1)   structure within the home group
   (2)   structure between home groups
   (3)   structure between the large group and small groups

I wrote earlier of the biblical relationship between ministries in the large group and in the small group. It is not enough to have only cell or home groups. In the Bible these entities are found as a part of a larger group, a congregation meeting for worship. Though culture and history play their part in forming the specific structure, the small group–large group relationship is maintained in all the churches in this study. In fact, the large group is extremely important to the vitality of the small group.

Authors writing on the subject of cell group or small group ministries have created many definitions—each adding something to our understanding. I believe an operational definition of a biblical home group must take into account the relationship of the large and small groups. Biblically, each played a part in developing the disciples' spiritual life.

Dr. Ralph Neighbour, Jr., has worked tirelessly for many years facilitating cell church birth and growth around the world. Most of his work describes what cell churches are and how they can be managed. In an early edition of *Cell Church Magazine*, Neighbour defines the cell church:

> A "cell group" church is built on the fact that all Christians are ministers, and there is no "professional clergy" hired to do the work of ministry. According to Ephesians 4, God has provided "gifted men" to equip "believers who are gifted" to do the work of ministry. Such a church is not built around the assembly of all its members, but the clustering of believers to become "Basic Christian Communities" which do the work of ministry from cell groups that meet in homes. These cells then cluster for area congregation activities, and assemble regionally for "celebration" times. The life of the church is in its cells, not in a building. While it has weekly worship events, the focus of the church is in the home cells.[2]

This definition considers that church life is focused on the small group while being a part of the larger group, the worshiping congregation. His definition finds its roots in biblical data. I have developed my own definition incorporating some of the elements of the above and seeking to be faithful to the biblical structure relating small and large groups.

> A home group consists of 5 to 15 people meeting together regularly to fulfill the one-another commands of Scripture, while being integrally related to a local church, and having an outward focus on the world with the overarching purpose of glorifying God.

When we look at a large urban area, we wonder how the gospel can penetrate into all those apartments, barrios, people groups, and neighborhoods. It is through structure that the task is divided into smaller pieces and made more doable.

The most carefully structured churches of this study are in Accra. Among those, the churches of the Deeper Christian Life Ministry have the highest level of organization. Because of this, I am devoting considerable space to describing their organization.

Accra Churches
Church structures in a hierarchical society

The importance of structure for the Accra churches is reinforced by information from the questionnaire, particularly question 23 discussed in the leadership chapter. Sixty-six percent of the Accra respondents chose answer 'a,' indicating that order is the key value in the ideal home group. That percentage is more than double any of the other sites.

Accra — Deeper Christian Life Ministry
A structure trying to anticipate needs

The Deeper Christian Life Ministry in Accra has published a booklet, *Biblical Basis For Home Caring Fellowship*, in which job descriptions are given for each leadership level. Adult ministries in this denomination are based on the home groups. The first division is based on gender. Adult groups and leadership levels are divided between men and women. They also have children and youth home groups, not divided along gender lines.

All home groups in the Deeper Christian Life Ministry meet on the same day (Sunday), at the same hour, and study the same material. The meetings last 1½ hours, beginning at 5:30 P.M. and ending at 7:00 P.M. The structure for each meeting is given in all the publications. Pages 19–20 of the above mentioned booklet show one example:

a. Opening prayer   3 minutes
b. Choruses   5 minutes
c. Testimonies   10 minutes

   Nature [of testimonies]: What God does for an individual, especially within the period of attendance of the Deeper Life Programme.

   Control: The Home Leader is expected to control the testimonies or run commentaries as the case may be on all as need be.

d. Follow-up report and prayer requests   12 minutes
e. Praise, worship, and intercession   15 minutes
f. Bible discussion   30 minutes
g. Prayers (on what we studied)   5 minutes
h. Follow-up schedules   7 minutes
i. Benediction   3 minutes[3]

In the groups we attended, this format was followed with little variation. An important aspect of being a leader, Pastor Oladimeji told me, concerns the use of time. "Honor it. We feel that we must have precise time management. The time in each group is carefully planned and they all use it the same way."

The material used in the Bible discussion was the same for each group and adapted for children or young people. Much of the material used in this church comes from the mother organization in Lagos, Nigeria. However, Pastor Oladimeji also prepares material for the home groups and leadership training.

Leadership Levels. The following shows the levels of leadership in the men's track, but there is a similar women's track. The women's home groups have women leaders, who in turn are led by female area, zone, and district leaders.

Leadership Levels for Deeper Christian Life Home Group Ministry

National Supervisor leads the 12 districts in Accra

↑

District Leader supervises 4 zones

↑

Zone Leader supervises 4 to 6 areas

↑

Area Leader supervises 4 to 6 home groups

↑

Home Group Leader (Approximately 600 home groups)

Figure 1

The first level of leadership is the home group leader. The book mentioned earlier gives a list of 31 duties and responsibilities of home leaders, a tribute to the refinement of their organization. Without naming all 31 responsibilities, the list can be divided into the following categories:

1. Responsibilities to the people in the home group
2. Personal holiness
3. Administrative responsibilities
4. Looking for and developing new leaders

Thirteen of these responsibilities can be characterized as administrative. Record keeping is important, because in this way superiors can deal with any problems or changes. The home leader is under the authority of the area and zone leaders, and an upward line of communication is expected. A report giving a summary of attendance, general trend of events in the home group, and a record of visitors and problems encountered is to be made immediately after each week's meeting.

The home group leader must always be present to lead the group. However, the home leader can "notify the zone leader at least seven days before any absence except in a case of emergency." Home leaders have responsibilities to keep their spiritual life on track. They also have duties to those in the home group in terms of visitation as well as teaching, since they are expected to visit every member each week.

The next level of authority is the area leader. Most area leaders now supervise only four to six groups, and they are seeking to make four the maximum. Area leaders visit each home group every week. They spend only 10 or 15 minutes in each session before moving to the next, but the visit is organized so they see a different aspect of each group each week.

Few people own cars. The home groups are within walking distance of each other so the home group leader and the area leader can usually manage these visits without public transportation. These visits (even though required) bring about a high level of personal contact. When I met with 30 or 40 of the top church leaders, they agreed that though the system sounds rather strict, the emphasis is on developing networks of caring relationships to evangelize and make disciples.

Area leaders meet regularly with home group leaders and then summarize their reports for the zone leader. The area leader may at times substitute for a home group leader in case of an absence. Through reports, visits, and conversations with the home group leader, the area leader identifies problems. This person will then either deal with the problem at that level or bring it to the zone leader, the next level of organization.

One of the major tasks of the area leader is to work with the home group leader to decide when and where a new group will be started. The home leader has the best sense of timing about when a group is ready to multiply, but the decision is not made alone. The area leader works with both the zone leader and home group leader to decide who will lead the new group. One of the major obstacles in creating new home groups is lack of leadership. Although they do have an excellent system for training leaders, the ministry is growing so fast they are having difficulty keeping up with that growth.

Zone leaders are responsible for 4 to 6 area leaders, and they summarize the reports of the area leaders for the district coordinator. They also visit various home groups although they will not visit every home group in their zone.

The Deeper Christian Life Ministry has divided Accra into 12 districts, each with a district coordinator. The district coordinator is a pastor of that entire area of the city. He supervises the zone leaders and area leaders in his district. He summarizes the reports that come to him and gives them to the national coordinator, Pastor Oladimeji. The district coordinators (or the zone leaders within the district) pastor the local churches in their districts.

Within two days of the Sunday home group meetings, the district coordinators put their summarized reports on the desk of the national coordinator. Information gathered and summarized in the weekly reports includes attendance, offering, number of visits made, people saved, and a description of any problems that may have occurred.

Meetings. Besides the weekly home group meetings, people meet in their local churches three Sundays a month for worship. On the fourth Sunday three districts combine for a celebration service. For the fifth Sunday all the districts meet together at central headquarters. The reason for the combined services, according to Pastor Oladimeji, is to maintain the highest possible standards throughout the ministry.

Following is a schedule for a typical week:

1. Sunday morning—'Search the Scriptures' service
2. Sunday afternoon—home groups
3. Monday—zone level Bible study
4. Wednesday—Pastor Oladimeji meets with district coordinators and zone leaders
5. Thursday evening—citywide 'Revival and Evangelism Training' service
6. Every other Saturday—home group leader training
7. Alternate Saturdays—door-to-door evangelism

Money. With the exception of the national coordinator and some limited office help, this ministry is entirely run by laity. No one receives remuneration. All the churches rent halls for their Sunday worship services. Currently, the national headquarters is also in a rented facility. They are in the process of building a central building for the monthly district meetings. That facility will house their offices and be the central location for various social ministries.

Offerings taken in the home groups are carefully counted and reported to the higher level. These gifts are put in a central bank account to meet financial needs of members. The home group leader is the first level to approve a member's need. From there it goes up to the district coordinator who will see that the need is met. Though it sounds rather laborious, the process can be accomplished quickly.

The structure I have spoken of here may seem excessive but the church is growing rapidly. Beckham speaks of the predictability factor.

When we hear the words 'predictability' and 'constancy of purpose,' we often think 'control' and 'loss of freedom.' Some may ask, "If every cell follows the same format, materials, and tracks, doesn't this limit the work of the Holy Spirit? Isn't this just another cookie cutter approach to church life?" This is not so! Our danger today is the lack of a predictable framework. Constant change only gives the illusion of progress and freedom.[4]

The Deeper Christian Life Ministry with its high level of predictability has made it possible for a larger number of members to move into home group leadership. When people know exactly what to do and expect, they are more willing to become leaders.

While the Deeper Life Christian Ministry is completely based on home groups, the Baptists and the Evangelical Presbyterian Churches of Ghana are churches in the more traditional mold who are implementing home group ministries to cope with growth. They use different terminology and are less structured.

Accra — Calvary Baptist Church
Combining Ghanaian and Western structural forms
for a creative structure

The Baptists call their home groups sheepfolds. They have 200 sheepfolds distributed in seven areas. Sheepfold size varies from five or six to more than 30. Pastor Fred Deegbe indicated that about half the congregation attended one of these groups. While the church is not totally home group based, the leadership is seeking to increase their numbers and importance to the church body.

Karen and I attended the opening service of a new satellite congregation. About 30 home groups in a local area of Accra came together to form this new congregation. On that first Sunday 299 people were present.

The difference between a satellite congregation and a new church is seen by how the new group relates to the mother church. In the satellite congregation model the members of the satellite are still members of the mother church. A new church is totally independent of the mother church. This independence has created problems in the past. Some of the churches have moved into areas of doctrine and practice that the Baptist leadership felt were counterproductive and even dysfunctional. With a satellite congregation the relationship between the mother church and the satellite is close and should inhibit any move into error. Also, because Calvary Baptist Church is a prestigious downtown church, many people do not want to sever their ties to this church. By forming satellite congregations, they can alleviate this reluctance.

Calvary Baptist has four satellite congregations including the newly opened one we attended. The pastors see home group ministry as key to future growth. They have even changed their Sunday school. Previously it was divided along either age or interest groups. Now they have divided it along geographical areas. People who live close to each other attend Sunday school together. In the beginning there was some resistance. However, one of the benefits has been that people are developing stronger relationships with people who live nearby. When someone is absent or has difficulties, another person from the Sunday school can more easily follow up the contact. Since they made this change the Sunday school has doubled, and Sunday school classes are becoming more like home groups.

Sheepfolds include both men and women. Furthermore, both men and women lead the mixed groups. People in the groups are brought together by geography and language. They live near each other and speak the same language. The meetings are not highly structured but include praise, prayer, and Bible study. Bible discussion normally takes about two-thirds of any given meeting. Structures are in place for leaders to receive formal training and to relate to each other.

Accra — Evangelical Presbyterian Church of Ghana
The traditional approach to church structure

The principal difference between this church and the others in Ghana is that people usually come into the home groups through the larger Sunday celebration service. These churches are the first I have found that make this direction the normal process. People in the home groups invite their friends to the Sunday meeting, which is more evangelistic. Some, however, do come directly to the home group meeting.

Once people make a commitment to Christ, receive baptismal instruction, and are baptized, they are assigned to a home group. The churches now require their members to be a part of a home group and they take attendance. The spiritual and material care happens at the home group level, making it imperative for church members to be a part of the small group. The average or ideal size is 12–15, at most 20, since one-half or a little more come at any one time. Therefore, the number of people in the home group will be similar to that of the other Accra churches—ten or less.

After a visit to a home group the leader gave me a somewhat typical schedule they use. A welcome and time of praise and worship takes up approximately the first 17 minutes; Bible study about 35; testimonies, prayer, and offering another 25; and refreshments and announcements occupy the last 13 or so minutes.

All the Accra churches struggle with time constraints. Public transportation is not always reliable, which often makes people late for home group meetings. This engenders an attitude that says, "I won't be on time even if I try, so I might as well not worry about it." The leaders are trying to encourage people to be on time.

Another problem is getting people to leave their current group to begin a new group. People who have been together for several months have grown in their personal relationship and do not want to leave to start another group. Dr. Osie-Bonsu told of a solution tried by the Baptists. They have a home group called Genesis. When they were ready to multiply, they called the next group Genesis 2. After that they started Genesis 3. By maintaining continuity of name, they have maintained a feeling of relational continuity with the original group and with each other.

Another difficulty in multiplying new groups is that of locating places to meet. Houses are small and often have extended families living in them. There is also the problem of trust. House residents are not eager to show their goods to strangers who may come into the home group. People have been victimized by thieves who pretended that they desired to be a part of the home group.

The Accra churches all launched home group ministries to deal with the rapid growth they were already experiencing. The home groups, while helping with the necessary pastoral care of the believers, have also accelerated the growth patterns into new areas.

Caracas Churches
Mature and basic structures appropriate for the task

One mistake made in ministry is that of trying to transfer to a full-blown home group system without taking the time to work out a structure for the given context. The Caracas and Accra churches in this study are older churches and are the most well organized. They have developed structures that work in their contexts because they have had time to work out the system.

Nelly Sanchez, the home group coordinator of the Dios Admirable Church in Caracas, leads a home group in her own home, directs one of the church's four zones, and coordinates the entire ministry. She recently retired from an administrative post at a university and now has time to give to this work. She uses the term apprentice for the home group 'assistant' leader. This person is there not only to assist the leader but also to prepare to lead a future group. Nelly personally oversees five home groups and visits each one at least every six weeks. She phones the home group leaders each week.

Each home group leader turns in weekly one-page reports. Attendance, number of visitors, number of people doing one-on-one discipleship, and number of people in the baptism class are key elements of the report. The area leader summarizes the reports of his or her home group leaders each month and gives them to the home group coordinator. She sets annual goals, and these reports help her ascertain progress toward those goals.

The four zones are called tribes within the church structure. So far they have the tribes of Judah, Levi, Ephraim, and Reuben. This system is similar to the Baptist churches in Accra. This 'tribal' structure has implications in two areas. First, it gives the home group ministry a tie to the Bible. People feel a part of their spiritual forebears. Second, it draws the church together. The tribe is a network of home groups. The tribes together constitute a nation, which is the church. The home group ministry of Dios Admirable also has meetings for prayer and to train home group leaders.

The modest structure of Dios Admirable gives way to that of Las Acacias, the megachurch. There the 400 home groups are divided among 14 sectors. Each sector is divided into parishes that are in turn divided into nuclei. With some help from Mirtha Villafañe, I have drawn a schematic of what her sector, Sector Este, looks like structurally.

Structure of Sector Este

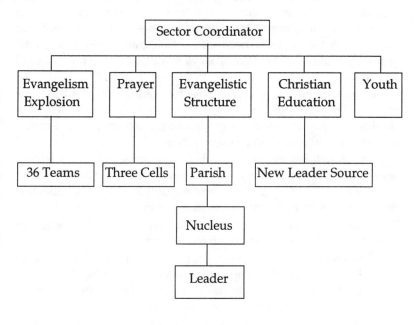

Figure 2[5]

The home group ministry shows up under the evangelistic structure. However, each heading contributes to and is a part of the home group growth. A nucleus consists of two to five home groups, a parish has two to five nuclei, and the sector has two to five parishes. The sector coordinator reports to the church's general manager. As the ministry grows new sectors are created.

Mirtha has been a sector coordinator for three years. She came up through the ranks beginning as an assistant home group leader shortly after she was saved seven years ago. Presently she oversees 36 home groups with a goal to grow to 92 by next year. These numbers include the three youth home groups that were recently added in her sector and which she hopes will grow to ten next year. This church has its young people in the home group structure instead of the traditional youth group.

Chicago — New Life Community Church
Carefully defined and simple

This church has 50 home groups with new ones being added regularly. Zone pastors who are full-time or part-time pastoral staff oversee the home groups. One of the three zones is a youth zone. Zones have followed along social networks, not geography, so when a home group multiplies, the new group stays in the same zone regardless of location.

In addition to a youth zone, New Life Church divides the home groups into the following categories: general groups (adults, both singles and couples), women's groups, men's groups, Spanish-speaking groups, and a support recovery group.

The church has defined the roles of the home group ministry in several of their publications. By carefully defining the basic vocabulary, they have added clarity in terms of church focus. The following definitions are from *Renewal Through Restoration*:

Zone Pastor	Full-time person who oversees a zone of home groups composed of up to 350 people.
Team Leader	Leader who assists the zone pastor in supporting a cluster of up to five home groups (about 75 people). The team leader will usually be an intern working towards full-time ministry.
Shepherd	Person who leads a weekly home group of 6–16 people. The shepherd watches over the spiritual health and growth of the group. The term home group leader is often used for this person.
Undershepherd	Person in training to lead a home group. He or she assists the shepherd in leading and caring for the home group.
Apprentice	Person preparing to be an undershepherd. He or she is usually completing training material.
Mentor	Person in the group who is discipling a younger believer. All those involved in the above roles should be active mentors.
Co-mentor	Person who is assisting a mentor in the discipleship of a young believer. Usually, these people are gaining practical experience before they begin mentoring.
Student disciple	Young disciple in a discipleship relationship with an older believer who is teaching him or her the spiritual basics.[6]

Good church structure frees people to do ministry. It should not be used to control and suppress. Finding the appropriate structure is a process, not a ready-made package that a church can open and apply to their situation.

New Life Community Church publishes a list of the home groups in their Sunday bulletin. It lists the home group leader, day and time of meeting, and a phone number. Each week at the celebration service the senior pastor and the zone leaders encourage the congregation to participate in home groups. According to their office staff, 65 percent of the adult and youth membership participate in one of these small groups.

Moscow — Rosa Church
A new church with a structure in process

Rosa, the newest church in the study, is in the process of developing structure. Their congregation of 1,200 to 1,400 attendees is divided into 65 home groups within 10 Moscow zones. About one-half of the congregation participates in a home group. Their meetings tend to be smaller than others with six to eight people considered optimal. When a group grows to 12 they try to multiply.

New freedoms in Russia give the church the authority to meet publicly. Home groups are not really new; rather it is the large celebration service meeting openly without constraint that is new. This fact affects home group ministry. The tradition of the large Orthodox churches predate modern communism, and people desire to return to these large group gatherings. Some Orthodox churches have introduced home groups as they, too, realize the importance of the small group–large group relationship. So the small gathering is a place where people can enter and move on to the church (the large group), but it also works the other way. People can first enter the church through the large group and later enter the smaller.

This church has looked at models from America and Korea and prayerfully considered how these examples might work for them. They recognize the need to refine their current system. Beckham gives examples of churches that developed their home group programs. They all moved ahead, faltered, regrouped, and advanced again. Home groups failed, especially in the early stages.

According to Karen Hurston, who grew up in Yoido Full Gospel Church, this initial group of 200 processed through several cycles before the infrastructure for the remnant was complete. She comments that 'with few exceptions, those first groups collapsed.' Dr. Cho then gave attention to special problems which had caused the groups to fail and proceeded to strengthen the cell infrastructure.[7]

The Rosa Church is transitioning to home groups. However, because the church is young and the mentality already changed to the home group style, they should be able fairly quickly to find a structure that works in their context.

The dependable and inexpensive public transportation does create an interesting wrinkle in the structure of this church. Home groups are put together in geographical zones. However, a person living in one zone can attend a home group outside that zone because of the desire to be with friends. But I did not find any groups where the majority of people come from another zone.

Bombay — New Life Fellowship
A structure for the fast-growing megachurch

The Rosa Church in Moscow is not the only church in transition. This megachurch in the megacity, New Life Fellowship of Bombay, is making some interesting changes in its infrastructure in order to better deal with its size. I will describe what the leaders are transitioning toward, even though it is not yet completely in place.

The church is currently divided into 25 zones each with its own zone pastor. They are in the process of dividing the city into 15 zones based on population. Each zone will have approximately one million people. The zone pastor will have more autonomy in the way ministry is done within that zone. He will also have to recruit the workers, teachers, and evangelists that he needs.

Funding, both collections and disbursements, will be kept within the zone. Each zone will locate its own celebration centers and keep its own records. Although it sounds as if each zone is an autonomous local church, that is not quite the case. The members and leaders still belong to the New Life Fellowship Church of Bombay. Also, the five-man senior staff will continue to lead the citywide church.

Four senior leaders currently supervise four Bombay regions. The new structure frees them up to use their gifts in any area of the city or nation. Because their gifts vary, this should strengthen the church citywide as their strengths are shared across all 15 zones.

Bombay is creatively using computers for the Kingdom. Each of the 15 zones will be linked to the others via a computer connection to be used for two purposes. First, prayer needs will be shared across the zones via the computer linkup. Plans call for a 24-hour prayer chain in each center. A second use of these regionalized computer centers will be to keep track of the home groups and people. Because new groups start daily, it is difficult to know how many are functioning at any point in time.

One pastor who is already doing this showed me his computer printouts. He knows the needs in the groups from the printouts. He takes the necessary action in terms of giving help, putting out a prayer request, or signaling the appropriate person to act. Because this church functions in a large modern city, the high-tech option is viable, even desirable. This system can also help the leadership keep track of the various language and people groups inside their home groups.

Questionnaire Evaluation (see Appendix B)

I asked how people viewed the relationship of the cell group to the church in question 22. Most of the responses were either 'a'—The cell group is the church, or 'b'—The cell group is supervised by the church. Accra (78 percent), Bombay (86 percent) and Caracas (81 percent) were similar with a clear majority going to 'b'. Respondents in those groups clearly perceived a strong relationship between the larger church body and the smaller home group.

The Chicago church gave 38 percent to 'a' and 59 percent to 'b.' While the percentage is not as overwhelming as above, most people acknowledge a strong relationship between the large church body and the home group.

Moscow had the opposite results with 'a' at 86 percent and 'b' at 12 percent. The Moscow church is enjoying new freedoms in a once highly structured culture. I observed loyalty to both the large congregation and the small home group, but their emotional church life takes place in the small groups.

Question 32 deals with the perceived relationship of the cell group leaders with each other and with the local church leadership. The two main categories were (1) structural and organizational relationships, and (2) personal or informal relationships. A higher than normal percentage of respondents did not answer, but from those who did, Accra had 48 percent organizational and 25 percent personal. That fits with Accra's strong structural orientation. Chicago tilted in the opposite direction with 27 percent organizational and 41 percent more relational, which was similar to Bombay (19 and 55 percent). Moscow was 5 percent organizational and 74 percent relational, again fitting the loose structure of the Rosa church. Caracas was quite evenly divided.

Key Points

- Structure comes out of vision and enables vision to happen.
- The purpose of structure is to manage and facilitate ministry, not to control it.
- Structure grows and develops appropriate to ministry needs. Changes and adjustments are normal.
- Structure is affected by context—transportation, political context, national traditions, and social level.
- Optimum home group size varies with culture.
- All home groups in this study were a part of a larger celebration or local church service.
- Structure provides prototypes that allow for sustained growth.

Endnotes

[1].   Ken Blanchard, "Turning Vision Into Reality, an interview with Ken Blanchard," *Leadership* (Spring 1996): 118.

[2].   Ralph Neighbour, Jr., "What is a 'Cell Group' Church?" *Cell Church Magazine*, vol. 1, no. 1 (1991): 2.

[3].   *Biblical Basis For Home Caring Fellowship* (Accra: Deeper Christian Life Ministry, n.d.), 19–20.

[4].   William A. Beckham, *The Second Reformation* (Houston: Touch Publications, 1995), 176.

[5].   *Informe Año* (Caracas: Las Acacias Church, 1995).

[6].   Home Group Conference '96, *Renewal through Restoration* (Chicago: New Life Community Church, n.d.).

[7].   William A. Beckham, *The Second Reformation* (Houston: Touch Publications, 1995).

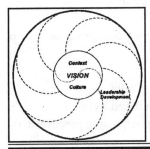

CHAPTER 5

Leadership Development
Fulfilling the Vision

In his leadership training manual, Rev. Fred Deegbe of Accra wrote:

Leadership is needed to accomplish a purpose. To get something done. An important part of God's plan is that His work will be done by people, guided and empowered by the Holy Spirit. God chooses people, and gives them specific tasks to do, in order to accomplish His purpose.[1]

Every leader interviewed agreed that good leadership is necessary for home group ministries to succeed. Not only is qualified leadership needed, but there also needs to be a continuing source of new leadership. Much of the energy of each member of the senior leadership is spent finding and developing new leaders.

Caracas Churches
Developing leaders in areas of perceived need

From question 18 on the questionnaire we learned that 23 percent of the respondents are currently leading home groups while 69 percent are not. The other eight percent did not answer that question.

Caracas — Dios Admirable
Godliness is the first order of leadership

Home group ministry as a major emphasis and the leadership development accompanying it is fairly new at Dios Admirable. As the home group ministry began to bear fruit and grow, many new people were needed in leadership positions. The home group ministry director, Nelly Sanchez, relates that leaders were surveyed. They were given a list of 52 possible areas where they felt a need for training and were asked to choose 12. They could also write in items not on the list.

The priority needs have since been or soon will be taught to the home leaders.

(1) How to facilitate sharing—group dynamics
(2) How to lead a meeting
(3) Recruiting methods—how to get new people into the group
(4) How to start new groups
(5) Training apprentice leaders
(6) Identifying and developing spiritual gifts
(7) Christian liberty—praying through it and living it
(8) How to make disciples—how does discipleship function in the home groups

Home group leaders meet monthly for two hours. One hour is spent in dealing with vision and the other in training. The hour spent in training with all the home group leaders together deals with the above topics. The other hour is divided up into 'tribes' for sharing challenges, prayer, and vision as the home group leaders' needs are considered.

People volunteer for leadership. However, volunteering does not necessarily mean a person will actually become a leader. A potential leader must already be in a home group. That person must also have completed the church's training on how to prepare and lead a Bible study, as well as its discipleship class. Finally, the potential leader must begin as an apprentice. People have definitely risen to that challenge, considering the number of apprentices in the Caracas churches.

Caracas — Las Acacias
Leaders produce leaders

Sam Olson stated that home groups are the ground floor to all ministry. People who are in ministry, whether paid staff or volunteer, come out of the home groups. His vision is for an expanded home group ministry, and the key is a trained leadership. He trains his own home group leaders, but his efforts encompass more than that.

There are two ways to train leaders. First, within the church. General leadership training is available to all church members no matter what their educational level. The training was developed by a specialist and is an ongoing three-year program. About 300 people are involved. This basic training becomes the platform for further training in other specialized areas, especially professional ministry.

Second, there is a seminary in town of which I am chairman of the board. In 1982-83, five denominational leaders started the seminary. It meets 5 or 6 days a week and has morning, afternoon, and evening classes. About 200 students from 70 churches are enrolled. The board represents 10 to 15 denominations.[2]

He feels the Las Acacias church is a good model of decentralized leadership. The church is divided into small 'pieces' led by different individuals, which helps to moderate the societal tendency toward strong dictatorial leadership.

Mirtha Villafañe,[3] whose sector is one of the fastest growing in the city, said of her role in leadership development, "I am developing leaders. I am also a pastor or shepherd to them. One thing I enforce and encourage is that they must delegate." She has leadership training every Monday evening, and she is usually the trainer. She feels that good training helps bring unity. Her sector has 36 home groups and they are starting four to six new ones per month. At that rate they should reach the goal of 92 home groups by the end of the year. Mirtha credits leadership development and prayer as the two main reasons for growth.

Groups do fail. When Mirtha became sector coordinator three years ago, there were four home groups. "All sick," she stated. She prayed that the Lord would work in them. He did and they all closed down. "From there," she said, "we have grown to our present level of 36 groups." Leadership is often the problem in failure, as well as the key to success. She gave an example of a 26-year-old woman leading a group of women who were over 50 years of age. This did not work because the leader could not lead people who had so much more life experience than she did. Mirtha recognizes the need for different kinds of groups to reach various parts of society.

Each Tuesday evening is given to some form of home group leadership development activity:

(1) One Tuesday, all nucleus, parish, and sector leaders meet with the senior pastor.

(2) One Tuesday, all nucleus and parish leaders meet with their sector leader.

(3) One Tuesday, all home group and nucleus leaders meet with their parish leader.

(4) One Tuesday, all home group leaders meet with their nucleus leader.

I attended a meeting of a parish leader with the nucleus and home group. The meeting format was that of a home group. The main difference was the sharing time, which dealt with the victories and challenges facing the home group leaders. I asked several leaders about the benefit of the meeting. They said they encourage one another to stay with the ministry and also discover new ideas.

Chicago — New Life Community Church
Personal caring, an important part in developing new leaders

Tony, a mature Christian, has been at New Life Church for more than 20 years. Karen and I attended the home group he leads with his wife, Linda. He had a relaxed attitude with the young men present and with us. He greeted us warmly, with a big hug. He joked back and forth with the younger men. Then he skillfully turned the conversation to more serious matters.

"Look at this," Tony said to me, "the Lord has given us three assistants in our group." All three are preparing to lead home groups because his group is large and growing. It is evident to Tony that leadership growth is key to home group growth.

In the weeks that followed I stayed in touch with Tony's group. At least two new groups have multiplied from the group we saw, and his small living room remains crowded with new people. Tony is an effective leader who finds himself working as a counselor or mentor with the new home groups that have multiplied from his.

Question 18 on the questionnaire indicated that Tony is one of 29 percent of the respondents leading a home group while 71 percent are not. The fact that I did the questionnaire in a home group leaders' seminar as well as in seven cell groups puts this number a little high in proportion to the actual number of leaders.

"Home group leaders are the heroes of our church," stated Dave Garrett. Each new home group with its leader is dedicated in front of the entire Sunday morning celebration service. Twice a year all the home group leaders and assistants are presented and commissioned in the Sunday morning celebration service.

One key to having good home group leaders is the zone pastor. Zone pastors are responsible for the home leaders' preparation, but the senior pastor, the zone pastor, seminars, relevant reading, and outside specialists all contribute to the development of the leaders. The zone pastor meets twice a month with the leaders in his zone for ongoing training. He reviews the weekly reports to know the victories and challenges and then calls each group leader each week.

In further conversation with both Tony and Dave, I learned that each had changed his ministry focus since beginning home group ministry. Tony stated that he spends more time training the people in his group who will become group leaders. He is a model and mentor for them. Dave said, "My focus has changed. Now I am helping groups multiply. My job as a zone pastor is to be a resource for the group leaders. They are great leaders and I am able to cheer them on."

Besides meeting with the zone pastors, the home group leaders have an all-day seminar twice a year. The church rents a hotel conference room. Everyone involved in home group leadership attends—pastoral staff, team leaders, home group leaders and their assistants, and even those who are looking into that ministry. Often people from other churches and even other countries attend.

The effect of this mix of personal care and supervision mixed with more formal teaching is that people move into home group leadership quickly and effectively. Most of the people in the group Ralph now leads are new Christians. He has known the Lord about three years, but in his home group he is the senior member in the faith. This relatively new Christian can model effective leadership because of the leadership he has seen modeled.

Moscow — Rosa Church
People want a leader who will co-suffer with them

According to question 18, 26 percent of the respondents in Moscow are home group leaders while 74 percent are not. Some of the leaders are zone leaders as well as home group leaders.

We attended the Saturday evening leaders' meeting for the Rosa Church. This weekly assembly is the principal forum to develop leaders. One purpose for the meeting is to instill the church's vision into the leaders. Another is training. Over 100 leaders attended that meeting, which had many elements of a celebration service. The session began with 45 minutes of worship followed by a one-hour exhortation by Pastor Pavel, speaking of the necessity for leaders to judge themselves and keep their lives pure. Seven zone leaders gave progress reports and prayer needs. After each report, the entire group prayed for the leader. The meeting ended three hours after it started, typical of most other meetings in this church.

We also attended a zone meeting where the home group leaders met with the zone leader. This zone, in southeast Moscow, is one of the most active, having ten home groups. In this meeting they also spent time in prayer and worship. Two questions we asked this group dealt with leadership. First, "What are you, as a leader, doing differently now from when you started?" and second, "What kind of training have you received?"

These leaders are young in years and relatively new in the faith. All referred to their youth and how nervous they were in the beginning.

I was nervous and the fellowship was dry. I prepared a lot of special teaching. I tried to force-feed people and I would think, "Why can't they understand?" Now I let the Holy Spirit lead, and I feel anointed and find it much easier to teach. I give more personal examples now, and I have become more patient.

Two people were mentioned to us as productive home group planters. They had each started three or more groups, and the leadership seemed a bit puzzled. The woman was exceptionally shy, and the man had trouble expressing himself. We met both people but were able to attend only one of the groups. I was impressed that it is not outstanding speaking gifts that bring a new home group into existence. Caring and prayer, dealt with in other chapters, are the keys to starting new groups. These leaders allowed other people to participate, recognizing that others had gifts that needed to be used. And they were focused, faithfully leading their home groups and not expecting to be moved into another role or 'promotion.'

Home group leaders here also learn from each other. They visit other home groups and interact with each other by telephone. Their reports enable the senior leadership to give help in areas of felt need.

They have had to deal with failed home groups and leadership. One of the problems with new leadership has been immaturity. Pavel and Marina, as senior leaders in the church, did not have much experience in selecting and developing leaders. Sometimes the leaders were not growing in the Word. Others were living in sin. Now they are focusing careful attention on the zone leaders.

Leaders face special problems in Moscow. People tend to turn to God and the church when there is serious trouble, but when life is normal they stay away. Alcoholism is a huge problem, and it often leads to abusive husbands. A high level of commitment is demanded of the home group leader, so sometimes leaders are too troubled with their own lives to become really involved with serving group members.

Pastor Pavel wants to bring more people onto the church staff. While this church is primarily led by volunteers, he feels ministry will be strengthened with three more full-time staff. He is looking for people who have come through the home group system.

In contrast to the Russian model above, I talked to an American missionary who is seeking to build a home group ministry. He said he came to facilitate church planting efforts based on small groups. He has worked with Russian Christians in the project, but it has not gone well. He was trying to teach something he had not done in Russia. Also, with the Russian aversion to slogans and written goals, he may have erred in being too programmatic. Now he has changed his tactics. He is working with Russians to begin a couple of home groups in his area with the goal that they will be the beginning of a local church and become models for future home groups.

Accra Churches
Leaders model leadership when they release people for ministry

The majority of the Accra church respondents were home group leaders—72 percent—while only 26 percent were not (question 18). The most likely explanation for the large percentage is that most of my contact with people able to fill out the questionnaire was in the context of home group leader meetings. Literacy was also a problem at the grass roots level.

Accra — Calvary Baptist Church
Biblical leadership facilitates people in fruitful ministry

One important aspect of a home group ministry, according to Pastor Deegbe, is that people need to be freed up for ministry. He said, "A leader cannot keep stepping in, or people will not accept the new leader—nor will the leaders be able to become models of good leadership." He feels that the structure must encourage people to minister and let them serve without unnecessary interference from higher leadership levels.

Because the Baptist leadership is spread out in home group ministry, the leaders have better opportunity to facilitate people for ministry. The zone leaders are deacons in the church, who also undergo training and participate in the development of the home group leaders at Calvary Baptist.

Rev. Deegbe's thirteen-page leadership training manual contains practical aspects but grows out of a biblical base.

> The best way to develop our own abilities is to begin at once to help others to develop theirs. Timothy was not instructed to become fully trained and at some point he would

be a leader who could take charge of others. He was guided into the beautiful truth that good leaders remain teachable and involved in the lives of their people.[4]

Rev. Deegbe not only teaches the facts of good leadership, he models it as well. I have been impressed that the leadership of the churches in this study are all teachable. They are continually seeking to better their ministry, their leadership, and every part of their lives.

Accra — Deeper Christian Life Ministry
Leadership is hard work

Leadership education is highly organized. Before a person can become a home group leader he or she must move through three levels of classes:

(1) Beginners (9 weeks). This course deals with Christian life basics such as salvation, devotional time, evangelism, baptism.

(2) Intermediate (9 weeks). This is a basic doctrines course that focuses on Bible knowledge.

(3) Prelim (5 weeks). This is the last class a person takes before becoming a home group leader. It deals with practical issues about how to be a leader.

When this series of courses is completed, the potential leader has an oral examination. Many do not pass and are encouraged to retake the class. Every month a new program begins, as an old one is being completed. In that way a new group of leaders is ready each month. Once a person has passed and is assigned a home group, biweekly training follows for all leaders.

How does a home group leader become an area leader? The home group leader is expected to do two things in the home group. First, 'develop a Timothy' who will take over the group. Second, lead the home group for two years. After that the zone and district leaders evaluate the group. They pray about it and want to know if it has grown and borne fruit. Becoming a zone or district leader follows a similar process.

Home group leaders are expected to follow the goals and vision laid down by the higher leadership. Discipline is invoked when workers fall into sin. Besides the usual lists of sins one finds in Paul's writings, they mentioned disobedience to the leadership, no growth in the home group, and striking one's wife. One district coordinator gave the following example:

A home group leader moved in with a person that the area and zone leaders felt was evil. They thought the home group leader would be influenced for evil so they told him he should move out. He refused. His life then became influenced by the evil so he was removed from being a home leader.

Leaders who are relieved of their leadership role can return to service after a period of time. The time is not stated but when the supervisory leadership feels the person being disciplined is ready, he or she will enter into service at the same level. During the discipline period certain assignments, readings, and counseling may be a part of the restoration process.

The Evangelical Presbyterian Church of Ghana
Good leadership is shared leadership

Rev. Major Mensah-Dharty, moderator of the denomination, had wise words about leadership. "People will gravitate to a good leader and stay away from a not-so-good leader. In that way, some groups will grow and their offspring may not. Also, others besides the designated leader should lead in a home group."

We visited several home groups from this denomination, both from the Madina and Kotobabi churches. The leadership we observed in the home groups was shared. The Bible discussions were animated with nearly everyone participating. The leader kept the study on track and raised questions from time to time but allowed people to carry on the discussion with a degree of freedom.

Each Sunday evening the home group leaders meet together when the pastor teaches them the lesson for that week. The lesson material they were using when we were there was from a booklet, *How to Handle Conflicts*, published by their denominational press.[5]

Not only pastors teach the leaders. Dr. Seth Gbewonyo, a lay person, taught at an all-day session for leaders. He pointed out Andrew's leadership qualities; planning ahead, showing interest in others, and using initiative. Dr. Gbewonyo encouraged leaders to share responsibility with others. One denominational leader stated that previously, pastors tended to do everything and sometimes they dominated the people, so churches were losing members. Today, with leadership shared and more people involved, the churches are growing.

Bombay — New Life Fellowship
A leader both serves and fellowships with the Father

We spent over an hour with Pastor Joseph and his senior staff. Pastor Joseph began by giving us some historical perspective of what today appears to be one of the world's great megachurches.[6]

In the 1960s we had good teaching from the outside as well as our own. We had praise and worship but two things were lacking. The church was not growing and leadership was not developing.

The theme of serving and letting go came through clearly as this godly pastor spoke out of his vast experience.

The leader should give others freedom to develop and not try to dictate. The leader must get underneath people and lift them up to prepare them for ministry. Ministry must be based on the fivefold pillars of Ephesians 4:11–16. The types of leaders mentioned there are for the building up of the body of Christ for ministry.

Leaders develop like the natural aptitudes found in a child. It is a process. The key to leadership is not the Bible school or seminary but the church. Leaders in the local church evaluate character, gifting, and ministry ability, as well as Bible and theological knowledge. And a learner's attitude is important. As soon as a leader stops learning he is finished.

How do the senior leaders keep up with the growth?

Humanly, we cannot cope with the fast growth just now. We are checking to see if the groups reported are real and if they have leaders. We are trying to bring it all down to a manageable level. If someone is leading three or more groups then he or she should be in the process of releasing one of the groups. If a person has a job and a family then one or, at most, two groups, is enough for a leader. If the person is full-time, then five or six is maximum.

Bombay, like Accra, had a high percentage of home group leaders filling in the questionnaire. In both places local leaders supervised the questionnaire collection. Question 18 showed that 59.5 percent of the respondents are currently leading home groups.

Sister Hilda, a house group leader for seven years as well as a zone leader, spoke about the challenges she faces. One of the biggest is that those coming from a Hindu background often compromise and worship idols. Much family and community pressure is applied. Furthermore, there is persecution from militant Hindus. Another challenge is the lack of leaders.

The leaders receive training and supervision. I queried Pastor Willie Soans about discipline—what leaders were disciplined for and how this was handled. He indicated that discipline is handled at the appropriate level and just to the extent of the problem. If it only concerns people in the local setting, the house church deals with it. If it is serious, then the area pastor will be brought in. "There have been times when we have asked people to sit out for a time," he indicated. One leader sat out for three months due to gossiping but that person was restored.

One of their great concerns is anything that affects unity. I was impressed while in Bombay at the efforts made to maintain a spirit of oneness. Unity is an active leadership function in New Life Fellowship.

When the higher leadership levels hear that something is amiss, they investigate. For instance, they have discovered divisive teachings that needed correcting. A person teaching error was confronted and asked to sit out for several months. In the end, that person left. However, others have been open to correction and have been restored. Their goal is always restoration.

Much of the evangelism and other ministry is done in teams. They try to be careful with single leaders. Evangelists and other leaders often attend the home group meetings, which helps alleviate concern when unmarried people lead. They feel an unmarried leader should not counsel and should not even enter a house alone.

Pastor Willie and the other senior leaders are seeking to develop effective leadership training methods for this largely lay-led, fast-growing church. Pastor Willie teaches home group leaders and is developing a manual for church leadership.

Questionnaire Evaluation

Several of the questions in the research questionnaire deal with leadership. In question 33, I asked people to list three qualities of a good home group leader. My question was open-ended and people simply listed qualities as they thought of them. I later created categories based on the answers. The answers were tabulated in five specific categories, with a sixth labeled "other."

"Caring, compassionate, sensitivity to people" came out the over-all number one category. From Moscow, with a high of 93 percent, to Accra where 64 percent of the people marked that category, the importance of caring was emphasized by the majority. This fits in with Marina's comment that people of the Rosa Church in Moscow want a leader who will co-suffer with them.

A second category of leadership qualities that rated high was the leader's "growing relationship with God." From the 76 percent of Bombay and Moscow to 54 percent in Caracas, well over half the respondents put this category in second place.

One category little mentioned was Bible/theological knowledge. While as many as 60 percent mentioned it in Bombay, making it the number three category there, elsewhere it came out fourth or fifth. I doubt that anyone considers Bible knowledge unimportant. Rather, people see relationships as more important—relationships with other people and with God.

Where do churches find the needed supply of home group leaders (question 29)? New leaders come from the home groups whether the church leadership or the home group selects them. In all the churches except Accra, the majority of home group leaders were recruited by the church leadership (Bombay 95 percent, Caracas 75 percent, Chicago 69 percent, and Moscow 52 percent). In Accra only 39 percent said leaders were approached by church leadership while 39 percent said that the people in the home group choose their own leaders.

While the Accra churches have been described as highly organized with a pyramidal structure, this percentage may seem to moderate that conclusion. I suggest that at the home group level where personal relationships are the most important, the collective quality plays a more important role. Hofstede's value rankings put West Africa high in both collective and power distance areas.

The ideal of all the home group coordinators or pastors is that each home group has a leader and an apprentice or assistant leader. He or she serves as a back-up for the leader (who may sometimes be absent) and also receives training for leadership. Of course, the ideal is not always realized. Question 31 notes the percentages of home groups that have apprentices: Chicago 80 percent, Moscow 76 percent, Bombay 64 percent, Caracas 63 percent, Accra 53 percent.

Each of the churches in this study had well organized programs to train home group leaders. In answering question 30 about the training of leaders, most answered that the church leadership trained the home group leaders (Accra 95 percent, Caracas 75 percent, Bombay 81 percent, Chicago 60 percent, and Moscow 55 percent). Chicago tabulated 23 percent and Moscow 21 percent for learning by observing or modeling.

The case studies in the questionnaire, questions 36 through 42, reflect leadership style and the decision-making process. Questions 36 and 37 ask how the material is chosen for the home groups. In Chicago,

Moscow, and Bombay the material is chosen by the home group leader. In Chicago the home group would discuss it but the leader would ultimately decide. While this reflects a high power distance, it may also reflect the many new Christians who desire a more leader-focused home group, especially in the area of choosing materials.

In Caracas the home groups themselves decide on the materials to be studied. Caracas is extremely high on the collectivity scale and also has the most mature Christians in terms of the length of time they have been believers. Although the groups decide, the senior leadership in the churches gives options from which to choose. The high power distance is shown as the senior leadership sets the parameters for the decision.

In Accra the home study materials are part of the church program. The churches surveyed there are good examples of congregations that have highly structured programs, but these are programs that happen primarily in home groups. While the groups have a say in choosing their leaders, control is maintained in the area of selecting what will be studied and how the leaders will be trained.

Questions 39, 40, and 41 deal with the way in which the leader confronts others in the group. Direct confrontation in the meeting was the majority response. However, differences enter into the evaluation when we consider the secondary responses. In question 39 the percentages that favored direct response were Moscow 83, Chicago 68, Accra 67, Caracas 65, and Bombay 55. Twenty percent of Chicago's group felt the response should be indirect; i.e., ask a question of another individual rather than correcting directly. In Bombay 26 percent of the people indicated this should be dealt with outside the meeting. Questions 40 and 41 reflect similar attitudes. In 41, some groups gave a high secondary response to working through a third person, usually another leader (Accra 33 percent, Bombay and Moscow 24 percent). The point here is that there are a variety of ways to deal with error or with difficult people. When dealing with challenges leaders trained within the culture will have a better understanding of how to handle difficulties than those outside.

When I was testing the questionnaire I found suburban Americans did not quite know how to answer question 42 concerning a crisis situation of death from AIDS. When they answered they mentioned the use of instruments available to them every day—the phone for dialing 911 and using their cars for transportation. Some mentioned schedules that could only be stretched so far. This may be appropriate in suburban America. However, when an African international student answered, he knew exactly what to do in Africa. The whole home group comforts the bereaved, then goes together with the family to be at the home. Indeed, leadership is a function of culture.

I also asked about ideal leadership styles that I felt would reflect the host cultures. Question 23 asked people to choose which of four statements best described the ideal home group. The Accra churches tabulated 66 percent for "orderly/rules." Their highly structured and church directed programs would seem to indicate, in Hofstede's terms, a high uncertainty avoidance dealt with through a high power distance or strong leadership. Caracas and Bombay came out highest in "authority/leader," 38 and 60 percent respectively. While a high score in "orderly/rules" indicates an outside authority such as the church hierarchy (not present) or the written material, a high "authority/leader" score indicates a strong leader who is present. The Chicago high was 31 percent for "father/chaotic." This indicates few rules. The leader is seen as a father figure and the members will follow that person. Finally, Moscow's highest rank showed 38 percent for "equality/flexible." This may be partly because of the respondents' youth and partly due to a reaction to Russian history.

Many of the percentages here do not follow the stereotypes of what the cultures might be expected to show. The main reason for this is that while the home group reflects culture at some points, it also moderates extreme aspects. American culture on Hofstede's scale is the most individualistic culture in the world, but that has been moderated as people work together in the home groups. Venezuela has one of the highest power distances in the world, but in the home group everyone's ideas are considered. The Spirit of God working through small groups of people can moderate cultural extremes in society.

Key Points

- Home groups provide both a source and the need for continued new leadership.
- Effective senior leadership builds up and encourages ministry, not dictating or controlling.
- Leadership is a process and is learned by doing.
- Leaders need to be learners in process.
- Leaders may be young but should not be immature.
- Leadership style in the small group reflects the emphasis of the large celebration group.

- Home groups moderate extremes of culture and affect leadership functions.
- Biblical leadership is servant based.

Endnotes

1.   Fred Deegbe, "Leadership Training" (Accra: Calvary Baptist Church, n.d.), 1.

2.   Sam Olson, interview by author, Caracas, Venezuela, 19 March 1996.

3.   Villafañe, Mirtha, interview by author, Caracas, Venezuela, 19 March 1996.

4.   Fred Deegbe, "Leadership Training" (Accra: Calvary Baptist Church, n.d.), 5.

5.   Alex Dzameshie, *How to Handle Conflicts, Group Discussion Edition* (Accra: Bible Study & Prayer Fellowship, E. P. Church of Ghana, 1995).

6.   S. Joseph, interview by author with senior leadership, Bombay, 30 January 1996. Present were S. Joseph, Willie Soans, Shelton Davidson, Jerry D'Souze, and Shekar Kallianpur.

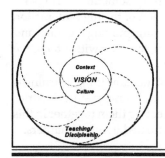

CHAPTER 6

Teaching/Discipleship
Applying Truth to Everyday Living

In a home meeting with some home group leaders, zone pastors, and evangelists, they were telling us their story. They had not known the Word of God, but when the Spirit of God fell upon them they had a burning hunger to learn it. Two women, Catherine and Marina, were among the first in this movement. They learned of a place 25 kilometers away where the Bible was being taught and traveled there every week to satisfy this inward hunger. Marina states, "My life began to change. God was setting us free by the Word. Some people returned to praying to Mary but we didn't." The result of this great moving of the Spirit of God in Bombay 20 years ago was a hunger for the Word of God.

Home group programs around the world focus on the Bible. The Bible teaches about all the other home group activities. People pray, fellowship, worship, care for one another, evangelize, and learn the Bible because of biblical injunctions to do so.

Home groups are a modality for effective adult learning because the adults are in dialogue with their peers. Primarily the process for adult learning is one of participation. In the case of the new Christian, prayer, witnessing, and understanding Bible truths are new ideals for their lives. They do not learn these things only by listening. They also observe others with greater skill and knowledge than they have. Next they make their beginning attempts, which may often be tentative and poorly done. But eventually, working with others in the home group, they acquire these skills. Peer input continues as the people in the home group develop in similar areas in their spiritual walk. Vella states, "A major fact in motivation is that advice or praise from a peer carries more weight than advice, correction, or praise from an outsider or a manager."[1]

The one-another commands of Scripture—"Love one another," "Instruct one another, " "Accept one another"—encourage this kind of interactive approach to learning. Involvement is the key to the process.

Mono-directional teaching in the home group sometimes brings results. In such cases good results are a function of the high interaction in other parts of the home group such as sharing, praying together, and continual contact during the week. However, teaching with interactive methods results in greater understanding.

While teaching and discipleship are not the same thing, learning is an important part of being a disciple. In terms of home group ministries they are closely related concepts, so I am treating them together in this chapter. Other aspects of discipleship are treated in other chapters.

Caracas
Teaching from a cognitive base

From their basic discipleship all the way to higher level leadership development, both Caracas churches have emphasized teaching. They assume that if one is to grow in the Christian life, one needs cognitive input. These churches give a variety of opportunities for people to continue their study in how to be growing disciples.

Caracas — Dios Admirable
In teaching, what the disciple hears is important, not only what the teacher says.[2]

Almost all 18 adults present had a printed copy of the lesson. As the leader worked her way through the lesson on forgiveness, she asked an application question. "What is the most important characteristic we have studied here?" The answers were not slow in coming.

"Leave revenge to the Lord."

"Treat your enemy with love. This is not easy and, at times, impossible."

"If my enemy needs help I cannot give it. I cannot forgive. Am I too cruel?" (Everyone laughed and the discussion continued.)

These people were taking Scripture seriously. What does it mean to forgive and how does that apply in their lives? They deal with bosses who take advantage of them, employees who cheat, spouses who have wronged them, and rebellious children. And in their society, revenge is more highly regarded than forgiveness. This home group was a place where these people could interact with the Bible as they came to understand the implications for their lives.

In the discussion on leaving revenge to the Lord, the leader pointed out that we should not hope or wait expectantly for vengeance to come. We can only deal with our own attitude. She asked people to list benefits they received when they forgave someone. "You feel clean," one man responded. Another person said, "You have inner peace because your burden is taken away. Since we have been doing this study, God has brought deliverance in my family." (This response was from a woman learning to forgive her father who antagonizes her.)

The Bible lesson in this group lasted for one hour and fifteen minutes. Aside from a few minutes of sharing and prayer, Bible study dominated the time. A noticeable characteristic was the animated participation in discussion time. Humor was evident, helping keep people relaxed and enabling them to absorb some biblical truths that directly confronted their culture.

Successful home groups deal with culture from the biblical perspective. While the style of the home group may conform to the culture, the content will conform to Scripture. When Scripture contradicts a cultural norm (forgiveness instead of revenge) the fact that people are in a culturally appropriate setting will help them accept truth conflicting with their culture.

Pastor Liévano feels the people need to gain a deeper understanding of the Bible. Bible study, therefore, is the key element of the home group ministry. They offer material from four different sources. He creates study questions based on the Sunday sermon and puts them in the church bulletin. He also makes available lessons developed by Campus Crusade for Christ, CBInternational, and the Peru Evangelical Free Church.

Many Christians hesitate to lead a small group because they do not know how to create a Bible study. They are overwhelmed with the idea of preparing what they think will be a "sermon." When good materials are available, along with instruction in their use, people without a formal biblical education are more willing to participate in that task.

The seven-lesson booklet that Liévano wrote entitled (in English) *Basic Groups of Christian Discipleship* indicates the importance he places on the discipleship aspect of home groups. In the proposed 60-minute program, he gives 30 minutes to Bible Study.[3]

The home group ministry is only one avenue by which Dios Admirable makes disciples. There are several levels of classes, some of which are necessary before the church allows a person to lead a home group. The first level is what Liévano calls the initial discipleship class. This six-week class takes place before the Sunday celebration service when most training levels are programmed, but this level can also be done in the home group.

Following the initial class are two intermediate levels, after which a person studies for baptism. The next step is a Navigator 2:7 training course. This level is training for ministry, and the home group leaders receive their first level of training here. Ministry training for home leaders continues in the Sunday evening sessions.

Since teaching is the key element in this church, the home groups are a main part of the discipleship program. When asked what benefit they received from the home groups, the aspect of discipleship was evident. "I have learned to read and understand the Bible." "I used to read the Bible but did not understand it, but now I can understand it and even share what it says with others."

Caracas — Las Acacias
Teaching style and content is modeled by senior leaders

Sam Olson's sermon on the Sunday morning we visited his church was about leadership. He used the life of Joshua to give some biblical instruction to leaders. The 50-minute exegetical sermon took the major part of the Sunday morning service, emphasizing the importance this church places on teaching. That importance is reflected in the church's home groups. The leader of one cell we attended dealt with the biblical material of the Sunday sermon, applying the teaching to everyday life. The Bible study lasted about 45 minutes, over one-half the home group's total time.

Teaching drives the home groups in Caracas. The emphasis on teaching as the central focus applies to both churches; one charismatic, and one non-charismatic. They evangelize, pray, care for one another, and worship God, but their activities revolve around the teaching ministry.

Moscow — Rosa Church
Teaching from a prayer base

If the churches in the Caracas site put the most emphasis on formal teaching in comparison to other home group activities, the Moscow site probably puts the least. The Rosa Church puts comparatively more time and effort into non-teaching activities. However, learning does take place. The higher levels of leadership emphasize teaching. Leadership training sessions on Saturday and the celebration services on both Thursday and Sunday have long preaching and teaching times.

The Rosa Church is new, the leadership is new, and they have not established traditions. So the home groups have developed a different pattern. The senior pastor is an evangelist and a motivator. When he teaches the leadership, a substantial part of the teaching involves motivation toward a deeper Christian life, a more fruitful ministry, and encouragement to keep on serving even though the ministry is difficult. He is a product of the underground church and knows the cost and the joy of being a Christian in Russia. He was a part of the prayer and fasting in 1986 that helped lead to the loss of power by communism. He continually models teaching through serving. He is available to the zone leaders and all the church leaders when they need him.

At the Saturday evening leaders' meeting, Pastor Pavel taught for an hour. His teaching concerned sin and the necessity for a leader to walk in the Spirit. "We are saved by grace but God hates sin. If you have sin in your life, are you letting God deal with it?" He encouraged the leaders to judge themselves so that God would not judge them.

Pastor Pavel later told me that this was not the usual way he taught the leaders. Dealing with grace is easier than dealing with strict truth, but he felt his teaching must be balanced. He is aware that the existing freedom could dissolve. In the underground church the level of purity was high because the price for being a Christian was high. Now it is easier to be a Christian, and sin begins to creep in.

One of the differences that impressed me in the Moscow and Caracas churches is the way teaching takes place in relation to other aspects of the Christian life, such as prayer. In Caracas, the teaching is the basis for prayer, while in Moscow the teaching comes out of prayer. In the home group meetings in Moscow most of the time will be spent in prayer, while in Caracas it is in teaching.

Vladimir taught the Bible study in the home group he led with his wife, Masha. He referred to a few notes as he worked his way through several Bible passages. His teaching was a reflection of Pastor Pavel's although he looked at some different verses. Most of the time in that group was spent in prayer, and the teaching time was a preparation for the prayer time. Home group leaders usually teach the pastor's lesson. They have no standardized materials.

Moscow — Other Groups
Learning may come from traditional models

One morning we invited pastors and leaders who are working with home groups to meet together with us for a time of interaction on various home group approaches in Moscow. Many groups in Moscow are implementing some type of home group ministries. The models they use are often imports from the United States, and some groups are having difficulties. The problem may be less with the model and more with the fact that foreigners are trying to implement it without fully understanding the context.

Our experience in Madagascar with the turning of the bones illustrates the point. We knew what Scripture taught concerning this ritual of taking the bones out of the tombs for veneration. However, we had never done it, never felt family pressures to be involved, and never been told we were traitors to our nation for not doing it. But Malagasy who had experienced it, and through conviction of God's word and prayer decided not to be involved, were able to help others in a way we could not.

We talked to other people in Moscow who are in some way working with home group ministries. A few Orthodox churches have begun a type of home group ministry. Their groups are focused on Bible study. One active member of such a group told me that they have three types of home group meetings, two of which focus on teaching. Everyone in the groups has gone through a membership process to enter the Orthodox Church. The church assigns them to a home group with others who joined the church with them.

Bible study is exegetical, verse by verse, teaching Scripture content. Meetings last about two hours with Bible study, drinking tea, and fellowship being the main activities. The home group leader is appointed by the church and reports to the church, but the Bible discussion may be led by a different person.

Andrei Petrov is a young Baptist pastor working in one of the large new Baptist churches that started after Billy Graham's Moscow crusade in 1989. They are only beginning to prepare for a home group ministry, but that preparation will depend heavily on teaching. He believes that first the teachers must be prepared, a step currently in process. Each group will have a different focus, divided up into Bible study, evangelism, and prayer groups.

Alexander Fedichkin pastors a church that began home groups about three years ago. He points out the necessity of community within the home group. "Part of the community," he stated, "includes teaching. The pastor teaches the home group leaders who teach in the groups." His church has many new believers who have become leaders. But because they lead and teach in a home group, sometimes they do not want to follow the larger church leadership.

Accra
Teaching from an organizational base
The Accra churches in the study have developed materials that lay people can use to lead their home groups. Both the Deeper Christian Life Ministry and the Evangelical Presbyterians of Ghana publish

material that all their groups use. The Baptists print study questions in the bulletin, which are widely used in the home groups. This more structured orientation to content has the advantage of giving the lay person usable material that takes minimal supervision, allowing lay people to serve as supervisors.

Two problems were mentioned by churches using uniform materials. First, since different groups proceed through the material at various speeds, fast groups may become bored and slow ones may feel pressured. The second problem concerns depth of spiritual level. Different people have different spiritual needs. The leadership realizes a need for wisdom in choosing the right approach.

Evangelical Presbyterian Church of Ghana
Practical teaching meets daily issues

Felicia Dade is the women's ministry director for this denomination. She states that home groups are the most efficient way to teach the Bible to people. The home groups are only a short walking distance from where people live, making Bible study readily available.

Special home groups deal with women's issues. Felicia relates that women form the largest force of the farming community in Ghana and are also a force in the church. A church that does not accommodate women will not progress. Therefore, their church has developed material for women's home groups. Topics include a series on marriage, home management, and vocational training. They stress the importance of Christian marriage so they have materials to teach women preparing for marriage, as well as materials for married women and child raising.

While the church has materials published in the Ewe and English languages, they minister in five other languages as well. Having the printed materials in the local languages helps facilitate teaching in the home groups, leading to greater growth, but printed materials for home group ministries assume literacy. This church, as well as others, is dealing with the problem of illiteracy. Cassettes have helped non-literates as well as literates with Bible lessons. Non-literates are not separated into their own groups since they are an integral part of the family, neighborhood, and society.

Dr. Gbewonyo invited us to attend a home group in his home at Legon, the university community where he teaches microbiology. Professors and non-university people attended the home group. That evening's lesson came from a booklet entitled, *The Christian and Culture*, written by one of the church leaders.

They discussed the names of God in the traditional religions of Ghana. Following that they examined the same topic from the biblical names for God.

1. What attributes do the traditionalists give to God?

2. Mention the attributes that Christians give to God. How do they compare with the traditionalist's view?

3. Ewe names in traditional culture, as well as Christian tradition, portray the nature of God. Mention some and explain how.[4]

The question, "Do traditionalists worship the same God as the Christians?" sparked a lively discussion. One man asked if Muslims worshipped the same God as the Christians. These issues touch people every day as they interact with traditionalists, Muslims, and a host of cultural issues influenced by these religions. Fetishes, charms, and witchcraft belong to much of daily life. The home group provides a place for people to find biblical answers to their questions.

Ghana — Deeper Christian Life Ministry
Teaching in a context of oral communication

Education is important to Pastor Oladimeji. Although he is largely self-taught, he reads widely and requires the leaders in the movement to read. Because he comes from Nigeria and because of the diversity of languages in both nations, English is the common language although he speaks some vernacular languages. In large groups, teaching takes place in English with simultaneous translation into four or five other languages. The same thing may happen at the home group level. Though emphasizing English standardizes materials, it does have disadvantages. In the home group meeting, it tends to prevent those who do not speak English from actively participating.

We attended the combined district meeting for the Sunday morning worship service where Pastor Oladimeji was the preacher. His sermon was a theological teaching lasting about one hour and fifteen minutes with the theme of bibliology. This sort of oratory seemed appropriate in a society that appreciates speech-making and honors people who have these skills. The points were carefully outlined and dealt with in a didactic way, though he did use stories and humor to illustrate some points.

1. The Bible builds and bathes the believer.

2. The Bible molds and makes the believer.

3. The Bible helps and heals the believer.

4. The Bible saves and sanctifies the believer.

5. The Bible provides and protects the believer.

6. The Bible guides and guards the believer.

7. The Bible uplifts and upholds the believer.

The home groups we visited demonstrated some of the same one-way communication modeled in the large group meeting. Leaders did seek to draw people out, encouraging them to interact. However, when people were silent they reverted to the mono-directional format. Part of the challenge in these groups is that they are highly programmed. A certain amount of time is given to cover a certain amount of material. That material was taught to the leaders in the same way they teach it to the home group. Home leaders with more skill do an excellent job of getting people to interact.

Bombay — New Life Fellowship
Teaching also depends on prayer and worship

In the weekly three-hour prayer meeting for the Sunday celebration service, Vinod, a young Gujarati man, prayed that the Word would be preached accurately and clearly. He also asked that it would bear fruit. People in Bombay are increasingly hungry for the Word of God.

Pastor Paul gave a short, practical exhortation from Acts 3 in the Sunday celebration. He noted that at the hour when most people would have finished a big meal and settled down for a nap, Peter was on his way to the temple to pray. Because he was in touch with God, God was able to use him. Later he read from Acts 16. At midnight Paul and Silas sang and praised the Lord. In the midst of persecution their response was one of worship.

Both stories presented people in touch with God who knew how to take advantage of a situation to glorify God, but each case was hazardous. Peter could have been jailed for his efforts and Paul and Silas *were* jailed, a practical application for people who live in a hostile context. Preaching, teaching, and the accompanying fruit can all cause people to be jailed or persecuted. Pastor Paul exhorted, "They were not afraid. Don't be afraid of any jail."

After the shorter exhortation, Pastor Willie Soans gave a longer, one-hour sermon. Before he stood up to speak, the children were dismissed to Sunday School, a common practice for the Sunday service in the church. Pastor Willie's sermon was also in English, translated into Hindi. His sermon dealt with prayer—nothing will happen without prayer, and prayerlessness is sin. He gave an invitation asking people to seek God's face, looking for Him to work in a special way. Nearly all 500 people present came forward.

The content of the two teaching sessions mentioned above is typical of the content in the home groups. People receive from the large group and relay it and discuss it further in the home groups. We attended a home group taught by one of the mature Christian women. Marina is an experienced teacher. She spoke on the Christian's spiritual armor in Ephesians 6 and often referred back to the Sunday message on prayer.

There seemed to be little, if any, prepared printed materials for the Bombay church. That may be due to diversity of language and people groups. Printed materials are available in English to the home group leaders. Those materials, prepared and taught by Pastor Willie, deal with leadership and teaching. They are not lessons that can be assimilated and re-taught to a home group.

Much of the teaching in New Life Fellowship is in real-life situations. People learn to evangelize as they go with evangelistic teams to the slums. In all the many ways people evangelize, the newer believers are learning by being a part of the process. Likewise with prayer and worship, the teaching is a 'learning by doing' process. While less time may be given to formal teaching, learning is taking place.

Chicago — New Life Community Church
Teaching is personal

We were sitting in Tony and Linda's home group when the phone rang. Linda disappeared into another room to answer, reappearing much later. Later she shared the prayer request with us. A woman she is mentoring in a women's home group was scheduled to be baptized the following Sunday but some problems had developed. She was receiving opposition from close family members who were members of a different church. She needed counsel and encouragement. She was baptized the next Sunday and by that commitment gave a powerful positive testimony.

Personal mentoring is a core value at New Life Community Church and often takes place in the context of the home group. Everyone who has been mentored is encouraged to mentor another person, newer in the faith. A specific, organized body of teaching material exists for that purpose, making mentoring accessible to everyone. The material is published by the church and is entitled *First Steps*, a series of three booklets.[5] When a mentor has led someone through the material, that person is ready to mentor someone else.

While most of the mentoring in the church is happening at a basic Christian life level, it does not stop there. Zone pastors mentor the team leaders and home group leaders in their jurisdiction, team leaders mentor home group leaders, and home group leaders mentor their apprentices. Here the mentoring process is even more personal than in the home group. Usually it involves a weekly one-on-one meeting.

Accountability takes place at the home group level. Each week the mentor and mentoree fill out the report forms telling how often they met, what studies they completed, and verifying that they prayed together. If difficulties arise the home group leaders, team leader, or zone pastor can lend the necessary support. Mentoring is a quiet but pervasive aspect of spiritual development in the church. Everyone who completes a mentoring course is publicly recognized in the Sunday celebration service at some point during the home group cycle.

Bible study is a key element in the home groups of New Life Community Church. Many groups use material from the Sunday sermon. When Gus opened a new home group he led a Bible lesson on attitude, making several references to Pastor Mark's sermon.

This church has some gifted teachers. The zone pastors lead home groups and model culturally appropriate and biblically sound teaching methods for young adults. They are touching the generation X population with the appropriate teaching style. Generation Xers tend to be preoccupied with healing their own emotional wounds. Because they are focused on their own needs they can feel inadequate to help others. One of the major aspects of the ministry of home group leaders and mentors is to move people from 'consumers' to 'contributors.'

The danger of becoming preoccupied with one's own hurts, needs, or concerns looms as a real threat. However, it is positively dealt with at every level of church life by the emphasis on outreach. As people focus outward, their healing begins. Over time, biblical solutions to their problems are put into place, and they become more able to focus on others. This is a key to adult learning as Vella[6] points out, "The approach to adult learning...holds that adults have enough life experience to be in dialogue with any teacher, about any subject, and will learn new knowledge or attitudes or skills best in relation to that life experience."

Wuthnow[7] also speaks to the issue of community.

I must admit that I would worry if I thought these groups caused people to focus only on their inner emotional needs or to spend their time only with members of their own groups. I would also worry if the evidence showed that these groups pulled people away from their families or caused divisions with their loved ones. But the evidence was largely favorable, suggesting that small groups may help to integrate people with their families or neighborhoods and to make them more aware of the wider society. In this sense, small groups cultivate community…

Questionnaire Evaluation

Discipleship was the main purpose of the home groups for the largest percentage of respondents.

Questions 14, 15, and 24 all touched on discipleship. Question 15 asked about the purpose for the home group. Of the six possible categories the percentages for discipleship were: Moscow 74 percent, Accra 62 percent, Caracas 56 percent, Bombay 55 percent, and Chicago 50 percent. These percentages are the highest of any of the possibilities, showing that at all sites a majority of respondents felt the purpose of the home group was discipleship.

Question 14 asked why the respondent was in the home group. I divided the answers into eight categories, of which discipleship was one. The responses to this question are not so clear cut. Those specifically mentioning discipleship were: Accra 52 percent, Caracas 40 percent, Chicago 32 percent, Bombay 21 percent, Moscow 10 percent. Thirty-one percent of Moscow respondents mentioned answers that signified convenience of the home group location, time, or lifestyle. Bombay gave 14 percent to "evangelism" and "relationship building" while also giving 21 percent to "accountability/leading a group." Bombay had a high percentage of home group leaders—60 percent of those surveyed.

In question 24, I asked people to list their home group activities and how much time they gave to each. Most of the people who responded mentioned teaching or Bible instruction. Answers indicating the ranges of the average time for teaching are as follows: Accra: 45–60 minutes, Caracas 30–45 minutes, Chicago 30–40 minutes, Bombay 20–30 minutes. Few people from Moscow answered question 24. The reason may be because their home groups are unstructured enough that they cannot predict with accuracy how much time will be given to any one activity. But in a three-hour home group usually at least 30 minutes will be given to Bible study.

Culture impacts home group ministry in the area of teaching. In societies where the public education system is highly structured, education programs in churches may reflect that. But the churches researched are also coming out of the culture in an attempt to involve everyone in the learning process. Churches having a strong emphasis on teaching in the large group also tend to stress that in the small groups. However, the home groups include the important dynamic of feedback and sharing. Teaching styles are in process in all the research sites, affecting and being affected by the culture.

Key Points

•   Applying biblical truth to everyday practical living is the primary purpose of home group teaching and discipleship.

•   Changed lives is the principal goal of the teaching process.

•   Adults learn best in dialogue.

•   Printed materials for home groups can expand the potential of lay leadership participation.

•   Significant personal relationships enhance learning.

•   Personal participation in home group activities is key to the process of learning.

•   Culture affects learning styles.

Endnotes

[1].   Jane Vella, *Learning To Listen, Learning To Teach* (San Francisco: Jossey-Bass, 1994), 108.

[2].   Donald K. Smith, *Creating Understanding* (Grand Rapids: Zondervan, 1992), 65. I have adapted this statement from Smith who wrote a communication proposition stating, "Communication is what is heard, not only what is said."

[3].   Francisco Liévano, *Grupos Basicos De Discipulado Cristiano [Basic Groups of Christian Discipleship]* (Caracas: Dios Admirable Church, n.d.), 16.

[4].   Elom Dovlo and E. K. Agozie, *The Christian and Culture* (Accra: Bible Study & Prayer Fellowship, E.P. Church of Ghana, 1995), 2.

[5].   *First Steps: New Life Series Book One, Two, and Three* (Chicago: New Life Community Church, 1994).

[6].   Jane Vella, *Learning To Listen, Learning To Teach* (San Francisco: Jossey-Bass, 1994), 3.

[7].   Robert Wuthnow, *Sharing the Journey* (New York: Free Press, 1994), 346–347.

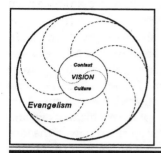

CHAPTER 7

Evangelism
Fueling Growth

Team members speaking multiple languages spread out across Asia's largest slum to share the Good News of Christ. Ghanaian Christians quit their jobs and resettle in new areas of their nation to begin new home groups. An announcement on a bulletin board in Chicago helps form a ministry team to evangelize a hospital. Videos used in discussion groups reach the upper class in Venezuela. A hurting friend is invited to a small group meeting in Moscow.

The importance of evangelism in the home group based churches in this study is difficult to overstate. It is modeled and practiced at every level of leadership from the senior pastor to the various home group leaders. The fact that all the churches in the study are growing is a tribute to the idea that home group based churches are effective in evangelism. "If you don't evangelize, all you will have is transfer growth," noted Pastor S. Joseph of Bombay.

In most of the home groups we asked the question, "Who is the newest Christian and how long have you been a Christian?" Responses were revealing. They ranged from "yesterday" to "about a year," but more answers were closer to "yesterday." We met many people in the groups who were converted to Christ within the three months just before our visit.

Bombay
Focused and fruitful evangelism in a multicultural city

About 25 of us climbed the steep, narrow stairway to the upper room in a small building the church used for a preschool. We spent two hours in fervent worship together before hitting the streets of Kondivati, Asia's largest slum, for team evangelism.

It was late morning by the time the evangelism started. The youngest member of the team was still in her teens. The oldest was a retired dentist. Altogether the team members spoke at least a dozen languages, necessary in this area of Bombay where people come from all parts of India.

The spiritual battle waged within the shade cast by three Hindu temples. Pastor Bonny, like a general, directed his troops. He designated certain people to go door to door. Then he gathered the rest in an open place along two busy, narrow streets. The team began singing Christian songs in Hindi, and people gathered. Certain members staged a skit illustrating a biblical truth about the problem of evil and its power that can only be broken by greater spiritual power, the love of Jesus. The crowd grew. Some young men who had been gambling drifted over to watch. People perched on the roofs of shacks to get a better view.

The skit ended and the team members spread out in all directions, talking to people in small groups, sharing Christ. I counted 11 or 12 circles of people talking with one or two team members each. Pastor Bonny was explaining events to me when a woman approached to ask a question. He mentioned that she spoke Teligu, and he called over a Teligu speaker on the team to talk with her. Pastor Bonny speaks six or seven languages, as do many of the team members. However, in Bombay, no one could possibly speak all the needed languages.

"Look!" Pastor Bonny said as he pointed discreetly to some people who were praying to receive Christ. "And look over there!" Again heads bowed as more angels rejoiced (see Luke 15:10). They would get names and addresses from the people they contacted this day and return for follow-up visits within a week. At that point they would organize home groups. Activities similar to what I have described happen almost daily in various parts of Bombay.

Karen and I met with one group of leaders who work in the Kalina area. Here the main languages are Hindi, English, and Konkoni. We wondered how they were received when they were evangelizing, but they stressed that they wanted to share the good news of Jesus regardless. Hindus usually welcome them to their homes and they have good opportunity to share. With Roman Catholics, the second largest religion in that area, they have to say as much as possible within the first two minutes. Catholics are apprehensive because the priests have warned them about cults who go door-to-door.

Another barrier in door-to-door evangelism is the doorman or concierge at the apartments through which visitors must pass to gain entrance. They deal with that barrier by preaching to the doorman or concierge first. Also, they often preach in the apartment buildings where they live, so access is no problem. Though Christians are free to preach, pressures are brought to bear on them. The best schools and hospitals are run by Christians, mostly Roman Catholic, and evangelicals want to have their children in the best schools. "Proselytizing" is not a good way to accomplish that. But opposition can work for the evangelist. When opposition is too strident it piques the curiosity of the people, who then want to know more.

The most effective means of personal evangelism is through networks of neighbors. When a neighbor has a special need such as major illness, marriage problems, job loss, or children's schooling, the Christians know about it. They go to the home and ask if they can pray for them. The religious world view of India encourages people to accept and appreciate the prayers of others, including evangelicals. When prayer is answered, people often become more open to the gospel.

Dicto became a full-time evangelist in 1995. He is asking the Lord for 50 souls this year. By the end of January he had already brought eight people to Christ so he felt God was going to answer his prayer. He is also asking God that he will be able to start 10 new house groups during the year. He had already started one new group that someone else had taken over.

I asked Dicto about the effect of the healing and exorcism ministry in evangelism. In most meetings, both large and small, people pray for the sick and demon-possessed. Usually this prayer happens after the meeting when a few remain to pray. People are healed and delivered, and through that testimony some have come to know Jesus. Dicto stated, however, that perhaps only 20 percent of these people actually become believers.

Generational curses must be dealt with. The power of demons attached to a particular idol is often passed from mother to daughter for generations, but the power of Christ can break those curses. Sister Hilda related the story of an older woman, a powerful prayer warrior today, who had been freed from such a curse. One of the current home group leaders, Lata, worshiped Hindu gods. After she was freed from that power, she started a group in another part of town. She, along with other helpers, had started 20 to 25 home groups. When I asked, "Who is the most recent convert?" the response was instantaneous. They pointed to a certain woman, saying, "She came to Christ yesterday."

Evangelism takes place in both the home groups and the celebration services since non-Christians are almost always present. I attended a Hindi-speaking worship service of about 70 or 80 people where an invitation was given. In other larger celebration services as well, there was usually an invitation for people to come to Christ.

In an interview, Jacob Serrao, who has seen the work in his area grow dramatically, stated some principles on which he bases his work. His first principle is to go where people are responsive. In such an area one can sow and reap in the same day. When Hindus or Catholics visit a church they may experience a lot of opposition from family or friends, but this is usually not present when they visit a home. So they meet with people in homes for at least six months. In that way they have fewer casualties. They anoint houses where they meet and ask that generational curses be broken. Then family and neighbors see the difference in the lives of the new converts and want to know more.

His second principle deals with focus. He feels that new Christians do not need a lot of rules. The home where they meet may still have idols in place. In one home, the occupants made liquor in another room. But the focus is on preaching Christ and making the gospel known, not on external things. In about two to three months the idols will be gone. Some people have removed the idols because they said Jesus spoke to them in a dream telling them to get rid of the images.

People who come to Christ have a hunger for the Word of God. Sanjay is an evangelist of New Life Fellowship who worked in the far northeast of India before coming to Bombay. He grew up in a devout Hindu home, hating Christians. He felt they were bringing Western traditions into India and thought that they paid people to become converts.

One day a person invited him to an evangelistic crusade, telling him there would be healings. He stood in the front row. When a blind man he knew received his sight and a crippled man was able to walk, he was affected and started reading the Bible. John 3:16 impressed him when it assured him that God loves the world, not just Christians. One evening he had a dream of Christ crucified, and he knew it was for his sins. He was so overcome that he cried and repented all night long. His life changed and he felt full of joy. He left a gang and began to witness to them. He also suffered persecution from his family, but God gave him grace to stand.

The three-pronged goal of New Life Fellowship—"Evangelize," "Equip," and "Establish"—emphasizes evangelism. "Evangelize" refers to direct evangelism but "establish" refers to multiplying house churches, both as the result of evangelism and as outposts from which further evangelism can be launched.

Accra
Where hospitality encourages evangelism

Expansion is given priority status in the Deeper Christian Life Ministry in Accra. They encourage people to quit their jobs and go to new areas to find jobs and begin evangelizing. Rev. Oladimeji remarked, "I started that way as a farmer." He came from Nigeria and supported himself for several years while beginning the work of the Deeper Christian Life Ministry in Ghana. Teachers, for example, will ask for transfers to places most people do not want to go. They do this as part of their missionary outreach while maintaining a government post and salary.

Outreach is primarily through the home groups. In the early years they had some evangelistic crusades in Ghana but not recently. Members invite others to the home groups. A person can belong to a home group and not be a member of the church, but cannot be a member of the church without being a participant in a home group.

Visitors come to the celebration services. At the service we attended visitors were asked to come to benches up front where they were given forms to fill out. After the service several people are designated to talk to the guests to obtain information, so they can visit them in their homes and bring them to a home group. In the groups we attended visitors were almost always present. They are encouraged to ask Jesus into their lives, and it is made clear to them that they need to repent.

There are also special times for evangelism. Members visit people in their neighborhoods on holidays and alternate Saturdays. In these visits they follow up contacts made at other meetings. People in Ghana are hospitable and usually welcome the Christians into their homes. This group has also created specialized ministries for outreach in schools, the military, and prisons. They have different groups for outreach to primary schools, secondary schools, universities, and teacher training schools.

For the Baptists as well, following family and personal friendship networks is the key to evangelistic outreach. People come into the Baptist home groups through follow-up by zone leaders and personal visitation. One of the major differences between Western cities and many African cities is that personal networks tend to be more geographical in the African cities. People know their neighbors well enough to share with them.

The Baptists (as well as Deeper Life Christian Ministry) have evangelistic teams for the zones. People are trained to do personal evangelism rather than crusade ministry. Pastor Deegbe emphasized grass roots training in evangelism. They always have visitors in the large worship services, and the church makes effective use of the celebration service to evangelize.

Although the Evangelical Presbyterian Church of Ghana has a different approach, their evangelism is also effective. They first bring people into the church body, give them teaching in Christian fundamentals, and then assign them to a home group.

Their evangelism is based on the needs of the people. Fear of the devil and demons is an expressed need in Accra. However, when people come to Christ and know the power of the Holy Spirit they throw away their fetishes. This church has a deliverance team that deals with spiritual bondage throughout the city where zone leaders need this kind of help.

Throwing away fetishes or destroying idols is a powerful testimony. One man informed his friend that he had become a Christian and was going to throw away his fetishes. His friend was afraid for him lest he die, but the man testified that Jesus is more powerful than Satan. The friend replied, "If you are still alive in three months, I will throw mine away, too." Three months later the Christian returned and assured his friend, "See, I am still alive."

Evangelism is a big part of what the Evangelical Presbyterian Church of Ghana home groups are all about. They build quality and depth into people's lives, but they are also equipped to do personal evangelism, which happens through already-existing personal social networks.

Chicago
A passion for evangelism

Much of what this church is about hinges around evangelism. While the form varies with the diversity of home groups, evangelism permeates the church. Pastor Mark evangelizes at every opportunity, and in so doing, he sets the example.

This church was experiencing growth before the transition into home groups. But before the groups started, the church was pastor-centered and keeping up with the growth was exhausting him. As the church grew, serious questions arose: "How are these people going to become fruitful followers of Christ? Where is leadership going to come from to maintain the growth?" So the church was driven to a home group model because of their evangelistic growth. At the same time the groups serve as a basis for expanded evangelistic growth.

This scenario is not uncommon. Many churches experiencing growth are driven to a home group model in order to sustain growth—

not just numerical but spiritual growth as well. Church growth advocates report that 60 percent of a traditional congregation may be inactive.[1] If that is the case, as the church grows it may only produce larger numbers of inactive members.

In the staff meetings, in the home groups, and in interviews we heard many stories about personal evangelistic efforts and results. These people pray for the lost, and we met several unsaved people who were brought to the home group by a member.

Dave Z. has a burden for ministry. He works at a large hospital that employs more than 3,000 people. "God has given me a vision for this work. I have made contacts through my job. Some of those people are Christians and are interested in a home group. I want to form a ministry team to reach the hospital." He began by putting an announcement on the bulletin board and talking to people. He is leading the new home group that will focus on the hospital. When the launch date was set for the new home group, everyone in the original group was encouraged to attend the opening meeting, and arrangements were made for rides.

New Life Community Church has been creative in their evangelism. Church members have bought spot announcements on a local MTV channel, telling about the church. And we met people in two home groups who came because of those announcements.

Caracas
Evangelizing along interpersonal networks, bringing glory to God

Pastor Liévano of the Dios Admirable Church is a gifted evangelist and skilled promoter. With his wisdom and age, he has the respect and ability to lead the church. His vision is driven by evangelism, with home groups as a part of that vision. If disciples are growing in the Lord, he believes they will be bringing new people into the Kingdom. That is best accomplished by home groups.

One of the men in the church stated that at least 75 percent of the new converts have come through the home group ministry. He also reported that 90 percent of the active ministry of the church happens through the home groups. Their organizational diagram shows that the home groups are only one program of the church. However, in reality the home groups are the dynamic leading edge in evangelism and discipleship.

Nelly Sanchez strongly encourages people to be "instruments of God in their home groups." In her group she reminds them of the group's goals. "We are to invite people here and win them to Christ." In-depth personal relationships are important in Latin culture. Nelly prays, keeps alert to the world around her, and follows her network of friends. One contact is a woman who lives in the penthouse in her apartment building and parks next to her. She discovered that they both walk for exercise and invited the woman to walk with her. As she built the relationship she showed the Jesus video to the woman and her children. Today the woman comes to the home group, but Nelly has not yet had contact with the woman's husband.

One woman who was saved and discipled in Nelly's group now leads her own group. Two young people came to Christ there. They shared with their mother and today a group in their home is reaching into that neighborhood. Nelly also has home groups for the unbeliever. Non-Christians may attend the home groups with Christians, but the simple evangelistic groups try to eliminate Christian jargon.

Dios Admirable plants churches by using the home groups that cluster in an area where there is no nearby church. Pastor Liévano stated that they were about ready to start a new church. They have a cluster of four home groups and are seeking a hall to rent for the Sunday celebration service. But they do not rely solely on home groups. Street preaching, radio, and special meetings are also involved in outreach.

Cesar Zamora is a businessman who leads a home group. He offered to stop by the apartment where I was staying and take me to his home group. He called us from his cell phone when he arrived at our building. Cesar started the group a year ago and it has grown to its current level of 10–15 people. One of the members is preparing to lead the group within the next few weeks, freeing Cesar to begin another group elsewhere.

The lesson that evening dealt with evangelism. The film was a Campus Crusade movie filmed in the United States and dubbed into Spanish. I wondered how people would react since the context was United States suburban and not Latin urban. However, they were able to see the basic principles and seemed to enjoy what they learned from the film. To bring in new people, they have special social activities, serve cake, and show videos. Their results are impressive as they reach the upper classes with the gospel.

Las Acacias Church operates in a similar way. "Evangelism Explosion" teams are sent into places where no home groups exist. They do saturation evangelism in those new areas. I was told of one area where they had no Christians or home groups. After doing saturation evangelism they now have two home groups with about 20 believers.

Although evangelism is active in the Caracas churches, I am impressed that it seems to be done in preparation for discipleship. Evangelism is always the forerunner to discipleship in Caracas.

Moscow
Balancing home group with celebration service to accomplish effective evangelism

I presented a series of questions to home group leaders whom I could not personally interview. Several of those questions involved the place of evangelism. In Moscow, they do door-to-door evangelism in the apartments. They also witness on the streets at various events. However, most said that inviting friends is the main source for home group growth, giving more contacts than all the other methods combined. Most people in the Rosa Church are relatively new Christians (57 percent have been Christians less than two years). They still have many non-Christian friends and family, so evangelistic contact is not difficult.

Sergei told us that they had gone throughout a neighborhood and invited people to view the Jesus film. The hall was full of people but they were mostly children and young people. They preached the gospel and had a good meeting. However, none of the home group growth came though that special outreach. Another time they went door to door and invited people to a puppet show. Through these means they find they can reach youth but not the adults.

One barrier they face in evangelism is rampant alcoholism among men. One home group member gave a testimony about an alcoholic he had witnessed to for a long time. He spends a lot of time with him and senses the Holy Spirit is working in this man's life, changing him little by little. The home group member wanted prayer for wisdom and spiritual power to help his alcoholic friend.

I asked all the leaders how new home groups come into being. In every case evangelism was at the source and was done through an existing home group. When that group grew, another group was started with the apprentice leader either taking the new group or staying with the existing one.

The celebration service is also important in evangelism. One Sunday morning we attended such a service. One of the members sat by us to translate. After the sermon several people stood and spoke about various ministries. One young man welcomed visitors, gave his testimony, and then invited people who wanted a living relationship with Jesus Christ to come forward. Seven people went to the front. Several Christians took them to one side of the auditorium where they quietly talked and prayed with them while the service continued. Each one who came forward was given a New Testament.

In addition to those who come to Christ in the celebration service, many more are contacted because of that service. Visitors fill out a form giving their phone number and address. These people are later contacted by zone leaders. The list of home groups, with a phone number and the nearest metro stop, is also displayed on the overhead projector. People who are not in a home group can contact someone at that phone number. People attend home groups along social networks which, in Moscow, are not primarily within geographical areas. Some prefer to choose a group and travel quite a distance to be with people they know.

When we asked why people came to Rosa Church one man responded, "I found people genuinely interested in me and my problems. I was saved in a home group, one of the first groups in the church." We heard similar testimonies in other home groups we visited.

Questionnaire Evaluation

Questions 8, 9, 16, 25, 26 and 28 all relate to evangelism. Question 9 was largely ignored by those from Moscow. Otherwise the questions were answered by a high enough percentage of the populations surveyed to give some interesting and practical information.

If networks are the key to evangelism then the people in the home groups should be the result of those interpersonal networks. Question 7 asked about the types of relationships between members of the home group. The following chart gives a summary of the distribution.

Type of Relationship	Accra	Bombay	Caracas	Chicago	Moscow
Family	1-3: 40%	1-3: 21%	1-3: 44%	1-3: 24%	1-3: 37%
Colleagues	1-2: 7%	2-4: 14%	1 : 12%	1 : 7%	1 : 2%
Church	7-12: 28% 14-20: 35%	10-15: 50%	9-14: 56%	5-10:45%	1-4: 23% 10-15: 24%
Neighbors	1-6: 39% 8-12: 22%	10-15: 36%	3-7: 29%	1-5: 25%	1-4: 23% 10-15: 24%
Other Friends	1-4: 37%	5: 7%	4-8: 23%	1-4: 35%	0

Figure 1: Current Home Group Relationship to Site

Within each square there are two numbers. The number on the left is a range of answers from the respondents. The number on the right is the percentage of the respondents who answered in that range. For instance, looking at the church relationships in Bombay, the number "10–15 : 50%" means that 50 percent of the respondents indicated that 10 to 15 of the people in their home group were also in their church. The total percentages are over 100 percent because people in the home groups often have multiple types of relationships. A person may be both a neighbor and attend the same church as the respondent. This chart tells us where the primary network relationships are.

The primary relationship is the church. Approximately one-half of the people in the home groups are also in church with the other home group members. "Neighbors" was the type of relationship ranked highest in Accra (61 percent) and Moscow (47 percent) and was relatively high in Bombay (36 percent). Even in Caracas and Chicago, the numbers are high enough to see that growth will come through neighborhood relationships.

Network relationships were reinforced by answers to question 16, "How did you become part of the cell group? Can you name the individual(s) who brought you into this group?" In Bombay 43 percent and in Accra 47 percent named the individual(s) responsible for their participation in the group. The other three sites had much higher percentages (Caracas 65 percent, Chicago 68 percent, and Moscow 71 percent). The difference can perhaps be explained from the larger number of home group leaders filling out the questionnaire in Bombay and Accra.

Accra had 34 percent of the people placed by the church leadership—a function of a highly organized church. When people have passed through the training they are placed in a group. Usually they are placed near their homes and the new home group members will be neighbors, but the initiative comes from the church structure. Being placed by the church leadership was in second place in Bombay (17 percent) and Caracas (10 percent) and was a close third for Chicago (12 percent). Moscow only showed 5 percent in that category. The exceptional case of Moscow can be explained largely by the fact that it is a new church still forming.

In question 9, I asked people to list *potential* group members giving the same categories as in question 7.

Type of Relationship	Accra	Bombay	Caracas	Chicago	Moscow
Family	1-5: 54%	1-5: 36%	1-5: 55%	1-5: 44%	0
Colleagues	1-4: 44%	1-3: 14%	1-6: 35%	1-5: 48%	0
Church	1-4: 28%	2-8: 36%	2-5: 25%	1-5: 33%	0
Neighbors	1-6: 69%	1-6: 29% 8-12: 21%	1-6: 48%	1-6: 52%	0
Other Friends	1-6: 35%	1-5: 21%	1-5: 35%	1-5: 32%	0

Figure 2: Potential Home Group Relationship to Site

There are healthy ranges of potential contacts for all the sites. The percentages for potential home group members coming out of the church are lower, while friendship, family, and neighbor contacts are usually higher. Potential only suggests possibility, but realization of the possibilities is a first step in the process of evangelism.

In question 25, I asked how many new people visited their group in the past six months, and in 26, how many stayed at least a month. The responses are summarized in the following chart.

	Question 25	Question 26
Sites:	No. of visitors: Percentage	Visitors who stayed a month: Percentage
Accra	3-6: 44%	1-4: 53% 6-8: 14%
Bombay	1-5: 68%	1-5: 64%
Caracas	2-4: 19% 6-10: 44%	1-4: 35% 5-8: 25%
Chicago	2-4: 19% 5-10: 32% 20: 9%	1-6: 45% 8-12: 25%
Moscow	3-5: 69%	1: 31% 2-5: 45%

Figure 3: Results of questions 25 and 26

The percentages listed on the right side of the columns are the percentage responding with those answers. For example, in Bombay 68 percent of the respondents recorded that between one and five visitors attended their home group while 64 percent said that between one and five people stayed at least a month. All sites show a continual flow of visitors with significant numbers staying at least a month.

In Question 38 a case study asks what respondents would do if they encountered a friend who needed to talk while they were on the way to a home group meeting. I divided the answers into five categories although most answers fell into one of three.

Site	1) Schedule another time to talk	2) Talk to friend now	3) Invite friend to meeting	4) Talk now but involve group (i.e., call)	5) Other
Accra	18	6	70	5	2
Bombay	27	27	39	0	4
Caracas	25	29	35	0	0
Chicago	11	30	47	10	0
Moscow	33	21	17	10	17

Figure 4: Question 38 - Case Study (Percentages)

In any culture personality differences will account for some variation. However, this question presents enough variation fitting with
other data from this study to give some indication of differences in
evangelism styles.

While every site except Moscow gave "3, invite the friend to the
meeting" the largest percentage, note the differences. Accra at 70
percent was the largest. Many people questioned in Accra are home
group leaders. They have a sense of their responsibility to the group as
leader, and the need to have the group grow. This factor derives, at
least in part, from the highly developed structures of the Accra churches.
Evangelism is affected by the strong emphasis on structure.

In Chicago evangelism comes from the context of caring. While 47
percent of the people would invite the friend to the group, another 30
percent would talk to him now regardless of the home group meeting.
Only 11 percent would make a later appointment. Most of the Moscow

respondents opted to make a later appointment. Home group time is spent mostly in prayer. With a three-hour meeting and a possible one-hour travel time each way, making another appointment is reasonable.

Bombay and Caracas results are fairly evenly distributed among the first three categories although inviting the friend to the home group is six to eight percent higher. Caracas respondents often mentioned all three possibilities in their responses. Seventy-one percent of the respondents in Bombay were home group leaders. There was a positive correlation between those who said they would make another appointment and those currently leading home groups.

Key Points

• Home group ministry must be involved in intentional, aggressive evangelism.

• Cultural factors play a key role in what is effective, relevant home group evangelism.

• Church leadership must model as well as teach evangelism in the home group.

• The celebration service and home group work together to enhance evangelism.

• Interpersonal social networks are the most effective avenues for evangelism in the home group.

• Prayer, worship, caring, and teaching are necessary disciplines that accompany home group evangelism.

• Evangelism is a process making the home group an effective outreach vehicle.

Endnote

1. See Peter Wagner in "Syllabus and Lecture Outlines for Classroom Use," *Church Growth Principles and Procedures* (Pasadena: Fuller Theological Seminary, 1980), page 13. Wagner designates 5 classes of workers from unpaid lay workers to various church staff people. He also has a sixth category called "consumers"—people who require care but can give nothing to the church. In the average church 60 percent are in this category. In an active church 36.5 percent are in this category and in a dying church 71 percent fall into this group. He references Donald McGavran, *Understanding Church Growth* (Grand Rapid: Eerdmans, 1970), page 286.

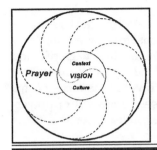

CHAPTER 8

Prayer
Making Evangelism Fruitful

Regarding the expansion of the gospel Paul wrote:

All over the world this gospel is bearing fruit and growing, just as it has been doing among you since the day you heard it and understood God's grace in all its truth (Colossians 1:6).

In the chapter on evangelism I wrote about aggressive evangelistic efforts, showing that the truth Paul declared in the early church is still true today. People are coming to Christ, the light is pushing back the darkness, and the Body is growing. However, evangelism is not the only reason behind this exciting growth. Prayer is a significant force making the evangelism fruitful. A. W. Tozer wrote,

A praying Christian is a constant threat to the stability of Satan's government. The Christian is a holy rebel loose in the world with access to the throne of God.[1]

Having served as a church planter for many years, I was impressed that as we prayed and mobilized people to pray, God worked—breaking down barriers, opening hearts to the Gospel, and building up the people of God as new churches came into existence. Prayer is hard work. The word translated "pray" in Philippians comes from the Greek word "agonize." Paul understood the effort necessary for prayer.

All the churches studied have strong prayer ministries, and the home groups are the basic units for prayer. Some of the churches have other places where they have longer and more specific prayer efforts, but even those are built upon the home group.

Separating prayer from other activities is difficult. We pray in order to evangelize, care for others, develop leadership, and even know God's will about vision. In the Christian life prayer should be a part of every activity. But when I speak of prayer in this chapter, I want to look at it mainly as an activity of the home group, even though of necessity, the discussion may sometimes spill onto other topics.

Moscow — Rosa Church
Prayer is the principal focus

The spirit of the home group ministry in Moscow can be summarized in the words of one member in her response to my question, "Why are you in the home group?" She replied, "We are here to glorify God and pray a lot. We pray for one another and the nation. We have Bible studies, but prayer is more important." Prayer is the focus of this church and everything else the church does comes out of prayer-centeredness. In the home groups we visited, at least one hour of the time was spent praying.

The first meeting we attended was a three-hour leadership training meeting on Saturday evening with 100 leaders present. The meeting opened with ten minutes of prayer. People prayed in soft voices simultaneously. The leader then lifted his voice and closed that part of the meeting. The first hour was given to prayer and worship, the second to the pastor's teaching. The final hour was given to sharing and prayer again.

The hour of prayer started with personal confession and repentance. The first part of the sharing consisted of reports from the various zone leaders. After each leader gave a report, which included needs and victories of the group as well as the leader, the pastor and a few others came forward to lay hands on that person as the entire group prayed. Each report took less than five minutes, sometimes only two or three minutes, while the prayer for that need almost always lasted five minutes or more. More general prayers were voiced for the home group leaders: that they would take the work seriously, that they would have a living relationship with the living God, and that they would not fall into an empty formalism with God or the home group.

The pastor gave a plea for prayer for youth, especially those who were going into the military. He recounted something of the difficulty of his own military experience where he was persecuted for his faith. "We should bring men into the church and pray for them before they go out with the military," he said as he led us in fervent prayer for young men doing their military obligation.

The following day we attended the celebration service. Part of that service was given to prayer as well. During the worship time a senior leader led in prayer for about 15 minutes. The prayer began with Romans 8:33, "Who will bring any charge against those whom God has chosen..." He prayed for the congregation, their needs and their spiritual growth, for their leaders, and the coming election. He asked for wisdom and the fear of the Lord to come on all people in government leadership. He mentioned the wickedness in the nation and asked God to preserve the land, the city, and his people. After 45 minutes of worship, another man led in prayer before the preacher brought the message. His plea was that the Word might change and bless us.

Two hours into the service, the man in charge of leading the prayer time stood. He had in his hands a wad of papers (written prayer requests passed forward during the service). Everyone stood and he prayed generally for those requests. His closing words were, "As with Lazarus you had the people remove the stone and you gave him new life. We are going to remove the stone." He then tore all the papers in two. People had continued to pray out loud but softly during this process.

Then people came forward for special prayer. A woman brought a baby who was ill. Another couple brought their infant for dedication. People who had family or friends in Chechnya stood as the leader led in prayer for those in Chechnya. Individuals stood who had a close friend or family member who was alcoholic, and prayer was offered for the problem of alcoholics and their families. A team of youth who witness on the streets was asked to stand and the church body prayed for them. The next 25–30 minutes was spent in prayer for the sick, together with testimonies of answered prayer. The service eventually ended at 1:30 P.M.

We learned more about the church prayer life in the meetings for zone and home group leaders. They always mentioned prayer as being important in their group. They also meet 30 minutes before each celebration service to pray for the service.

The zone leaders are organizing special prayer efforts as well. They are linking people up in a prayer chain where a person in the home group will pray daily for another group member. The second effort concerns home prayer groups in each zone. These special groups spend the entire time praying.

Each home group meeting we attended started with 15 minutes of prayer. Everyone in the group participated, either in actually leading or in various verbal responses to the leader. Before praying for individuals in the home group, they prayed for the church, the leadership, the pastor specifically, for unity, for national and city governments, and that the Kingdom would advance in their area.

When I asked what they were doing differently from when they started participating in the home groups, I found one answer particularly revealing.

We were children spiritually and came to the group with lots of questions. We met twice a week and talked about ourselves. We knew each other well. Now we have fewer questions and we pray more. Before, we prayed for everyday needs. Now we pray for spiritual growth.

One group had no Bible teacher and I asked about that. They stated that one of their prayer requests was that a Bible teacher would come to their home group. For now, they pray and drink tea, and pray some more. This group has a lending library that includes Christian books, cassettes, and videos to help provide teaching.

I asked people what they do to get new people to come. The usual response was, "Of course, we invite people, but mainly we pray."

The emphasis we experienced in the Rosa Church is also a part of other churches in Russia. They may not be as focused as Rosa, but prayer is important. Andrei Petrov, a Baptist pastor, sees spiritual healing, prayer, and tea as the three main parts of a home group. He feels that spiritually focused fellowship couched in prayer is the purpose for the home groups. Alexander Fedichkin, also a Baptist pastor, is trying to create home groups that will focus uniquely on prayer. A special prayer group would be a prayer center for each zone, drawing a few people from each of several home groups.

Caracas — Dios Admirable
Pray without ceasing

One of the first testimonies I heard in a home group dealt with prayer. The woman, a visitor to this home group, was telling about a morning she had spent in prayer with her home group. She said,

We are so busy in the day and tired at night. We tried to break that routine by giving a morning to prayer. I always thought it was difficult to pray for one hour. But we started at 8:00 A.M. Suddenly it was time to quit at 11:30 A.M.

The model for prayer in the home group ministry in Caracas was certainly different from that in Russia but no less intense. Each home group had a time of sharing and prayer. The prayer was not the major focus of the home group time because that time was primarily taken with Bible teaching and discussion. However, the place of prayer is strong in the home group ministry.

They start each new group with one to three months of prayer prior to opening the group. The home group host, leader, apprentice, and supervisor meet weekly at the proposed meeting time and place to pray. Sometimes the pastor or other home group leaders in the area will be a part of the prayer time. They pray for people to come to Christ and for the home group to be a strong witness in the area.

Less organized prayer also has had a part in starting home groups for Dios Admirable. Irma told how she and another woman prayed for two years that a group would start in her home. They prayed that people would come and fill the empty chairs. The four-year-old group now has eight to twelve people who participate.

The home group leader's wife shared an interesting story with us about answered prayer. She and two other women were praying together. One prophesied and another interpreted. They were to travel to the nation's largest prison, look for a certain man, and give him a message from the Lord, but they were only given his first name. The man had recently been shot in the back and almost died.

The women traveled that day to the prison and because one of the women is a senator, they were able to enter. However, there were thousands of prisoners and they only had a first name. One of the women went into the restroom to pray and ask for specific guidance. She was directed to another part of the prison, where they asked for the person by his first name. A man with that name was there so they asked him if he had been shot in the back and almost died. He was astounded and asked how they knew about him. They told him the Lord had sent them to give him a message from God—God wanted him to receive Jesus and be saved from his sins. They led him to the Lord and feel he will be an instrument of God to witness in that prison. Many pastors and Christians have already preached in that prison. Today about one-third of the prisoners are Christian, which has had a profound effect on the prison.

By the time I had an in-depth interview with Nelly Sanchez I was impressed by the significance of prayer in their ministry. I asked her what part prayer plays in the home group ministry, especially for her as the ministry director. Nelly stated that she and the four area coordinators pray for the home group leaders, members, and their families on the day they meet.

Several corporate meetings focus on prayer. Every second Sunday of the month the entire church meets for prayer from 2:00 P.M. to 6:00 P.M. While this meeting is not uniquely focused on home groups, much of the prayer need comes through home groups. The church publishes a weekly list of prayer requests and meets every Friday from 6:30 P.M. to 8:00 P.M. to pray through these requests. They also have occasional all-night prayer meetings.

The month of January is a month of prayer for the entire church, and prayer is the main activity of all church meetings. During that month all the home groups spend their meetings in prayer. Some of the home groups also dedicate one meeting a month for prayer.

Caracas — Las Acacias
Prayer is the important first step to effective ministry

"For Latins," Mirtha said, "prayer is important. The work is of God even though the programs are of men." She continued to share information about the prayer structure in the Las Acacias church. She reported that Venezuela is quite closed to the Lord and evangelism. Because of that, the Lord's work is hard and their main tool is prayer.

Her sector has three prayer coordinators. They work together constantly to develop new prayer strategies. In addition to the current 36 home groups in this sector, there are 14 prayer home groups that were created solely for the purpose of prayer. Sometimes these groups consist of elderly people who make prayer their ministry.

Every third Tuesday all the home group leaders, nuclei leaders, and parish leaders meet together and pray. Sometimes they rent a bus and go to an area where they plan an outreach with the purpose of starting home groups. They walk over that section and claim it for the Lord. Two years ago they began focusing prayer on one large area that had no evangelical witness. Today eight home groups are in operation there.

All home group leaders fast one day a month. Before opening a new group they pray for a month. Mirtha wants to be sure the host, the home group leader, and the others are serious. The leadership team for the prospective home group meets for a month to solidify the commitment. Sometimes they delay the opening of a home group in order to extend this period of prayer preparation.

Both churches in Caracas have demonstrated a strong prayer emphasis in the various large group meetings and the smaller, home group meetings. They have developed a prayer strategy that is effective, powerful, and fruitful.

Bombay — New Life Fellowship
Prayer is the spiritual battle

As we walked into the rented auditorium to attend the Bandra celebration service, the first thing I saw was an older gray-haired woman praying with a younger woman. One of the elders said the pastoral staff was in the back of the auditorium engaged in intercessory prayer. After the final prayer of the service, the elders of the church and others stayed to pray for individuals as they expressed special needs.

Several small groups laid hands on the sick and the needy as they prayed.

That evening we attended a celebration service in Hindi, in a poor part of the area. Some of the people who participated in the morning English-speaking service led the Hindi service. As in the morning worship, the primary prayer for people took place after the service when the leaders were called to pray for people's needs.

Two days later we attended a zone leaders' meeting in Chembur, in the eastern part of Bombay. The meeting was a prayer and praise report following a three-day evangelistic crusade in Satara, a city several hours away. After about 35 minutes of praise and singing, the meeting moved into testimonies. Many of the testimonies touched on direct answers to prayer although evangelism was the theme. This meeting spoke volumes about the church focus in terms of prayer and outreach.

The first person who spoke praised God for the great things He had done. Over 300 people attended the crusade the first day. "God is great," she said. "We saw signs and wonders and many came to Jesus. Many people heard the gospel and even many Hindus and Muslims gave their lives to Jesus."

One of the leaders mentioned what he thought was the greatest miracle that happened. "We enjoyed being together with each other. We sang in many languages and played games. We had joy in each other's company." People were open and they met little resistance, which he credited to answered prayer.

These testimonies terminated in an extensive time of prayer and praise. We were asked to share about some of the places we have worked as missionaries. After that people again gathered in several smaller groups for prayer. One woman and her husband asked Karen to pray for her as they have not been able to have children in their 12 years of marriage. Karen did. Afterwards the woman thanked Karen but assured her that they were following Jesus whether or not they had children.

In most of the house groups, the meeting was taken up mostly with worship, some sharing, and Bible teaching. Prayer was usually the final thing that happened and often occurred after the meeting was officially closed.

In Sister Hilda's home group session, we met from 7:00 P.M. to 9:00 P.M. The women prayed for a woman who had been troubled by a sense of evil. Sister Hilda said that when Christians return to their homes in the country, they are often coerced into paying homage to a

Hindu god. We were reminded that the battle is spiritual and must be fought with the weapons of the spirit. Prayer is the key weapon.

At another level certain prayer groups meet for intercession. Christians from different house groups in an area gather to pray for three hours each week. They pray for the coming Sunday celebration services, for the various ministries, and for personal needs. Another prayer meeting much like this is for home group leaders who live close to each other and gather to pray all night each Friday.

On Saturday the elders and pastors meet for prayer. This meeting prepares hearts for Sunday and they also pray for the material needs of the church and its members. I mention the details of the above prayer meetings to give an impression of how overtly the enemy works in this culture. People sense the power of evil even as they sense the power of the Spirit of God. Satan may have gone underground in some cultures, but not in Bombay.

Chicago — New Life Community Church
Senior leadership models prayer and fasting for home groups

Effective and specific prayer is powerfully modeled in this church. Pastor Mark graciously invited me to a staff meeting which included church staff at all levels as well as a few out-of-town visitors. The meeting began with a time of singing interspersed with prayer and praise, followed by people sharing from their ministries, but often Pastor Mark would stop the proceedings and ask that we pray for an individual.

One young man told of a close call that he and one of the other workers had as they walked through a gang-infested area near the church. Some gang members threatened them. He yelled, "We only have Jesus!" Gang members started shooting and the two workers ran. They escaped but someone else was hit and wounded. The group gathered around them to pray for continued protection for them in their ministry to the youth in that area of the city.

In a home group with Dave Garrett, he challenged the group to choose three unsaved people whom they saw as 'impossible' projects, people hardened to the gospel. He shared that he had chosen three and prayed for them. Then during a holiday he was able to lead one of his impossible cases, a close relative, to Christ. When he finished with his story the entire group clapped and cheered. The time ended with 15 minutes in what Dave called a holy huddle. We stood in a circle, holding hands and praying for each other.

Ralph told us that each person in his group has a one-day fast on a regular basis. The rest of the group supports that person with special prayer during the fast. The senior church leadership went on a 40-day liquid-only fast leading up to Easter and a special evangelistic crusade for the Chicago area. Several of the people joined the church leadership in the fast. Some fasted the entire time, while others fasted for different amounts of time from one day to two weeks. During that time, several new home groups opened and the celebration service attendance increased from 700 plus to more than 900.

Prayer requests in the home groups reflect the struggles of daily life. One man wanted to be a better parent. Another man prayed about his divorce. He talked about the pain of not having his four children at home. One woman has a teenage son who is trying to live for the Lord. He is often beaten up by gangs, but he wants to start a Bible study at his school. We prayed fervently for this boy who daily stares evil in the face. In John's group one of the new people has been beaten up by gangs—stabbed and shot. The group prayed he would have the strength to leave that lifestyle. We prayed about jobs, and we prayed specifically for the outreach of the group.

The prayer focus in New Life Church happens primarily within the home groups and with the senior leadership. However, prayer is also a part of the larger celebration services, especially as individuals kneel at the front to pray before and after the service. Prayer is modeled as a priority of this church.

Accra
Organized, fervent prayer is a part of every meeting

We attended a Saturday prayer retreat for the 31 home group leaders of the Madina congregation of the Evangelical Presbyterian Church of Ghana. The meeting started at 8:00 A.M. and ended at 1:30 P.M. Dr. Seth Gbewonyo, the home group coordinator for the church, led the activities for the day and gave a devotion. However, most of the time was spent praying. Sometimes people stood during prayer. Sometimes they sat on backless benches.

The well-organized time consisted of four major prayer segments, each led by a different person. These prayer times lasted about 30 minutes each and were interspersed with worship. The first part concerned self-examination; the second, personal concerns of home group leaders; the third section was focused on leadership; and the final major segment consisted of prayer for the church and the nation. This was an election year in Ghana so its citizens were concerned.

Representative prayer requests from this group show some of their cares.

- Pray that God will burden group members with a desire to visit people and help in any way possible.
- Pray about tardiness, that people will be on time for the meetings. Ask that God will remove the things that make them late.
- Pray that lessons will not be dull and leaders will be prepared.
- Pray for a right mentality on the part of the leaders toward the gifts and talents of home group members.
- A woman needed money to entertain and refresh people in her home.
- A man asked for help in memorizing Scripture so he can remember verses he needs to use.
- Another man desired freedom from debt. People owe him and he owes others. He cannot pay until he is paid.
- A man asked prayer for his unbelieving parents who only criticize Christians.
- A woman was killed by lightning. Her unbelieving family wants many fetishes so she is still not buried. The Christians want to bury her.
- A man's co-workers on the job cheat and pressure him to do likewise.
- Some of the people do not have steady employment.
- A person in the group talks too much.
- Pray that God's anointing and blessing would fall on the nation.
- Pray for peace and understanding between ruling and opposition parties.
- Pray for the president and all in authority.
- Pray for the Church universal that God's will be done in the Church.
- Pray for pastors and other church leaders.
- Pray that the work of the enemy will be destroyed—pray against Satan's efforts.

Throughout the home groups in the various churches in Accra, the prayer method was remarkably similar. People shared their requests briefly during a designated time. Everyone prayed aloud together. Often the leader spoke the requests one by one, leading the people through the topics of prayer.

Prayer plays a significant part in the home group ministry here. Although in the Deeper Christian Life ministry prayer is programmed into the meeting, there is variation and as much as 30 minutes may be given to prayer. When people in the home group trust each other, they accept one another in love and give support. They went home encouraged that their concerns had been given to God. He had heard their prayers and He would bring aid.

Questionnaire Evaluation

Question 24 reveals information about prayer in the churches of this study. The question asked people to list the activities of their cell group and how many minutes are given to each activity. Ten to twenty minutes is the average time each of the home groups spend in prayer. That amount of prayer for each group, multiplied by the number of home groups, amounts to significant prayer for the work of the Gospel.

The time range for prayer and the percentage of respondents for the various sites were as follows: Accra, 10–20 minutes, 27 percent of the responses; Bombay, 10–20 minutes, 61 percent of the responses; Chicago, 10–20 minutes, 55 percent of the responses; Caracas, 5–15 minutes, 67 percent of the responses; Moscow, no responses.

The uniformity of responses is remarkable considering how difficult it is for most people to think about how much time they give to any activity in the 'average' home meeting. Bombay, Chicago, and Caracas are quite similar. Accra respondents designated less time in their home groups for prayer. Their home group meetings are more highly programmed so they often wrote down how much time the program allows for prayer. Moscow questionnaires were mostly blank on this question because they feel they have no uniform structure for their meetings. However, as we have seen, this is not because they do not pray.

Key Points

- Prayer is a necessary basis for home groups members to grow in their relationship with God and each other.
- God works to expand his Kingdom, defeat Satan, and build his people as they pray in the home groups.
- In home groups, personal needs can be shared with a few trusted friends.
- Prayer demonstrates the unity of the home group with the larger church body.

- Home groups are the basis for wider prayer structures, both within the church and between churches.
- Corporate prayer is necessary for personal spiritual growth.
- Culture, as well as spiritual maturity, affects the requests people bring to God.

Endnote

[1].   A. W. Tozer, *That Incredible Christian* (Camp Hill, PA: Christian Publications, 1964), 71.

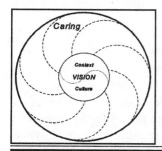

CHAPTER 9

Caring
The Integrating Factor

Aiding high school dropouts, counseling with a man who beats his wife, promoting plant husbandry, requiring premarital counseling, drinking tea together, announcing job opportunities during the worship service—these were only a few of the numerous ways the churches in this survey went about showing care.

In one way or another, caring touches every aspect of home group life. Some even use the name "care groups," emphasizing the importance of caring in the home group context. Caring also reflects the biblical command to show love through action.

> Dear children, let us not love with words or tongue but with actions and in truth (1 John 3:18).

When we relate to people over a period of time in a home group, we develop caring relationships that integrate all aspects of home group life. Fruitful home group ministry begins with a God-given vision. That vision itself is a function of the fact that God cares—for the lost and for his own people. We pray because we care, and we believe God works in us and through us when we pray. We preach the gospel and seek to reach others because God cares. Modeling is an important aspect of teaching in the home group, and caring is what shines through when we model Christ-like behavior.

Structure and leadership development are also touched by caring. Structures can become rigid and institutionalized, functioning for their own purposes and not for spiritual growth. However, as long as the leaders grow in loving relationships, that kind of rigidity is highly unlikely. Effective spiritual leaders are developed within a caring atmosphere. Modeling spiritual leadership includes obeying the many "one-another commands" of Scripture: to love one another, bear one another's burdens, show hospitality to one another.

Because caring is so integral to every other aspect of home ministry, writing about it as a separate factor can be difficult. However, our study shows enough data unique to caring that it merits a separate chapter.

Chicago — New Life Community Church
Caring is central to all they do

As I entered a small conference room to visit a staff meeting, I noticed a young man who did not look like pastoral staff. One of the church personnel had been ministering to him. When the meeting started, the staff member brought the man into the meeting where several of the pastors laid hands on him and prayed. The staff person then went with him into another room to continue ministry.

While certainly not all staff meetings begin this way, I think it illustrates the caring attitude of the staff that is modeled for the entire congregation. Caring is demonstrated and lived at every level in this church.

They show they care by listening. When Tony asked people to share in his group, he assured them, "You can share anything, good or bad (people laughed), as to what is going on in your life."

"My children are returning from a visit with their father," one woman offered. "Pray for me because that transition is always a challenge. I am new in this group and last week Tony asked me if I was ready to follow the Lord no matter what the cost. I want to. I have to trust the Lord for rent each month." Group members prayed for the woman, and special time was taken for her during and after the meeting. The total sharing time that evening lasted 45 minutes.

Caring continued after the group officially ended. Tony talked with his three undershepherds. His wife Linda visited with different people, giving encouragement with hugs. We walked to the car with Dave, who had come for the first time. As we approached the car we found two police cars almost blocking our way. They had a car pulled over and a group of young men were spread-eagled against the auto in the bitter cold. Perhaps the caring from the home groups will reach out and touch them one day.

Looking at the contact quotients, Tony's group had a total of 122 weekly contacts and 10 people had filled out the questionnaires. The CQ for his group is 12.2. That means that each person averages 12 contacts, either in person or by phone, with others in the group between meetings.

Caring is also shown by the time the home groups meet. Because people usually work during the day, most home groups meet in the evening. However, Roy leads a group for shift workers that meets in the morning after the people complete their night shifts. When I attended, it had grown to 12 people in less than six months.

Maria has a full-time job and is a single mom. Her energy and love is demonstrated as she leads a women's home group. When asked about what she is doing differently now than earlier, she commented on compassion. "My character has changed more than my methods. I have the gift of evangelism but I am learning more about mercy and compassion." This group had an extraordinarily high contact quotient of 18.2. One reason is Maria's energy and dedication to the group. However, other members are highly involved as well. They provide significant care for each other.

Kim and John shared about some of their contacts—people from their former way of life whom they are trying to reach with the gospel. Recently they confronted Frank who was slipping back into the street lifestyle. He had been shot and the bullet lodged in his heart. They are also trying to get together with another couple where the man is in drug rehabilitation. Yet another woman lives in a building where prostitutes work. They bang on her door trying to get money. These home group members have fruitful contact with a network of people who do not know Christ. Their relationships have resulted in fruitful evangelism.

Much can be learned about caring from observing the home group leaders.

1. They are encouragers. They affirm people and see the good in them. Even when some members have difficulties or have failed, the leaders see the positive side without minimizing the problem. They have often struggled with the same issues the others have and can give them useful input. They are on the phone or getting together with members between meetings.

2. They are flexible. Tony related that in a previous home group he had allowed two women to lead them on a 45-minute trail off the subject. He felt the digression, which concerned Jesus' words, "Whatever you ask in My name will be given you," was important. He plans to deal with this matter in the future. He is flexible but does not lose control.

3. They are practical. Cell group leaders deal with current issues in member's lives. Gus spoke up in a lesson that compared following God with following the ways of the world. "We confuse success with time spent on the job. Sometimes we take too much time for our job because we want to succeed but harm our families in the process."

4. They are friendly and hospitable. They make you feel welcome in a way that is genuine, not forced. They go out of their way to be friends and to accommodate you.

5. They are involved. They know what is going on in the lives of the people and they care. They have a high level of contact with the people in their group. At the end of one meeting, a man said, "I feel good about this!" He was referring to the teaching, but the group had shown great care for him. His wife had taken their four children and left him for another man. He was feeling lonely and wounded, but the group had taken time for him that night.

6. They are dedicated to their responsibility. They teach by modeling. Caring and responsibility are demonstrated in the daily lives of the leaders as well as many of the members. They are gently in control, making things move in a certain direction.

Accra
Developing caring relationships through neighbor contacts

Accra churches had the most well-developed structures, which influences their caring ministries. Caring shows up in the small details of daily life in Africa. It is a part of respect and perhaps a function of a traditional society where kinship ties remain strong. Even simple greetings are an important part of the caring as people daily show courtesy to those about them.

> Refusal to greet someone is taken as a sign of enmity, disrespect (especially, when children do not greet adults), pride, snobbery, etc. It signals refusal to acknowledge the person. African society frowns on such antisocial behavior. To greet is the most common and regularly observed moral norm.[1]

Accra — Deeper Christian Life Ministry
Caring for the basic needs of life—spiritual and material

Caring is a part of the name the Deeper Christian Life Ministry gives their small group ministry (Home Caring Fellowship). This church views humans as integrated beings and has developed a philosophy on that basis. The national director, Rev. Oladimeji, explained, "The HCF cares for every part and problem of man since these will affect the spiritual life sooner or later." They are structured to care for the people they serve, and that structure is both formal and effective.

An offering taken every Sunday evening in the HCF is kept separately for the specific physical needs of home group members. Hospital expenses, funeral costs, and funds for starting a new business are all examples of how these offerings can be used. Money collected in the home groups is turned into the church where funds from all groups are pooled and distributed based on a person's needs, not on what a home group has collected. The needs come to the home group leader who must okay the transaction and secure the zone leader's approval.

While we were with Pastor Oladimeji a call came from a pastor in a remote area of Ghana whose wife needed surgery. Immediate plans were made to bring her to Accra where the church cared for her expenses, her meals, and other physical needs as well as praying for her and ministering to her spiritually. They do not want people to think Christians do not take care of each other. So part of their witness is caring for those of their congregation who have severe need.

Another part of their caring relates to spreading the gospel. They send leaders to other cities to open new works. If those leaders cannot find jobs, they are given money to start up a small business.

Because they are involved in caring relationships, especially at important ritual ceremonies such as birth, death, circumcision, and marriage, Christians can witness from those platforms. Home groups have played a major part in funeral arrangements for members. Funerals are extremely important in Ghana, and the church makes great effort to support those who are mourning. A caring relationship offers an opportunity to preach the gospel to those who, in a crisis, may be more willing to listen.

The women's ministry of the church has a well developed training program to help people gain employable skills. Sewing, baking, hair styling, and plant husbandry are among skills taught to help women gain employment. They also seek to aid high school dropouts as well as those having difficulties with their exams. Further programs include secretarial skills, batik, and arts. Helping people who have come to Christ gain employment promotes church expansion as people gain the skills necessary to start businesses in new areas where they can begin a home group ministry.

In a discussion with senior leaders I asked about the kind of problems they experience in home groups. Marriage problems were at the top of the list. One instance they related was of a man who beat his wife. The home group leader normally deals with the problem at the home group level. If the problem cannot be handled by the home group leader, a zone or district leader may be called in to deal with the matter.

Senior leaders visit the home groups regularly so they can be alert to caring needs. Sometimes the home group leader needs care. The Bible study may become dry and home group members lose interest.

The supervisors then give help before the home group becomes stagnant or dead.

Accra — Calvary Baptist Church
Caring is the function of family

In this church all welfare issues come through the home groups. The pastors told me that while the church would exist even without the home groups, the quality of church life would be far different. They trust the home group leaders to know what is happening in their own groups. As with Deeper Life Christian Ministry, the home group leader is the first person who must approve welfare aid.

One interesting part of the caring ministry here concerns marriage. If a couple desires to be married in the church they communicate that first to the home group leader. That leader communicates the desire to the pastor. Dr. Osei-Bonsu, the pastor in charge of marriages, requires the couple to have six months of premarital counseling. In this way, the church cares for people by seeking to build stronger marriages.

After a church service I questioned a group of about 30 people involved in home group ministries. Their comments were significant. One woman said, "The shepherd has a personal relationship with the sheep. Everybody feels special. People want to come." A man said, "Our group helps each other with their blind spots." Their caring involves the tough love necessary to help people grow in difficult areas of their lives.

Another woman related that their group expresses unity by going to weddings, funerals, and births together. The home groups in this church are often composed of family members so attending these events would be logical. Home groups in Accra are more likely to consist of family members than at any other site.

Evangelical Presbyterian Church of Ghana
Struggles and caring bring growth

The senior leadership here requires everyone to belong to a home group and attendance is taken. The principal reason concerns their ability to care for the home members. One example illustrated the problem. A man who had some contact with the church died. The family approached the church, asking it to give the family 100,000 cedis toward the funeral. The leader told me, "We buried him but we did not pay the family as the man did nothing for the church." He was not in a home group.

Offerings are taken in home groups for the welfare of the members, and the church uses its resources to take care of its own people. A person must be in the home group to benefit from the church's "Welfare Union." They have developed a fairly structured method of determining how much a person receives for funeral expenses or other crisis needs. The criteria is based on how long a person has been a member, how active, or how close the relationship is with someone in the church. The home group leaders know who is active at the grass roots level, and the home group structure allows the church a more efficient use of its limited resources.

The prayer requests at leaders' meetings also demonstrate their desire to be active in caring. A repeated prayer request was for time and transportation to visit the people in their home groups. Women asked for enough money to have a hospitality ministry out of their homes. One pastor asked prayer for honest household help so his wife could be more actively involved in ministry.

I asked one home group what they wanted me to know about them. A woman replied, "We love one another. We are meeting in this kiosk. The owner closes her sewing business early on home group day to prepare to receive the group." As I looked around, I could see no indication that a few hours earlier the room had contained several seamstresses at work.

Martin Obeng, a worker for the Ghana Fellowship of Evangelical Students who accompanied us on many of our home group visits, was impressed at how well the groups worked. He felt that most people's concerns were in the area of money and health, and those are their areas of struggle and faith-testing.

Moscow — The Rosa Church
Drinking tea together, a necessary step in giving care

In a telephone interview with Sergey Kuzkov I asked what was culturally different in home group ministry in Russia in general and in Moscow specifically. One of the four things he mentioned involved caring. "Eating and drinking tea in small groups is important. People need to meet on days off such as Saturday or Sunday afternoon." That theme was reflected by most of the Russian leaders with whom I talked. Tea is important because that is where quiet people begin to talk and share their hearts.

We saw many examples of caregiving in the home groups we attended. One woman told the group that she was tired of playing church. She has been in church for three years and now wants to have fun. She is a single mom and often leaves her child with her mother. The group talked to her frankly about her relationship to God and her duty to her child. At one point she stomped out of the room in anger.

However, the group prayed and she returned. At another point in the discussion she turned to us and said in English, "They say I enjoy wallowing in my sin. I think they are right." The home group has been persistently caring for this young woman, and the battle is fought through prayer and caring.

People in the Moscow home groups often live at some distance from each other. Transportation is good so the personal and social networks are not as highly localized as in Accra. The telephones work well so there is continued contact by phone between home group meetings.

Andrei Petrov, a Baptist pastor in Moscow, noted that those they gained from the follow-up after the Billy Graham Crusade were almost all due to sustained caring relationships. As they became involved with people, they began to be integrated into the church.

Many personal testimonies we heard indicated that people bring their problems to the home group where they receive the help they need. This reflects the change one leader has seen in the groups. "When we began we were program oriented with heavy teaching involved in the group. We had little prayer and no relationship building. Now relationships are primary."

Bombay — New Life Fellowship
Seeing the needs and doing something about them

I was a little startled as I sat through the Sunday celebration service. The announcements caught my attention. Two announcements told of job opportunities and the contact person for the job. Here in a large worship service job offers were being publicly announced.

After that same service I saw and heard people praying for each other and discussing their problems. We left with the senior pastor, Jerry D'Souza and his wife, Bella. On the way out, pastor Jerry stopped to talk at some length to an older man quite poorly dressed. He told us later that the man was a street person he was working to rehabilitate.

Evidence of practical caring showed up in the home group leaders' meeting where they shared about the recent evangelistic crusade in Satara. One praise was for the driver of their bus. When they were returning home, they came across a serious accident. The police investigating the accident asked them to take an injured man and his wife to the hospital. Reggie continued the story.

We were like the good Samaritan. Even the police were surprised and pleased. One brother prayed for the sick in Urdu (they were Muslims). We gave them money and assured them we would inform their relatives. The injured man was surprised and touched. In spite of all of this delay we arrived on time.

Visiting is an important part of the home leaders' ministry. Dicto visits all his people every week. "I must eat at their table," he said, "so they know God is love." He takes someone with him. When two people are together the ministry is more powerful. Working together also protects them against rumor. Caring involves protecting the reputations of the workers.

Pastor Willie shared how they help their staff maintain strong family relationships. They encourage their staff to take days off to spend with their families. The evening we met with the leaders, Pastor Willie left early since his wife was away and he wanted to be with his children. Another time as he talked to us in his home, he sat on the floor helping one of his daughters make a clock because she was learning to tell time.

Caring involves wives in ministry partnerships with their husbands. This is modeled at the senior leadership level. Bev works with her husband, Pastor Willie. Pastor Jerry and Bella minister together as well. I talked to several zone and group leaders who view their ministry as a "husband-wife" team.

Caracas
Large modern cities require increased efforts in caring

The Bible study dealt with the command to overcome evil with good. A thoughtful discussion ensued as to how this might be accomplished. Finally, a woman offered an anecdote. She had need of food in the past and asked her neighbors for help. They refused. However, the time came when a neighbor needed help. She overcame the evil by generously giving what was needed.

Caring is a vital part of the home group ministry in Caracas. They help each other in the group and in the community. A partial list of needs met shows their spirit of servanthood.

- Reconciliation occurred between two people because of home group prayer and involvement.
- A person needing a job found employment.
- Members visited retirement homes and gave food and other necessities to the poor.
- After prayer, a woman who had not been able to have a child became pregnant.

- Home group involvement helped people who had no place to move find lodging.
- Because of caring concern in the life of a new believer he decided to attend the baptism class.

Pastor Olson has goals that revolve around a burden to help in social services. His vision includes help in economic development, health care, counseling, drug, and alcohol rehabilitation.

People in this fast paced city have little free time. When they meet in the home groups they want the time to be efficiently used. But relationships take time so people often use the phone. One area leader encouraged all the home group leaders to call each other and pray for one another during the week, and in the meeting he set up a structure for doing that.

City life influences people toward anonymity. It becomes easy for people to lose track of each other. Even among home group members that may happen, but these Christians actively and intentionally seek to know what is happening and help as they are able.

Questionnaire Evaluation

The home furnishes the appropriate setting for maximum relationship building. The combined total of all sites in this study reveals that nearly 91 percent of the home groups actually meet in homes.

Children are often kept in the meetings, emphasizing the family atmosphere. Question 12 reveals that in 38 percent of the responses people said children were kept in the meeting while only 14 percent said the children were kept at home. In 28 percent of the groups there were no children, but the majority of those who had children brought them to the home groups. I am often asked, "What do people do with children in the home group ministries you have seen?" This is never an easy question to respond to because the answers are diverse. But in many areas of the world people keep their children in the home group.

Question 13 asked, "Do you have older children who participate in your home group meetings?" Taken separately the sites showed wide variation. The combined data reveals that two-thirds responded "No." However, Accra has home groups for both children and youth, and all the sites have youth home groups.

In Question 27 people overwhelmingly indicated that they share highly personal problems in their home groups with the confidence that members will pray while maintaining confidentiality. Out of a combined positive total of 91 percent, 46 percent answered "strongly agree" and 45 percent "agree." The data varied little between the five sites. A follow-up question asked how many in their home group have shared serious personal problems within the previous six months. The numbers varied but almost everyone could list three to five people who had shared critical situations. In Moscow the numbers tended toward a higher range.

A look again at question 33 is revealing. People were asked to list three qualities of a good home group leader. Three sites listed caring as the most important quality: Moscow 93 percent, Chicago 87 percent, and Caracas 67 percent. In the other two sites caring came out a strong second with Bombay at 71 percent and Accra 64 percent.

Differences can be explained culturally. Moscow and Chicago indicated caring as an important function. Here human relationships are broken and that brokenness is evident in the society. While sin, a broken relationship with God, is the theological reason for that brokenness, people see the human aspect of the disaster around them. In Accra and Bombay where human and material action is seen more in spiritual terms it is not surprising to see that the relationship with God takes precedence.

In question 42 I stated a crisis situation and the respondents told what they would do in that situation. I then classified their answers in five categories. The first category indicates both material and spiritual help with maximum interaction. The second category is for those who said they would offer spiritual support such as prayer. The third category indicates people divided in their responsibilities, some stopping to deal with the problem and others continuing the home group. The fourth category is a case where the leader takes control. Accra showed a significantly high leadership orientation with 62 percent indicating that the leadership should take charge. The other sites indicated they would offer spiritual support, usually by praying: Moscow 86 percent, Chicago 40 percent, Bombay and Caracas 33 percent each, and Accra 30 percent.

People demonstrate care in differing ways at the various locales. In Accra the care is more leadership oriented and less time driven. The first reaction in Moscow would be to pray. Prayer is high in all the sites but Chicago and Bombay would each contribute significant material support as well.

One indication of potential caring is network density. Question 11 furnishes information necessary to construct a network analysis for each home group by indicating how many contacts each person had with the others in the group. That information is used to designate a "Contact Quotient" or CQ. The CQ can be calculated for each home group, church, and site, by dividing the number of contacts by the number of people in the group. The answer is the average number of contacts each person has per week. The higher the CQ the more often people contact others in their home groups. The CQ for each site was: Accra: 38.6, Caracas 32.3, Bombay 27.9, Moscow 20.6, and Chicago 15.4.

As might be expected, the more face-to-face societies had greater personal contact. This figure does not discriminate between the number of people contacted and how many contacts are made. For instance, contacting one person 10 times or ten people one time each is the same in the CQ measurement. While Chicago and Moscow have the lowest CQ, they have the highest percentage (question 33) who designated caring as a leader quality—Moscow 93 percent and Chicago 89 percent. One conclusion is that the more face-to-face societies of Accra and Bombay have home groups that are a part of their natural social networks and much contact throughout the week follows logically. Chicago and Moscow represent more fractured societies and sense a greater need for caring in their leaders.

Key Points

• Caring integrates other home group ministries in practical ways.

• Caring develops out of relationships. It is an incarnational ministry.

• Caring is an important home group leader quality.

• Caring results in effective evangelism and discipleship.

• Caring is universal in need but cultural in its local expression.

• Caring is a process, needing time to bear fruit.

• Caring involvement is the principal difference between the large celebration group and an effective home group.

• Caring must be intentional; it does not just happen.

Endnote

1.   Elom Dovlo and E. K. Agozie, *The Christian and Culture* (Accra: Bible Study & Prayer Fellowship, E. P. Church of Ghana, 1995), 13.

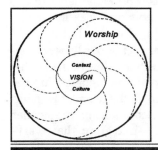

CHAPTER 10

Worship
Recognizing Who God Is

Chapter 7 of Revelation depicts a glorious worship scene. Worshipers from every nation, tribe, and language are gathered around the throne, focused on God, acknowledging his attributes as they praise Him in word and action.

The worship in the churches described in this book also reflects God's greatness and worthiness as the people praise Him. In Ghana, worship was expressed in a powerful way during a day of prayer through five hours of standing or sitting on backless benches. In one Moscow church, worshipers up front waved flags and banners and others did ballet-style dancing, while in a more traditional Orthodox Church, people praised God with liturgy and icons. The worship time in Bombay interspersed prayer, testimonies, preaching, and singing, during which girls with tambourines performed choreographed routines. In Caracas worship reflected biblical truth as more time focused on Bible study.

But, however expressed, worship is strong in all the sites studied— vibrant worship, normally using the vernacular language and familiar cultural forms, such as instruments and appropriate movements and visuals. Songs were in a style that the people understood as worship.

If caring is the integrative factor of home group ministry, worship is the soul. The Samaritan woman in John 4 wanted to know where we should worship. Each of the churches we researched exists in a culture that focuses on the place of worship. Often that focus is on a building, such as a temple or cathedral. Yet almost none of the churches in this study own a building in which they can worship. Although they might like to have a worship facility, the building is not their focus. They seek to worship God in spirit and in truth.

Worship is a part of both larger and smaller groups, but the large group tends to be the focus of worship and as such influences the worship of the home group.

Therefore, I urge you, brothers, in view of God's mercy, to offer your bodies as living sacrifices, holy and pleasing to God—this is your spiritual act of worship (Romans 12:1).

In light of Paul's injunction above, every act of our lives is to be counted as worship. However, there are different levels. Thus, this chapter deals with both corporate worship and the relationship between large group and small group worship. In the realm of worship the relationship between the large group celebration and the smaller home group is evident although the different-sized groups have varying functions. Beckham says,

Large group worship provides a setting for inspiration, information, revelation and celebration. Small group community allows application, edification, incarnation and preparation.

Those experiencing true worship while celebrating God's greatness will be drawn back into the experience of God's love within warm, intimate cell meetings. This is the rhythm of worship between cell and celebration that is possible in the cell church.[1]

Worship in both small and large group reflects two attributes of God, transcendence and immanence. Transcendence speaks of God, high and holy, lifted up. Old Testament saints who saw Him expected to die. We worship a God who is above the earth, pure, eternal, all knowing and all powerful. We bow down before Him because He is worthy.

Immanence speaks of his relationship to people. He dwells in us, wants to fellowship with us, and sent his own Son so that we might be his children. Here is God our Father, who sustains us, cares for us, and gives us strength, guidance, wisdom, and help. His Son is Immanuel, "God with us."

In the large group we tend to focus our worship on his transcendence and in the small group, his immanence. Beckham gives more implications of the relationship between God's transcendence and immanence in chapter 8.[2] Worship is awesome in its holiness and intimacy. Because He is God, He is holy but at the same time we can have an intimate relationship with Him.

In this study, we see how people worship God inside their culture. Some cultural forms (such as dancing, women's head coverings, clapping, standing, sitting, and the use of certain musical instruments) express sincere worship in one context but may communicate something quite different in another cultural setting.

This chapter will be treated differently than the others. It can only deal with the outward expressions of worship since God alone sees the heart. The danger in analyzing worship is that we may lose its mystery and wonder. But I trust that the cultural comparisons of worship mentioned here will help increase our reverence and sense of worship.

Culture profoundly affects the way worship is expressed. Because of that fact, I will use a grid of signal systems to look at worship in the home group and the larger celebration service and see how they relate. Dr. Donald K. Smith in his book, *Creating Understanding*, gives us some propositions that govern all human communication. While worship transcends human communication, we can only examine it from the human perspective and express it in human forms of communication. Smith states two propositions on which much of this chapter is built.

- All human communication occurs through the use of twelve signal systems.
- Usage of the signal systems is a function of culture; thus they are used differently in different cultures.[3]

The twelve signal systems Smith deals with are:

1. Verbal—speech
2. Written—symbols representing speech
3. Numeric—numbers and number systems
4. Pictorial—two-dimensional representations
5. Artifactual—three-dimensional representations
6. Audio—use of nonverbal sounds and silence
7. Kinesic—body motions, facial expressions, posture
8. Optical—light and color
9. Tactile—touch, the sense of "feel"
10. Spatial—utilization of space
11. Temporal—utilization of time
12. Olfactory—taste and smell[4]

In any communication, one, and usually several, of the signal systems are used together. Language, tone of voice, touch, facial expression, space between individuals—all combine to communicate. When we worship God we also use the signal systems together, consciously and unconsciously.

The above list of signal systems is given in the order of consciousness of use—those more consciously used at the top descending to those less consciously used at the bottom. However, when two signal systems contradict each other in communication, the less consciously used system is more readily believed. Elizabeth Roberts in her humorous guide to Russia gives such an example.

In church little old ladies come up and smack your hands if you are standing with them clasped absent-mindedly behind you during prayers for this is taken as a sign, like having your fingers crossed, that you are excluding yourself from the proceedings.[5]

That example of miscommunication happened to an American friend of mine who was standing (no chairs in the Orthodox Church) intently seeking to be involved in the worship, but for personal comfort he had clasped his hands behind him. A little old lady did indeed smack his hands. Whatever else the rest of him may have been communicating, his posture (kinesic) said he was not worshiping.

Each of the twelve signal systems has its own grammar and vocabulary when used to communicate. We usually recognize these in verbal language, but the reason the others can be used to communicate is because there is a commonality of meaning within each signal system so meaning can be mediated between people.

Only God knows our hearts. We worship in spirit. We know, of course, that a form of worship can be expressed without true worship taking place. But the richness of God's creation is seen by the way these 12 systems can be used by his people to worship Him.

Accra
Worship comes from the knowledge of spiritual realities

Forty-five of us stood, singing joyfully, clapping in various rhythms, swaying to the music with hands raised in praise to the Lord. I understood nothing of the language since the worship was in Ewe, but more than words were expressed. The music and movement were clear worship languages.

This was not a church service but the beginning of a day of prayer for the home group leaders in the Madina Chapel of the Evangelical Presbyterian Church of Ghana. The first hour of that time was spent specifically in worship. The only instruments accompanying the singing were six or seven drums of different sizes. Everyone knew the words so they needed no books or overhead projector.

Interspersed with the singing came times of spoken praise. Individuals spontaneously led out in audible praise to the Lord, sometimes in soft voices together and at other times with one person leading, drawing people together in their spirits. We all sensed the truth of being one body and reflecting the unity Christ prayed for his disciples in John 17. Worship and prayer was expressed in a powerful way throughout five hours spent either standing or sitting on backless benches.

Calvary Baptist Church, perhaps because it is so large, had a more professional-style worship service. The worship band, choir, and soloists were all highly skilled. Their use of song, instruments, and movement drew the worshipers to the throne of God, but there was a nice balance of spontaneity also. Singing was done both in English and the vernacular, but when people sang in the vernacular the singing seemed livelier with more body movement.

During the offering in some churches people came forward moving rhythmically to the music as they placed their money in Ghanaian baskets held by ushers. These worshipers expressed their joy with great energy as they gave to the Lord. Martin Obeng stated that it was important for people to have this time to actively worship the Lord during the offering. In fact, the dance was part of their offering.

The corporate worship in these churches had high audience participation. At Calvary Baptist Church during a song expressing great joy, people from the audience and choir came to the front of the church to express their joy by dancing. This time of praise lasted 10 to 15 minutes. After the song the worship leader asked the audience to "Give the Lord a big clap." People participated enthusiastically as they clapped, waved their hands, stomped their feet, and cheered for the Lord.

While there were times of spontaneity, there was also evidence of rehearsed planning. The worship team leading the congregation in their hymns and praise songs had rehearsed. The leader knew which songs to announce and had an appropriate comment on each. The highlight of the worship service at Calvary Baptist was the choir. Highly professional, well rehearsed, and talented, the choir focused on God and his love and greatness, helping us worship Him.

The verbal language in these descriptions was Ewe in the first case and English and Ewe in the second. Churches use English because it is a common language for greater numbers, but they use the vernacular language because that communicates at the emotional as well as the cognitive level. Instrumental music and singing rang out in the unique style of Accra and West Africa with drums, rhythm, and clapping. Clapping to the music usually involved several simultaneous and different rhythms. Kinesic motion was joyfully demonstrated by movement to the music and by dancing before the Lord.

People dressed in a certain way (artifactual) and used particular colors (optical). Many wore traditional African styles. Others dressed in the Western way. Those in traditional style included a sprinkling of Ghanaian Kente cloth. All dressed as well as possible since how one dresses is important in Ghana and speaks of respect and honor. One dresses well to meet a King. People were packed closely together as they worshiped, and they touched each other when communicating— a normal tactical communication style in Ghana.

Comparing the signal systems in the two situations revealed that home groups reflected the large group worship. Home groups in Accra lasted from one to one-and-a-half hours. About one-third of the time was given to worship. Many of the home groups met outside in the courtyards. The neighbors listened to the singing, praises, and prayers as evidenced by their body language, clapping, and rhythmically moving to the music, even singing quietly along with songs they knew. The neighbors would sometimes listen to the Bible study discussion, but the worship really caught their attention.

Women often covered their heads when they worshiped. Both in the homes and courtyards people sat close to each other (spatial). One decoration we saw in several homes was the Ghanaian pictorial representation which they translate as "Except God." It was a silent reminder to all who saw it that only God can accomplish something worthwhile.

Worship is pervasive in Accra from animistic practices in homes to the Muslims praying in the parks. Fetishes are a serious problem in the local culture. Christians come to church and to the home group to meet God. True worship for them is an acknowledgment of who God is and of God's victory over both daily obstacles and cosmic forces.

Moscow — The Rosa Church
Worship is integral to all activities

Sunday morning dawned cold and wet. After an hour-and-a-half trip on one bus and two metros, we received warm greetings by several people as we entered the theater where Rosa church meets. Young men and women greeters stationed along the way expressed worship and praise as people entered. "Greetings, God loves you!" one greeter affirmed as she shook our hands. "Peace to you. Welcome," said another. Speaking with expression (verbal), using body language and smiles (kinesic), shaking hands and standing close to talk (tactile and spatial)—these signal systems were already in use as people prepared to worship.

The large theater seats 1,500. People were still arriving as the worship time began at 10:35 A.M. During the first hour of the service people continued to enter, longer than would be acceptable in an American church.

Most people stood during worship, but not everyone. Songs in Russian were flashed on the overhead as the worship band began.

Several people at the front held aloft flags or banners which they waved during the singing. Others were doing ballet-type dancing in front of the stage (a very different cultural dance form than that in Ghana). On one side several children joined hands, dancing in a circle.

The audience sang and clapped to the rhythm of the music, and people raised their hands in praise. After 50 minutes of singing and praise, a man came forward to read Scripture and lead in prayer. Then we sang some more. The praise time lasted for one hour and ten minutes, followed by the sermon.

Home groups reflect the large group priorities. One thing the home group leaders are doing differently now is giving more time to worship. Previously they spent more time on prepared lessons, but now a larger portion of time is spent on spontaneous worship. Part of the reason may be the lack of teachers. Some home groups have no Bible teacher so they focus entirely on prayer and worship.

There is no truly 'typical' home group meeting but averages are stated here to give an idea of how time is apportioned. In the average three-hour home group meeting, a minimum of 30 minutes is devoted to praise and worship, followed by 30 minutes of Bible study. One hour is spent praying and one hour in fellowship, drinking tea.

Most of the signal systems were evident in the home group atmosphere. In many homes we saw Bible verses and Christian posters on the wall. Homes are usually small so people were packed close. In some places they sat on the bed as well as in chairs. A lot of hugging and touching took place as people greeted each other. Physical closeness seemed to reflect emotional closeness. The smell of tea and food added to the sense of unity.

The lively, free-spirited worship in the Rosa Church stands in contrast to other churches in Moscow. The majority religion in Russia is the Russian Orthodox church. We attended a weekday morning service in a small church being refurbished. Worshipers stood during the three-hour Orthodox service. The worship style was much more liturgical, with icons having an important function in assisting people in worship. However, worship became quite participatory as people read or quoted from the worship book, sang, bowed, and moved about the room during the service.

A number of things happened at the same time. One priest was leading the service from the front of the church. Another was hearing confession at one side. People walked in and out. In one wing funeral preparations were underway. Several people carried in benches to hold the coffin. The family entered with the coffin and placed lighted candles and flowers around it. In the back section, elements for communion were being prepared. This may be evidence of what Hall calls a polychronic culture.

While standing during the service (and being careful not to clasp my hands behind me), I was impressed that the Orthodox Church used all the signal systems to involve people in their worship service. Communion brought in the olfactory, and the use of the prayer book involved written and numeric systems. Using these signal systems cannot be equated with worship, but it does indicate good communication and maximum involvement.

Some Orthodox churches have started home-group-type ministries. These are divided into three kinds of meetings: (1) a Bible study which is verse-by-verse study of Scripture, (2) a preaching meeting where two members practice preaching to the group, and (3) a prayer meeting which is like an evening vespers service. They have both formal prayer and prayer for individual needs.

The purpose of these smaller groups is to provide mutual support for the members beyond what the priest gives, which includes helping people discover and use their gifts. The group is linked to the larger Orthodox Church administratively as the leader reports to the priest. Worship and prayer forms are also similar since icons are a part of the home group worship as well as large group gatherings.

The Baptist churches form yet another worship tradition. The service at the historic Central Baptist Church lasted two hours. Congregational hymns and communion were the primary ways people actively participated. The remaining time they sat and listened to the excellent choir and preaching. The service was signed for the deaf, which I had not seen elsewhere. The service seemed classical and professional. I was impressed with the intensity and solemnity of worship, communicated to me through silence, intent observation, and lack of movement. I had experienced this same phenomenon in Madagascar where people use silence and less movement as worship forms.

Twelve men served communion. When the pastor prayed over the bread, he lifted up a platter containing six large loaves of bread. The men gathered around, broke the bread into large bite-sized pieces, and passed it out to the worshipers. When the bread came to a row, the individuals stood, took a piece, meditated a few moments, ate it, stood quietly a few more minutes, then sat down. The wine came in a common cup. One deacon passed the silver cup and another stood by with a pitcher to refill it. Dress was important so people wore their best clothes. Many were dressed in somber colors and women usually had their heads covered.

Home groups are found in only a few of the newer Baptist churches. The struggle between faithfulness to a long and honorable tradition and an effort to seek the effective dynamic outreach brought by a home group ministry shows up in those Baptist churches that are starting home groups. Although the worship demonstrates the best of what is traditional, it is difficult to carry that traditional attitude into home groups. Baptist churches who have taken steps toward a home group ministry are dealing with issues of control as they sort out the balance between traditional and newer ministry forms.

The free-flowing worship of the Rosa Church is a new form taking root in a new church. The home group concept has no tradition to match, which may be why the church has attracted younger people and newer Christians. The more traditional churches have an older constituency.

Bombay — New Life Fellowship
Biblical worship in a spiritualistic society

Language, the first signal system, is an issue in the multicultural context of Bombay. Weekly celebration services are conducted in five languages in the Kalina area of Bombay. Once a month all those unite in an English celebration service, translated into Hindi. More languages are used at the home group level. The English-speaking Bandra Church was the first Sunday celebration service we attended.

As we entered the private school auditorium, several greeters warmly welcomed us with statements of praise to the Lord. The table at the front of the church held communion elements. Pinned to the tablecloth was a banner reading, "Jehovah Jireh, Gen. 22:8." The hall, which held 400 people, was about one-half full when the service began but filled up during the worship time.

The worship team involved three electric guitars, keyboard, flute, trumpet, five tambourines, a trap set, and four singers. One hour of worship time was interspersed with singing in English and Hindi, praises, prayers, and testimonies. An overhead projector was used to flash the words of the songs on a screen. Worshipers became actively involved as they clapped, waved, and moved during the music. Standing in the front rows across from the worship team, facing the front of the church, a group of six girls with tambourines performed choreographed routines during the singing. This was quite different from the dance in Accra or the ballet style in Russia. The church prayed especially for Muslims that Sunday since it was during Ramadan. They were praying through a 30-day Muslim prayer calendar. At the end of the first hour the pastor gave some words of encouragement especially motivating people to straighten out any broken relationships they had with others.

Sixteen men came forward to serve communion. They stood in a circle around the communion table, held hands, and prayed. The Indian flat bread (chapati), broken into smaller pieces and placed on 10 plates, was then served. People took the bread, again broke it into smaller pieces, ate some, and offered some to others. Soon the audience was taking and giving bread. People took advantage of this time to deal with any barriers between them, allowing believers to come to the Lord's table in unity. The common cup (ten of them) was then passed. Communion was a vivid worship time focusing on who Christ is. The men passed large plastic jars to take the offering after the communion service.

A quick glance at the list of 12 signal systems gives an idea of the unique Indian way they were used. Written, numeric, and pictorial systems were involved in the overhead images and the banners. Not only the multiple languages but also the dress (with a mix of saris, Punjabi suits, Western clothes, casual and more formal attire, and the use or non-use of jewelry and head coverings) communicated the diversity of people worshiping in unity. The length of time given to worship was a function of the temporal. Communion emphasized olfactory and spatial and tactile in a unique way. The signal systems were used in similar ways in home groups and the larger celebration service.

Though size varied, this brief description is fairly typical of the worship services we attended in Bombay. The home group meetings, special prayer meetings, and the leaders meetings began with a time of worship. Every meeting allotted significant time to worship which had, at a minimum, the elements of music, praise, and testimony. Sometimes someone played a guitar but the instrument of choice seemed to be the tambourine.

In home groups, we often sat together on the floor singing and praising God. The songs were those used in the larger worship services and people knew them. A colorful display of banners aided worship in the large celebration service, while Bible verse posters usually decorated the walls in homes. Primarily these were in English but a few were in Hindi.

Communion and offering were a part of the home groups designated as 'house churches,' groups with at least ten baptized believers. There the worship was more structured and the Bible teaching more formal. We asked about baptism. Once a person believes in Christ the church baptizes them quickly. This does not always happen in a formal service, but a few people from the home group may gather at the ocean on a weekday to baptize new converts.

Testimonies, including spiritual and physical healings, were an important part of every meeting. The host of one home, a 65-year-old man, shared how he had been an alcoholic. He sat in his little store at the front of the house and drank while the home group met, and in that way he heard bits and pieces from the meeting. He was religious but had no peace. "One year ago I came to Jesus and quit drinking," he related, "and last month I was delivered from cigarettes."

This pervasive worship strengthens the believer. We walked 200 meters along a narrow street going to one home group meeting. I gazed around at yet another part of town. Every few meters I saw a shrine decorated with garlands or other flowers. Some had incense burning. The number of shrines became oppressive, almost overpowering. We entered the small house, left our shoes by the door, joined other Christians, and soon started singing praises to God. The overwhelming oppressiveness began to lift.

Worship is a key factor in maintaining victory in the spiritual battle that overtly and continually surrounds the believer in Bombay. Later that night we left the home for the long trip to our hotel. We passed by all the shrines but now I saw them in a different light. We walked along, full of the joy of the Lord, thinking of the power of believers in home groups all over Bombay, praising and worshiping God.

Caracas
Worship is a reflection of biblical truth

People were still arriving for the home group when the meeting opened by reading from Psalm 63. Various conversations in the room quieted down as everyone listened to the Scripture. Nelly led in prayer and then a young woman began strumming the guitar. The song was written on a large 'story board' set where all could see. We began to quietly sing "Tempraro yo te buscaré..." gaining volume as the singing continued. People arrived for the next ten minutes while singing continued.

Signal systems have a different use in Caracas. Written and numeric systems play a larger role and time is organized differently. The kinesic is more subdued. Audio and language signals identify the meeting as a Latin culture. With the strong teaching emphasis, the verbal plays a greater part. The home groups I attended generally had short worship periods with more time focused on Bible study.

Bulletins helped tie the home group and celebration services together. They were a part of worship services in Caracas, some churches in Ghana, and in Chicago. They were useful where one language was used, literacy was high, and materials for the bulletins were available and affordable.

In one Caracas home group, Gloris, the group leader, led a Bible study using questions from the church bulletin. "What is the action in worshiping God? Do you always have satisfaction in worshiping God?" People responded to the first question with such answers as "Praying, singing, and the way we live." Someone chimed in, "Even the birds praise God the first thing in the morning. If the animals can praise Him, how much more should we." The discussion then turned to the ways people worship. They agreed that in the church, instruments can help to praise God. Some members admitted they did not enjoy the modern electronic instruments but still recognized their validity in worship.

The service I attended at the Dios Admirable Church was devoted entirely to worship as the church celebrated its thirtieth anniversary. The program—a choreographed singing presentation—made dramatic use of kinesic, optical, spatial, artifactual, audio, and verbal systems. A woman introduced the service by announcing that people could stand or sit and sing along or just listen. Twelve women and four men were in the singing group, six in the orchestra, and three women performed a classical dance routine with banners. The singers knelt, bowed, lifted hands, and moved as appropriate, reflecting ideas in the songs. Worship was the focus of the words, both spoken and sung. "All creation will sing to you. You are the King, pure and holy, without sin."

At the midpoint of the hour-and-a-half service, the deacons took the offering and made announcements. At the end the pastor spoke, giving an invitation urging people to yield themselves to God as part of worship.

Chicago — New Life Community Church
Involving all people in every aspect of worship

We walked into the high school auditorium to the strong beat of some lively music. The worship team, led by Asa App, consisted of four singers, two guitars, a saxophone, a keyboard, and a trap set with the appropriate sound system. I saw people singing and clapping to the beat while others raised hands in worship. Even as the worship started, some went to the front of the church and knelt at the stage area to pray. Throughout the audience several people worshiped with tambourines.

While all this was happening, people continued to enter the high school auditorium, which seats 1,000. A certain amount of noise stirred under the musical covering. Before locating a seat, people walked around and greeted each other, often with a hug. Sometimes they waved at people across the auditorium. These people, who live in the city with noise and multiple activities around them, can concentrate on worship even in the midst of moving around. Several signal systems were involving people with each other and directing the group toward unified worship. The style was particularly American with casual informality in dress and greeting.

The worship team had practiced and knew the music well. Worship continued for 30 to 40 minutes. Words were flashed on the overhead and the order was preplanned to coordinate with the message theme. At the end of some songs they gave worshipful applause to the Lord.

One phase of the Sunday morning celebration was what the traditional church calls announcements, but I hesitate to use the term here. Special events were featured. A new home group was beginning so the leader came up to be interviewed and then dedicated in prayer. She told how God led in starting the new group and presented a powerful challenge on the value of the home group. While leaders gave announcements, others passed offering boxes. They explained to visitors that this was not their obligation. Instead, they welcomed the visitors with printed material about the church.

This church has recently started a parallel worship service in Spanish. That service resulted from the increasing number of Spanish-speaking home groups. As their number has increased, the church has brought into full-time service the man who started that ministry. While language is obviously different, the other signal systems have important differences also. Even the distance between people as they stand talking to each other is different and can miscommunicate across two cultures.

While most home groups in this church have good Bible study and mentoring programs, worship coupled with prayer gives people the additional spiritual strength they need. The number of people in a home seems immaterial to the effectiveness of worship. Gus started a group with six people. One of those people played the guitar and led a 20-minute worship session. Maria's group, on the other hand, had 15 women present. She played the guitar and led singing that was equally worshipful. These groups, in common with many at New Life Community Church, used song sheets one of the members had made.

Lorene led the music for her husband John's group while she played the guitar. The seven children were brought into this part of the meeting and participated in the singing. One of the songs was a children's song. In many of the home groups we attended husbands and wives worked together using their complementary gifts in the ministry.

True worship must be in spirit and in truth but today, as in the Bible, it is expressed by human communication systems. Worship often becomes identified and even synonymous with the outward expression. Tozer says it well.

> We struggle to understand spiritual things by comparing them to natural ones; then little by little those natural things become identified with the spiritual completely and the spiritual suffers greatly as a consequence.

> One task of the illuminated Christian teacher is to internalize worship and raise the religious concepts of church people above the figures and allegories that enabled them to grasp those concepts in the first place. The figure is the box in which the shining jewel is carried; but it is surprisingly easy to mistake the box for the jewel and look for nothing more.[6]

As Tozer suggests, worship can become completely identified with whatever ritual or form is used in worship. Or as the Samaritan woman suggested, worship can be identified as a place. This chapter has dealt with the outward forms used to express worship in the churches researched, recognizing that research can never adequately deal with the true spiritual worship.

Worship in the churches studied has less emphasis on tradition. They minister in contexts where the traditional focus has been on a building. These churches seek to express worship in new ways—reference is often made to new wineskins. At the same time the worship takes place inside cultures where worship has been expressed in certain ways in the past. These surroundings do affect how things such as dress, musical instruments, body movements, silence, and the other signals of human communication are viewed in terms of worship.

Key Points

- Greater involvement in worship is reflected by intentional use of the maximum number of the 12 signal systems.
- Important cultural forms in worship influence both large group and home group worship.

- The cultural diversity of worship forms is reflected by the different uses of the signal systems applied to worship.
- Cultural forms of worship can become synonymous with worship, rather than as a way to express worship.
- Every part of our humanity—heart, soul, mind, and strength (Mark 12:30)—can be involved in worship in both the home group and the large group.
- The Spirit of God is the source of all true expressions of worship; individual, home group, and corporate.
- Worship in the home group tends to reflect God's immanence while worship in the large group reflects his transcendence.
- Worship is the soul of the home group meeting.
- Worship is the front line of spiritual warfare against outward satanic enemies and inward sins.

Endnote

1.   William A. Beckham, *The Second Reformation* (Houston: Touch Publications, 1995), 76.

2.   Ibid., 83–93.

3.   Donald K. Smith, *Creating Understanding* (Grand Rapids: Zondervan, 1992), 144.

4.   Ibid.

5.   Elizabeth Roberts, *Xenophobe's Guide to the Russians* (London: Ravette Books, 1993), 9.

6.   A. W. Tozer, *That Incredible Christian* (Camp Hill, PA: Christian Publications, 1964), 89.

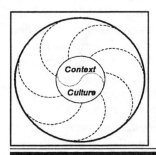

CHAPTER 11

Conclusion
Learning from the Home Group

By God's grace we became part of what one might call a larger "small group" community during this study, pilgrims together seeking to see how God is working in diverse home groups around the world. We were continually overwhelmed by the power of a learner attitude. As we honestly sought to learn, people invited us, not only into their homes, but also their lives. More than once we discovered we were the first foreigners a particular family had invited into their home. Though we have now concluded this study, the learning continues as yet others interact with us concerning this data and their own interest and experiences in small group ministry.

Cultural Diversity

Effective ministry must remain true to biblical principles while being appropriate for specific cultures. This has certainly proven true of home group methods. They cannot be transplanted to different cultures without considering the effect of culture on ministry. These differences were substantial in terms of Hofstede's four index continua.

The Chicago church was unique in this study since it uses a one-on-one discipleship program within the home group context. Chicago, a North American city, has a highly individualistic profile in the postmodern era. While cultural extremes are often modified by home groups, cultural tendencies still exist. The Chicago church tends toward the individualistic end of the continuum. Caracas, at the other extreme, has a strong sense of cultural collectivism. Although both contexts are urban where people are busy with full schedules, in Caracas people are more willing to meet in groups. Prayer groups, leadership development groups, and special leader groups, among others, all indicate a higher sense of the collective nature of the culture, and their home group ministry reflects that difference.

Adjustments in ministry were equally evident in terms of power distance. Home group members in Accra recognize leader authority and follow it. Some groups have two leaders—one recognized for age and wisdom, and the other for education and small group leadership skills. In Chicago, home group leaders call their members with offers of help, encouragement, and biblical wisdom. Although the Chicago leaders have less direct authority than the Ghanaian leaders, they do have indirect authority through influence on other lives.

High and low ambiguity avoidance is another important cultural feature revealing differences in home group ministries across cultures. Many home groups in Accra are highly structured, often with all activities planned down to the minute. People know what to expect and are generally content with this high degree of structure. Caracas, with the highest level of ambiguity avoidance, also has well planned and structured home groups. On the other hand, in Bombay, a culture with lower ambiguity avoidance, home groups are more free flowing. Leaders feel the need to be open to what God might do at any moment and generally resist attempts to structure their meetings.

We were surprised at the low level of ambiguity avoidance in the Moscow church, given the high level of structure in traditional Russian churches. This fact might be explained by youth in the church who have come out of a highly structured society and seek to express their freedom in Christ as a freedom from structure.

The degree of gender role separation also affects the way home groups function. Caracas reflects a culture with highly separated gender roles. Men usually play the dominant role in political and economical aspects of society. They tend to lead the churches at the senior level as elders and deacons. Women are the nurturers and are more concerned with the quality of life. They raise families and deal with the more relational aspects of society. Therefore, it is not surprising that the churches in Caracas have a higher percentage of women than other cities studied. Home groups deal with the quality of society, so women often lead home groups and some supervise and train home group leaders.

Cultures with blurred gender roles tend to have a greater mix of both male and female home group participation and leadership. In this study, the Bombay church demonstrated less separation between the genders than Caracas, especially at the grass roots level. Sometimes men lead, sometimes women lead, and at other times a man and woman work together to head up the group. Home group membership seemed to vary. Some groups were mixed. Others were predominantly male or female. Men and women served at the various stages of church leadership up to the level of elders. Much the same could also be said about the Moscow church and its home groups, which tended toward egalitarian values in terms of gender roles.

Impressions

We were a bit surprised at the number of churches in this study that owned no property. A passion for the lost, reflected by focusing on the city rather than a church building, characterized these fast-growing congregations. As the price of property skyrockets around the world, some of these churches are unable to buy or build. Instead they rent, but this causes hassles. They must continually be searching for meeting places, making frequent moves the norm.

Another result of growth is the multi-site church. We saw models of this in Bombay and Accra. The Chicago and Moscow churches are in the beginning stages of becoming multi-site churches. This pattern may be a future option for growing urban churches. Certainly the high costs of property and buildings as well as stringent building codes hold implications for church growth in urban areas.

All of the churches studied valued home groups because of the ministry that flows out of interpersonal relationship networks. From the senior leadership throughout the membership of each church, we found people making efforts to build relationships—never an easy task. The enemy seeks to separate people and destroy relationships, both those with God and with other people. Christ came to re-establish relationships, but building relationships requires time and trust. In many areas of the world, trust has been destroyed. Religious, political, and ethnic barriers have destroyed the trust on which relationships have been built. People working together in the home groups establish relationships and trust as they demonstrate love and care to the fractured world around them. How relationships are expressed, how conflict is dealt with, and how care is accomplished varied between cultures, but all churches valued their relationships more than programs.

The strong relationship between the home group and the larger worshiping congregation was reinforced in our minds. While the various factors look different in the five cultures, each has a small group and large group interactive dynamic, and both are important for spiritual growth. The home group integrates the larger congregational life into the neighborhoods.

Prayer is a lifestyle of Christians that we expected to find in home groups. The small groups involve people in prayer with their neighbors, friends, coworkers, and family, but prayer in home groups also leads to more prayer in the larger group. Although we expected the prayer emphasis, we were surprised to discover how important worship is in the home group ministry. It seems more intimate and personal in the small groups, while being more transcendent and dynamic in the large group. We learned, not only more about worship, but more about the God we worship as we experienced worship in its cultural variations.

While we suspected evangelism was a key to home group ministries, we were surprised at the force of its importance. The churches in this study do not divide the ministry into the lost and the saved with special home groups for each. In any given group, one might find a mix of non-Christians, new Christians, and more mature Christians. People come to know Christ in the home group with their friends or family who are already believers, and in the same group they grow in maturity.

The dynamic growth of the churches studied regularly results in the need for more leaders. Thus, each church places high value on home group leadership. A higher percentage of people are involved in ministry in a home group based church than in other churches, and this requires leadership training. The structure for training leaders is affected by the culture, but all these growing churches place high value on leader development.

The home groups that make up a church in a given city are themselves different from each other as they reflect the diversity of individual personalities with all the accompanying gifts, joys, sufferings, and problems. However, the diversity exists within the unity of God's church. We continually heard people expressing concern for unity in diversity. Churches are not trying to make everyone the same but rather to maintain unity, expressed in part by belonging to the larger group.

Implications For Practitioners

One major implication of this study should encourage the practitioner seeking to begin or enhance a home group ministry to find a church in a similar cultural context that has a home group ministry and study it. While in Moscow we had a meeting of several people, some Russian and some foreign, involved in leading home group ministries from a variety of churches. The Russians who attended desired to hear from other Russian Christians about their group ministry experiences. They recognized the need to learn from those whose cultural understanding was similar. No model should simply be copied but much can be learned from churches in similar cultures even though they may differ theologically.

Church leaders from a variety of denominations in Accra expressed appreciation for what they learned from each other when they came together around this research project. They built each other up as they shared with us and with one another about their groups. It was an important time, not only for learning from people in the same culture, but also helping each other in ministry.

Method is important even though it has not been the primary focus of this book. Most of the books that deal with home groups (cell groups, Bible study groups, care groups, etc.) deal primarily with method. Churches should first consider identity, mission, and how the basic factors discussed in this book will be worked out in their context. The books on method have given us significant help. However, method needs to consider culture and context. Once the basic factors are understood, books on method can be read with greater profit.

Home group ministry is not an instant solution to church problems. Churches that are not functioning well without home groups will not automatically function effectively because of them. If a church is not growing because the Christians are not evangelizing, it is unlikely to grow when home groups are started. We have seen home groups revolutionize a church, but it was a process that took time.

Home groups, like other ministries, are a spiritual work. They provide an arena to give many people opportunity to grow and use their spiritual gifts. Such groups, as an integral part of the larger church, used by the Spirit of God to do his work in and through his people, are making an impact on the large urban areas of the world.

Possible Areas for Further Study

Even though this book is completed, the study is not. I hope this study will be only the first step in further research from people involved in home group ministries. Study could be done in several directions with great profit to the Church as the world becomes increasingly urban.

One type of study might be a longitudinal examination that would look at the same churches over a period of time. What will the churches of this study look like in three years? In five years? In ten? How will the home group ministries develop and change? Churches could profit by doing their own studies to see how they are interacting with their culture and the networks within that culture and subculture.

Scholars may desire to do comparative studies in regions that have built-in similarities. A study of urban areas in the Muslim world comes immediately to mind. How are home group ministries similar and different across the vast areas of the world from North Africa and the Middle East to Pakistan, Central Asia, and Indonesia—all of which are predominantly Muslim? How does the predominant religion affect the ministry? A similar type of study could encompass the Chinese world. How do home group ministries differ between Chinese in China and those in the dispersion? Comparative studies in the Latin world, Europe, and other more restricted areas would also be helpful in finding principles and methods for effective home group ministries.

Another kind of study concerns attitudinal measures. A range of attitudes and emotions toward the home group ministry would help people contrast the positive and negative areas in home group life. This type of reflection would be more in keeping with Hofstede's "Values Survey Module,"[1] which he used to collect his data.

Yet another area of study is in the area of network analysis and subcultures. I touched on that briefly as a method and have used the results of network thinking in this book and in my personal ministry. Home group ministries are largely a function of networks, and we need greater understanding of how networks function in society. Secular scholars have given us much help in putting together useful models. However, some writers have become so theoretical that application is difficult. Christian scholars and workers could make a valuable contribution with a combination of solid biblical exegesis and network analysis.

While much reflection must be done in the future to bring about better understanding of the underlying factors of home group work, John 13:34–35 embodies the ethos and outworking of such group ministry:

> A new command I give you: Love one another. As I have loved you, so you must love one another. All men will know that you are my disciples if you love one another.

Endnote

[1]   Geert Hofstede, *Culture's Consequences: International Differences in Work-Related Values*, abridged ed. (Beverly Hills, CA: Sage Publications, 1984), 283–286.

Bibliography

Books and Articles

Barna, George. *The Power of Vision: How You Can Capture and Apply God's Vision for Your Ministry.* Ventura, CA: Regal, 1992.

Beckham, William. *The Second Reformation: Reshaping the Church for the 21st Century.* Houston: Touch Publications, 1995.

Bird, Warren. "The Great Small-Group Takeover." *Christianity Today* 38, no. 2 (February 7, 1994): 25.

Blanchard, Ken. "Turning Vision Into Reality: an Interview with Ken Blanchard." *Leadership Magazine* (Spring): 1996.

Bouissevain, J. "Network Analysis: A Reappraisal." *Current Anthropology* 20 (1979): 392–394.

Burt, Ronald S., and Michael J. Minor, eds. *Applied Network Analysis: A Methodological Introduction.* Beverly Hills: Sage Publications, 1983.

Crowther. Geoff, et al. *India: Travel Survival Kit.* Victoria, Australia: Lonely Planet, 1993.

———. *Africa: On a Shoestring.* Victoria, Australia: Lonely Planet, 1995.

Deegbe, Fred. *Leadership Training.* Accra: Calvary Baptist Church, n.d.

Dovlo, Elom, and E. K. Agozie. *The Christian and Culture.* Accra: Bible Study & Prayer Fellowship, E. P. Church of Ghana, 1995.

Dzameshie, Alex. *How to Handle Conflicts.* Accra: Bible Study & Prayer Fellowship, E. P. Church of Ghana, 1995.

Fischer, Claude S. *To Dwell among Friends: Personal Networks in Town and City.* Chicago: University of Chicago, 1982.

———. *The Urban Experience.* 2nd ed. San Diego: Harcourt Brace Jovanovich, 1984.

George, Carl F. *Prepare Your Church for the Future.* Grand Rapids: Fleming H. Revell, 1991.

Gibbs, Eddie. *I Believe in Church Growth.* Grand Rapids: William B. Eerdmans, 1981.

Granovetter, Mark. "The Strength of Weak Ties: A Network Theory Revisited." In *Social Structure and Network Analysis*, eds. Peter V. Marsden and Nan Lin. Beverly Hills: Sage Publications, 1982.

Gulick, John. *The Humanity of Cities: An Introduction to Urban Societies*. New York: Bergin & Garvey, 1989.

Hall, Edward T. Hall. *Beyond Culture*. New York: Doubleday, 1976.

————. *The Dance of Life*. New York: Doubleday, 1983.

Heald, Tim. *Networks*. London: Hodder and Stoughton, 1983.

Hesselgrave, David J. *Dynamic Religious Movements: Case Studies of Rapidly Growing Religious Movements around the World*. Grand Rapids: Baker Book House, 1978.

Hofstede, Geert. *Culture's Consequences: International Differences in Work-Related Values*. Abridged ed. Beverly Hills: Sage Publications, 1984.

————. *Cultures and Organizations: Software of the Mind*. London: McGraw-Hill, 1991.

Icenogle, Gareth Weldon. *Biblical Foundations for Small Group Ministry: An Integrational Approach*. Downers Grove, IL: InterVarsity, 1994.

Isaacson, Alan. *Deeper Life: The Extraordinary Growth of the Deeper Life Bible Church*. London: Hodder and Stoughton, 1990.

Jobe, Mark. *First Steps: New Life Series Book One, Two, and Three*. Chicago: New Life Community Church, 1994.

Kabagarama, Daisy. *Breaking the Ice: A Guide to Understanding People from Other Cultures*, Boston: Allyn and Bacon, 1993.

Knoke, David, and James H. Kuklinski. *Network Analysis*. Beverly Hills: Sage Publications, 1982.

Liévano, Rev. Francisco. *Grupos Basicos De Discipulado Cristiano (Basic Groups of Christian Discipleship)*. Caracas: Dios Admirable Church, n.d.

Lundstrom, Karl Johann, Donald K. Smith, Samuel Kenyi, and Jonathan Frericks. *Communication for Development*. Geneva: Lutheran World Federation, 1990.

Macalister, Kim. "The X Generation." *HRMagazine* 35, no. 5 (May 1994): 66–71.

McCallister, Lynne, and Claude S. Fischer. "A Procedure for Studying Personal Networks." In *Applied Network Analysis,* eds. Ronald S. Burt and Michael J. Minor. Beverly Hills: Sage Publications, 1983.

McConnell, Doug. *Maps, Masses and Mission: Effective Networks for Urban Ministry.* Victoria, Australia: Bible College of Victoria, 1990.

McGavran, Donald A. *Understanding Church Growth.* 1st ed. Grand Rapids: Eerdmans, 1970.

Maguire, Lambert. *Understanding Social Networks.* Beverly Hills, London, New Delhi: Sage Publications, 1983.

Marsden, Peter V., and Nan Lin, eds. *Social Structure and Network Analysis.* Beverly Hills: Sage Publications, 1982.

Nanus, Burt. *Visionary Leadership.* San Francisco: Jossey-Bass, 1992.

Neighbour, Ralph W., Jr. *The Shepherd's Guidebook.* P. O. Box 19888, Houston, TX: Touch Ministries, Inc., 1988.

————. *Where Do We Go from Here.* Houston, TX: Touch Publications, 1990.

————. "What is a 'Cell Group' Church?" *Cell Church Magazine* 1, no. 1 (1991): 2.

Nickles, Beverly. "Russians Spread Joy In A Time Of Crisis." *Charisma Magazine* (January 1994): 34–39.

Oladimeji, Jide. *Biblical Basis For Home Caring Fellowship.* Accra: Deeper Christian Life Ministry, n.d.

Olson, Samuel. *Informe Año: Annual Report.* Caracas: Las Acacias Church, 1996.

Plueddemann, Jim and Carol. *Pilgrims in Progress: Growing through Groups.* Wheaton, IL: Harold Shaw, 1990.

Roberts, Elizabeth. *Xenophobe's Guide to the Russians.* London: Ravette Books, 1993.

Rogers, Everett M. *Diffusion of Innovations.* 3rd ed. New York: The Free Press, 1983.

Rogers, Everett M., and D. Lawrence Kincaid. *Communication Networks: Toward a New Paradigm for Research.* New York: The Free Press, 1981.

Smith, Donald K. *Creating Understanding*. Grand Rapids, MI: Zondervan, 1992.

Snyder, Howard A. *The Community of the King*. Downers Grove, IL: InterVarsity, 1977.

Sokolovsky, Jay, et al. "Personal Networks of Ex-Mental Patients in a Manhattan SRO Hotel." *Human Organization* 37, no. 1 (1978): 5–15.

Tan, David Mui Kok. "The Transition from a Program Based Design Church to a Cell Church." D.Min. diss., Fuller Theological Seminary, 1994.

Tapis, Andrés. "Reaching the First Post-Christian Generation." *Christianity Today* 38, no. 9 (September 12, 1994).

Tozer, A. W. *That Incredible Christian*. Camp Hill, PA: Christian Publications, 1964.

Valente, Thomas W. *Network Models of the Diffusion of Innovations*. Cresskill, NJ: Hampton Press, 1995.

Vella, Jane. *Learning to Listen, Learning to Teach: The Power of Dialogue in Educating Adults*. San Francisco: Jossey-Bass, 1994.

Wagner, C. Peter. *Your Church Can Be Healthy*. Nashville: Abingdon, 1979.

———. "Church Growth Principles and Procedures: Syllabus and Lecture Outlines." Pasadena: Fuller Theological Seminary, 1980, 13.

———. *Leading Your Church to Growth*. Ventura, CA: Regal Books, 1984.

Wuthnow, Robert. "How Small Groups Are Transforming Our Lives." *Christianity Today* 38, no. 2 (February 7, 1994): 20.

———. *Sharing the Journey: Support Groups and America's New Quest for Community*. New York: Free Press, 1994.

Wuthnow, Robert, ed. *I Come Away Stronger: How Small Groups Are Shaping American Religion*. Grand Rapids: Eerdmanns, 1994.

Interviews (by author)

Accra, Ghana

Dade, Rev. Felicia, director of women's ministries, Evangelical Presbyterian Church of Ghana. 20 February 1996.

Deegbe, Rev. Fred, senior pastor, Calvary Baptist Church. 18 February 1996.

Gbewonyo, Rt. Rev. (CDR) F. H., moderator, Evangelical Presbyterian Church of Ghana. 22 February 1996.

Gbewonyo, Dr. Seth, lay leader, Evangelical Presbyterian Church of Ghana and professor of microbiology. 20 February 1996.

Kwami, Rev. S. Y., pastor, Kotobabi Church, Evangelical Presbyterian Church of Ghana. 26 February 1996.

Obeng, Martin, Ghana Fellowship of Evangelical Students. 26 February 1996.

Oladimeji, Rev. Jide, national overseer, Deeper Christian Life Ministry. 16 February 1996.

Osei-Bonsu, Rev. Dr., assistant pastor, Calvary Baptist Church. 18 February 1996.

Otitiaku, Rev. Victor E., synod clerk, Evangelical Presbyterian Church of Ghana. 20 February 1996.

Quaye, Rev. (CDR) Philemon, Evangelical Presbyterian Church of Ghana. 20 February 1996.

Bombay, India — New Life Fellowship

Arawattigi, John Robert (Luther), evangelist. 1 February 1996.

Davidson, Shelton, senior leadership. 30 January 1996.

D'Souza, Jerry, senior leadership. 26 January 1996.

Joseph, S., founder and senior leader. 30 January 1996.

Kalianpur, Shakar, senior leadership. 30 January 1996

Pereira, Benedicto, evangelist. 30 January, 1 February 1996.

Quadros, Paul, district pastor. 5 February 1996.

Sagar, Jaikmur, district pastor. 2 February 1996.

Serrao, Bonny, district pastor/evangelist. 5 February 1996.

Serrao, Jacob, district pastor. 7 February 1996.

Soans, Reggie V., district pastor. 7 February 1996.

Soans, Willie, senior leadership. 30 January, 3 February 1996.

Caracas, Venezuela

Carrion, Gloris, home group leader, Dios Admirable Church. 13 March 1996.

Dawson, David, missionary, CBInternational. 18 March 1996.

Denlinger, Jeff, missionary, CBInternational. 14 March 1996.

Liévano, Rev. Francisco, senior pastor, Dios Admirable Church. 13 March 1996.

Olson, Rev. Samuel, senior pastor, Las Acacias Church. 19 March 1996.

Sanchez, Nelly, home group ministries director, Dios Admirable Church. 15 March 1996.

Seapy, Chet, missionary, Church Resource Ministries. 13 March 1996.

Suarez, Fausto, parish leader, Las Acacias Church. 19 March 1996.

Villafañe, Mirtha, sector leader, Las Acacias Church. 19 March 1996.

Zamor, César, home group leader, Dios Admirable Church. 14 March 1996.

Chicago, USA — New Life Community Church

Campos, Ralph, home group leader. 15 November 1995.

Franklin, John, home group leader. 10 January 1996.

Garratt, David, zone pastor. 16 November 1995.

Jobe, Mark, senior pastor. 18 September 1995, 20 May 1996.

Obregon, Roy, home group leader. 7 December 1995.

Pangikas, Maria, home group leader. 17 November 1995.

Wasso, Tony, home group leader. 15 December 1995.

Ziel, David, home group leader. 8 November 1995.

Moscow, Russia (only first names are given in some cases)

Fedichikin, Alexander, Baptist pastor. 7 May 1996.

Kuzkov, Sergey, Christian worker. 6 May 1996.

Law, George, vice president, Russian Ministries. 6 May 1996.

Nickles, Beverly, missionary, CBInternational. 27 April 1996.

Petrov, Andre, Baptist pastor. 7 May 1996.

Reit, Jon Vande, pastor. 6 May 1996.

Saveliev, Marina, senior pastor's wife, Rosa Church. 2 May 1996.

Saveliev, Pavel, senior pastor, Rosa Church. 2 May 1996.

Masha. 5 May 1996.

Nancy. 28 April 1996.

Sergei and Marina. 29 April 1996.

Valera and Lena. 30 April 1996.

Miscellaneous

Spain worker's E-mail forum: "Spanish Forum.47D." 22 April 1996.

Appendix A

Research Questionnaire

1. Name: _____
   a) Age: Under 20___, 20s___, 30s___, 40s___, 50s___, 60s___,
      More than 70____
   b) Gender: M   F   c) Married: Yes   No
   d) How many children: _____
   e) Type of work: _____
   f) What is your home language or your parents' home
      language? _____

2. Educational level: **Check one.**
   a) 0 through grammar school
   b) Grammar through high school
   c) More than high school

3. How long have you been a Christian? (State years or months) __

4. Where does your cell group usually meet? **Check one.**
   a) In a home
   b) In a church
   c) In someone's place of work or school
   d) Other

5. How often does your cell group meet? **Check one.**
   a) Once a week
   b) More than once a week
   c) Less than once a week

6. How many people attend your cell group, not including
   children too small to participate if they attend? _____

7. Of the number who attend your cell group,
   a) How many are related to you (your spouse, children, or other family members)?
   b) How many are primarily work or school associates?
   c) How many attend the same church you do?
   d) How many do you know primarily because they live near you?
   e) How many are friends from other situations?

8. What are you doing to recruit new cell group members?

9. How many adults can you target as potential cell group members from each of the following categories?
   a) How many family members?
   b) How many work/school associates?
   c) How many people from your church?
   d) How many people who live close to you?
   e) How many people from other situations?

11. How often do you have contact with each cell group member between meetings?
    List the first names of all the cell group members in the left hand column (N1, N2, etc.) then check the column in the same row that indicates how many times you have contact with each person. Example: I talk to Philip on the phone once a week and see him at church. So I check column 2.

Weekly contacts with person listed	0	1	2	3	4	5	6	7	More than 7
Names: Philip			✓						
N1									
N2									
N3									
N4									
N5									
N6									
N7									
N8									
N9									
N10									
N11									
N12									
N13									
N14									
N15									

12. How does your cell group usually deal with small children?
    Check one.
    a) No children.
    b) Someone keeps the children at home while parents attend
        the cell group.
    c) Children are brought to the cell group and are kept in the
        meeting.
    d) Special arrangements are made for children either at the cell
        group meeting place or another place.

13. Do you have older children who participate in your cell group
    meeting?   Yes   No

14. Why are you in this cell group?

15. What is the purpose of the cell group?

16. How did you become a part of this cell group? Can you name
    the individual(s) who brought you into this group?

17. Have you ever considered quitting? If yes, why?

18. Are you currently leading a cell group?   Yes   No

19. If you are leading a cell group or have ever led cell groups, how
    long have you led them, total? _____

19a. How long have you been in the cell group you now attend?

    _____

19b. How long has this cell group been meeting since it originally
    started? _____

22. How does the cell ministry relate to the local church? **Choose one.**
    a) The cell group is the church.
    b) The cell group is supervised by the church.
    c) The cell group is loosely connected to the church but mostly independent.
    d) There is no relationship of the cell group to the church. It is independent.

23. Which of the following most closely describes the ideal cell group? **Choose one.**
    a) The group is orderly. Begins and ends on time. Each part of the meeting happens as it should. Rules will settle all aspects of cell group life. One person at a time speaks as the others listen.
    b) The leader is in charge and under the authority of the church. The assistant leader is the second in command. Problems are settled by the person in charge. People speak when they are encouraged to do so by the leader.
    c) Everyone in the cell group and their ideas mostly have equal value. Rules are flexible. No single person is in charge. Problems are solved and decisions are made by negotiating.
    d) The leader has the authority as a strong father. There are few formal rules. Several people may speak at the same time but everyone knows who is in charge.

24. List the principal activities of your cell group and the time for each activity.

25. In the past 6 months how many new people have attended your cell group?

26. How many of these people stayed for at least one month?

27. I could tell very personal problems to my cell group with the confidence they would pray for me, care for me, and not tell people outside the cell group. **Choose one.**
    a) Strongly agree b) Agree c) Disagree d) Strongly disagree

28. In the past 6 months how many people in your cell group have shared serious personal problems with the cell group?

29. How are cell group leaders selected? **Check the one usually true.**
    a) Approached by the local church leadership.
    b) Volunteer to the church to lead a cell group.
    c) They begin to lead their own cell group.
    d) The people in each cell group choose their own leader.
    e) Other.

30. How are cell group leaders trained to lead cells? **Check the one usually true.**
    a) The pastor or other church leaders train them.
    b) They learn on their own, i.e. read, attend seminars, etc.
    c) They learn by observing other cell group leaders.
    d) Other.

31. Does your cell group have an apprentice, someone in training for cell group leadership? Yes   No

32. What kind of ongoing relationship do cell group leaders have with each other and the local church?

33. List 3 qualities of a good cell group leader:
    a)
    b)
    c)

Case studies:

36. Your cell group has completed a series of Bible studies on the book of John. It is time to select the next Bible lessons. How will that decision be made?

37. It is time to select the next series of Bible studies in your group. The men want to study what the Bible says about leadership while the women want to study what the Bible says about family. How will the decision be made as to what to study?

38. You are on the way to your cell group meeting. You had to work late so you will be arriving late. You are about half way to the meeting place when you see William, a friend, whom you have not seen in some time. William desires to talk to you about something of importance to him. What will you do?

39. Sarah, a longtime member in the cell group, has just given a rather lengthy explanation of a Bible verse. Her explanation completely misses the point of the passage. What should Samuel, the leader, do?

40. Sarah, a longtime member in the cell group, has just given a rather lengthy explanation of a Bible verse. Her explanation completely misses the point of the passage. Samuel, the leader, seems a little unsure of what to do next. What should you do?

41. John has been in your group since the beginning. He has strong opinions on everything and tries to dominate the discussion with his opinions. He is a little older than most people in the group. How will the cell group deal with John?

42. Samuel is your cell group leader. Grace is a new women in the
group from the neighborhood. You are getting to know her.
Your cell group Bible study has gone a little long this evening
and you are late getting to the prayer time. Just as you are about
half way through the prayer time a great commotion is heard at
the entrance to the house. Everyone looks up from their prayers
to see what is happening. Grace's sister has come into the house
and is crying uncontrollably. Her husband's brother has just
died of AIDS in her home.

Describe the next few moments of what happens in the cell
group. What will Samuel do? What will Grace do? What will the
group do?

Appendix B

Questionnaire Evaluation

(N/A = not applicable; N/ans = not answered)
(Questions 10, 20, 21, 34, and 35 were discarded as questionnaire was tested)

	Accra		Bombay		Caracas		Chicago		Moscow	
1.a. Age:	No.	%	No.	%	No.	%	No.	%	No.	%
Under 20	1	0.8	1	2.4	5	10.4	11	9.7	--	--
20s	25	20.5	9	21.4	10	20.8	33	28.8	19	45.2
30s	49	40.2	16	38.1	5	10.4	41	36.0	7	16.7
40s	34	27.9	5	11.9	19	39.6	22	19.3	9	21.4
50s	11	9.0	7	16.7	6	12.5	3	2.6	4	9.5
60s	1	0.8	1	2.4	--	--	2	1.8	2	4.8
Over 70	--	--	--	--	3	6.3	--	--	1	2.4
N/ans	1	0.8	3	7.1	--	--	2	1.8	--	--
1.b. Gender:	No.	%	No.	%	No.	%	No.	%	No.	%
Male	91	74.6	24	57.1	11	22.9	49	43.0	15	35.7
Female	30	24.6	17	40.5	37	77.1	64	56.1	26	61.9
N/ans	1	0.8	1	2.4	--	--	1	0.9	1	2.4
1.c	No.	%	No.	%	No.	%	No.	%	No.	%
Married	74	60.7	28	66.7	21	43.8	50	43.9	16	38.1
Single	39	32.0	11	26.2	25	52.1	59	51.8	26	61.9
N/ans	9	7.3	3	7.1	2	4.1	5	4.3	--	--
1.d. No. of Children	No.	%	No.	%	No.	%	No.	%	No.	%
0	34	27.9	10	23.8	18	37.5	54	47.4	2	4.8
1	10	8.2	8	19.0	3	6.3	14	12.3	12	28.6
2	16	13.1	10	23.8	11	22.8	20	17.5	9	21.4
3	18	14.8	5	12.0	10	20.8	5	4.4	1	2.4
4	11	9.0	--	--	2	4.2	11	9.7	--	--
5	6	4.9	--	--	1	2.1	3	2.6	--	--
6	6	4.9	--	--	1	2.1	4	3.5	--	--
Greater than 6	1	0.8	1	2.4	1	2.1	--	--	--	--
N/A, N/ans	20	16.4	8	19.0	1	2.1	3	2.6	18	42.8
1.e.Type of Work	No.	%	No.	%	No.	%	No.	%	No.	%
Unemployed/retired	4	3.3	2	4.8	--	--	5	4.4	4	9.5
Student	9	7.4	2	4.8	10	20.8	15	13.2	7	16.7
Homemaker	2	1.6	6	14.2	4	8.3	7	6.1	6	14.3
Labor/factory	23	18.9	2	4.8	--	--	30	26.3	4	9.5
Trade/computer/office	60	49.2	12	28.6	4	8.3	40	35.1	11	26.2
Professional/self-employ.	22	18.0	17	40.4	23	47.9	12	10.5	6	14.3
N/ans	2	1.6	1	2.4	7	14.7	5	4.4	4	9.5
2. Educational Level	No.	%	No.	%	No.	%	No.	%	No.	%
Thru grammar school	44	36.1	3	7.1	4	8.3	6	5.3	2	4.8
Thru high school	50	41.0	15	35.7	8	16.7	38	33.3	22	52.4
Beyond high school	27	22.1	22	52.4	32	66.7	68	59.6	18	42.8
N/ans	1	0.8	2	4.8	4	8.3	2	1.8	--	--

	Accra		Bombay		Caracas		Chicago		Moscow	
3. Years a Christian	No.	%	No.	%	No.	%	No.	%	No.	%
0-1	1	0.8	2	4.8	2	4.2	15	13.2	12	28.6
2-3	12	9.8	6	14.3	6	12.5	13	11.4	22	52.4
4-5	15	12.3	12	28.5	7	14.6	17	14.9	6	14.2
6-10	36	29.5	16	38.1	9	18.7	25	21.9	1	2.4
11-15	33	27.1	2	4.8	9	18.7	17	14.9	--	--
16-20	13	10.7	3	7.1	5	10.4	15	13.2	--	--
Over 20	8	6.6	--	--	7	14.6	8	7.0	--	--
N/ans	4	3.2	1	2.4	3	6.3	4	3.5	1	2.4
4. Place of Meeting	No.	%	No.	%	No.	%	No.	%	No.	%
Home	108	88.5	37	88.1	47	97.9	90	78.9	42	100
Church	2	1.6	--	--	--	--	14	12.3	--	--
Work or school	12	9.9	5	11.9	--	--	6	5.3	--	--
Other	--	--	--	--	1	2.1	4	3.5	--	--
N/ans	--	--	--	--	--	--	--	--	--	--
5. Cell meeting frequency	No.	%	No.	%	No.	%	No.	%	No.	%
Weekly	117	95.9	32	76.2	47	97.9	108	94.8	42	100
More than weekly	5	4.1	9	21.4	1	2.1	3	2.6	--	--
Less than weekly	--	--	1	2.4	--	--	3	2.6	--	--
N/ans	--	--	--	--	--	--	--	--	--	--
6. No. in cell	No.	%	No.	%	No.	%	No.	%	No.	%
1-5	2	1.6	2	4.8	--	--	11	9.5	5	11.9
6-10	33	27.1	10	23.8	8	16.7	52	45.7	14	33.3
11-15	36	29.5	15	35.7	22	45.9	40	35.1	22	52.4
16-20	30	24.6	13	30.9	18	37.4	5	4.4	--	--
21-25	13	10.6	--	--	--	--	3	2.6	--	--
Greater than 25	8	6.6	2	4.8	--	--	2	1.8	--	--
N/ans	--	--	--	--	--	--	1	0.9	1	2.4
7.a. No. in cell related	No.	%	No.	%	No.	%	No.	%	No.	%
0	55	45.0	19	45.2	20	41.7	80	70.2	5	11.9
1-5	53	43.5	15	35.7	27	56.2	31	27.1	18	42.9
6-10	3	2.5	2	4.8	1	2.1	1	0.9	--	--
11-15	1	0.8	--	--	--	--	1	0.9	--	--
16-20	1	0.8	--	--	--	--	--	--	--	--
Greater than 20	--	--	1	2.4	--	--	--	--	--	--
N/ans	9	7.4	5	11.9	--	--	1	0.9	19	45.2
7.b. No. in cell work/sch.	No.	%	No.	%	No.	%	No.	%	No.	%
0	83	68	20	47.6	42	87.5	98	86.0	8	19.0
1-5	16	13.1	9	21.4	6	12.5	14	12.2	1	2.4
6-10	4	3.3	1	2.4	--	--	1	0.9	--	--
11-15	3	2.5	--	--	--	--	--	--	--	--
16-20	1	0.8	--	--	--	--	--	--	--	--
Greater than 20	--	--	1	2.4	--	--	--	--	--	--
N/ans	15	12.3	11	26.2	--	--	1	0.9	33	78.6

	Accra		Bombay		Caracas		Chicago		Moscow	
7.c.No. in cell same church	No.	%	No.	%	No.	%	No.	%	No.	%
0	1	0.8	3	7.1	7	14.6	10	8.8	--	--
1-5	12	9.8	2	4.8	4	8.3	19	16.7	9	21.4
6-10	26	21.3	8	19.1	19	39.6	57	50.0	10	23.8
11-15	30	24.6	11	26.2	15	31.3	20	17.5	12	28.6
16-20	29	23.8	10	23.8	3	6.2	3	2.6	--	--
Greater than 20	16	13.1	2	4.8	--	--	4	3.5	--	--
N/ans	8	6.6	6	14.2	--	--	1	0.9	11	26.2
7.d.No. in cell live close by	No.	%	No.	%	No.	%	No.	%	No.	%
0	24	19.7	7	16.7	17	35.4	68	59.6	5	11.9
1-5	41	33.6	3	7.1	21	43.8	29	25.4	10	23.8
6-10	27	22.1	9	21.5	5	10.4	12	10.6	2	4.8
11-15	11	9.1	10	23.8	5	10.4	4	3.5	8	19.0
16-20	7	5.7	3	7.1	--	--	--	--	--	--
Greater than 20	--	--	3	7.1	--	--	--	--	1	2.4
N/ans	12	9.8	7	16.7	--	--	1	0.9	16	38.1
7.e. No. in cell friends from other context	No.	%	No.	%	No.	%	No.	%	No.	%
0	58	47.4	23	54.8	26	54.1	60	52.6	--	--
1-5	46	37.8	3	7.1	13	27.1	43	37.7	--	--
6-10	3	2.5	--	--	6	12.5	6	5.3	--	--
11-15	--	--	--	--	3	6.3	3	2.6	--	--
16-20	2	1.6	1	2.4	--	--	--	--	--	--
Greater than 20	--	--	--	--	--	--	--	--	--	--
N/ans	13	10.7	15	35.7	--	--	2	1.8	42	100
8. Recruiting	No.	%	No.	%	No.	%	No.	%	No.	%
Nothing	--	--	--	--	3	6.3	12	10.5	1	2.4
Witnessing/inviting	101	82.8	27	64.2	23	47.8	70	61.4	26	61.9
Social events	--	--	1	2.4	1	2.1	9	7.9	1	2.4
Praying	5	4.1	6	14.3	1	2.1	6	5.3	--	--
Discipling	3	2.5	--	--	--	--	4	3.5	--	--
2 or more of above	9	7.4	6	14.3	2	4.2	8	7.0	5	11.9
Other	2	1.6	--	--	2	4.2	1	0.9	1	2.4
N/ans	2	1.6	2	4.8	16	33.3	4	3.5	8	19.0
9.a. Potential: family	No.	%	No.	%	No.	%	No.	%	No.	%
0	39	32.0	10	23.8	15	31.2	41	36.0	1	2.4
1-5	66	54.1	19	45.2	26	54.1	61	53.5	14	33.3
6-10	9	7.4	1	2.4	--	--	5	4.4	--	--
11-15	1	0.8	1	2.4	1	2.1	--	--	--	--
16-20	--	--	--	--	--	--	--	--	--	--
Greater than 20	1	0.8	1	2.4	--	--	--	--	--	--
N/ans	6	4.9	10	23.8	6	12.6	7	6.1	27	64.3

(For Question 11, see Appendix C)

	Accra		Bombay		Caracas		Chicago		Moscow	
	No.	%	No.	%	No.	%	No.	%	No.	%
9.b.Potential: work/school										
0	47	38.6	20	47.6	25	52.1	46	40.4	3	7.1
1-5	57	46.7	6	14.3	14	29.1	53	46.4	6	14.3
6-10	7	5.7	--	--	3	6.3	4	3.5	--	--
11-15	1	0.8	--	--	--	--	2	1.8	--	--
16-20	1	0.8	--	--	--	--	--	--	--	--
Greater than 20	1	0.8	1	2.4	--	--	1	0.9	--	--
N/ans	8	6.6	15	35.7	6	12.5	8	7.0	33	78.6
9.c. Potential: church										
0	38	31.1	9	21.4	26	54.2	51	44.7	3	7.1
1-5	33	27.1	17	40.5	12	25.0	38	33.3	--	--
6-10	13	10.7	5	11.9	1	2.1	10	8.8	--	--
11-15	11	9.0	--	--	1	2.1	1	0.9	--	--
16-20	6	4.9	--	--	--	--	--	--	--	--
Greater than 20	13	10.7	2	4.8	--	--	1	0.9	1	2.4
N/ans	8	6.5	9	21.4	8	16.6	13	11.4	38	90.5
9.d. Potential: live nearby										
0	14	11.5	8	19.0	16	33.3	34	29.8	2	4.8
1-5	72	59.0	14	33.3	21	43.8	57	50.0	9	21.4
6-10	20	16.4	5	11.9	4	8.3	11	9.6	--	--
11-15	3	2.5	3	7.1	--	--	2	1.8	--	--
16-20	2	1.6	--	--	1	2.1	--	--	--	--
Greater than 20	5	4.1	1	2.4	--	--	1	0.9	2	4.8
N/ans	6	4.9	11	26.3	6	12.5	9	7.9	29	69.0
9.e. Potential: other friends										
0	61	50.0	16	38.1	30	62.5	58	50.9	1	2.4
1-5	38	31.2	10	23.8	9	18.8	37	32.4	6	14.2
6-10	8	6.6	--	--	3	6.2	5	4.4	1	2.4
11-15	2	1.6	1	2.4	--	--	4	3.5	--	--
16-20	--	--	--	--	--	--	--	--	--	--
Greater than 20	--	--	--	--	--	--	--	--	1	2.4
N/ans	13	10.6	15	35.7	6	12.5	10	8.8	33	78.6
12. Children Present										
No children	43	35.2	3	7.1	15	31.2	60	52.6	5	11.9
Kept at home	14	11.5	1	2.4	3	6.3	3	2.6	20	47.6
Brought to Cell	45	36.9	26	61.9	23	47.9	19	16.7	12	28.6
Special arrangements	13	10.7	11	26.2	--	--	28	24.6	--	--
N/ans	7	5.7	1	2.4	7	14.6	4	3.5	5	11.9
13. Older Children										
Yes	29	23.8	15	35.7	16	33.3	17	14.9	25	59.5
No	87	71.3	25	59.5	27	56.2	93	81.6	15	35.7
N/ans	6	4.9	2	4.8	5	10.5	4	3.5	2	4.8

	Accra		Bombay		Caracas		Chicago		Moscow	
14. Why in cell	No.	%	No.	%	No.	%	No.	%	No.	%
Outreach/evangelism	10	8.2	6	14.3	1	2.1	5	4.4	4	9.5
Discipleship/growth	63	51.6	9	21.4	19	39.6	36	31.6	4	9.5
Accountability/to lead	17	13.9	9	21.4	2	4.2	17	14.9	2	4.8
Relationships	9	7.4	6	14.3	5	10.4	18	15.8	9	21.4
Worship/prayer	--	--	5	11.9	4	8.3	1	0.9	--	--
God's will, leading	--	--	1	2.4	--	--	16	14.0	6	14.3
Meets my needs/schedule	19	15.6	5	11.9	10	20.8	17	14.9	13	31.0
Other	4	3.3	--	--	5	10.4	1	0.9	3	7.1
N/ans	--	--	1	2.4	2	4.2	3	2.6	1	2.4
15. Purpose of cell	No.	%	No.	%	No.	%	No.	%	No.	%
Outreach/evangelism	28	23.0	8	19.0	16	33.3	20	17.5	6	14.3
Discipleship/growth	76	62.3	23	54.8	27	56.2	57	50.0	31	73.8
Accountability	4	3.3	--	--	1	2.1	6	5.3	--	--
Build relationships	12	9.8	6	14.3	1	2.1	22	19.3	3	7.1
Worship/prayer	1	0.8	3	7.1	2	4.2	4	3.5	1	2.4
Other	--	--	1	2.4	--	--	1	0.9	--	--
N/ans	1	0.8	1	2.4	1	2.1	4	3.5	1	2.4
16. How a part of cell	No.	%	No.	%	No.	%	No.	%	No.	%
I sought/started group	14	11.5	12	28.6	5	10.4	15	13.2	4	9.5
Placed by church leaders	42	34.4	7	16.7	5	10.4	14	12.3	2	4.8
Invited by someone	57	46.7	15	35.7	31	64.6	78	68.4	30	71.4
Other	1	0.8	1	2.4	3	6.3	4	3.5	6	14.3
N/ans	8	6.6	7	16.6	4	8.3	3	2.6	--	--
17. Quitting	No.	%	No.	%	No.	%	No.	%	No.	%
Yes	5	4.1	4	9.5	3	6.2	48	42.1	9	21.4
No	106	86.9	27	64.3	36	75.0	59	51.8	33	78.6
N/ans	11	9.0	11	26.2	9	18.8	7	6.1	--	--
18. Currently leading	No.	%	No.	%	No.	%	No.	%	No.	%
Yes	88	72.1	25	59.5	11	22.9	33	28.9	11	26.2
No	32	26.2	17	40.5	33	68.8	81	71.1	31	73.8
N/ans	2	1.7	--	--	4	8.3	--	--	--	--
19. Years as leader	No.	%	No.	%	No.	%	No.	%	No.	%
0	9	7.4	7	16.7	29	60.4	68	59.6	--	--
1 year or under	34	27.8	9	21.4	4	8.3	19	16.7	5	11.9
2	26	21.3	8	19.1	2	4.2	9	7.9	6	14.3
3	23	18.9	4	9.5	--	--	6	5.3	2	4.8
4	9	7.4	1	2.4	1	2.1	4	3.5	--	--
Greater than 4	11	9.0	4	9.5	--	--	4	3.5	--	--
N/ans	10	8.2	9	21.4	12	25.0	4	3.5	29	69.0

	Accra		Bombay		Caracas		Chicago		Moscow	
19.a. Years in cell group	No.	%	No.	%	No.	%	No.	%	No.	%
1 year or under	23	18.9	24	57.1	--	--	--	--	26	61.9
2	13	10.7	10	23.8	--	--	--	--	9	21.4
3	24	19.7	7	16.7	--	--	--	--	6	14.3
4	5	4.1	--	--	--	--	--	--	--	--
Greater than 4	8	6.6	--	--	--	--	--	--	--	--
N/ans	49	40.0	1	2.4	48	100	114	100	1	2.4
19.b. Years cell group mtg.	No.	%	No.	%	No.	%	No.	%	No.	%
1 year or under	12	9.8	19	45.2	--	--	--	--	20	47.6
2	8	6.6	8	19.0	--	--	--	--	7	16.7
3	20	16.4	12	28.6	--	--	--	--	11	26.2
4	10	8.2	--	--	--	--	--	--	--	--
Greater than 4	17	13.9	2	4.8	--	--	--	--	--	--
N/ans	55	45.1	1	2.4	48	100	114	100	4	9.5
22. How cell relates to local church	No.	%	No.	%	No.	%	No.	%	No.	%
Cell is church	26	21.3	6	14.3	7	14.6	43	37.7	36	85.7
Supervised by church	95	77.9	36	85.7	39	81.2	67	58.8	5	11.9
Cell loosely connected	1	0.8	--	--	--	--	3	2.6	--	--
No relation	--	--	--	--	1	2.1	--	--	--	--
N/ans	--	--	--	--	1	2.1	1	0.9	1	2.4
23. Ideal cell	No.	%	No.	%	No.	%	No.	%	No.	%
Orderly/rules	80	65.6	6	14.3	14	29.2	23	20.2	6	14.3
Authority/leader	32	26.2	25	59.5	18	37.5	27	23.7	9	21.4
Equality/flexible	3	2.5	3	7.2	11	22.9	22	19.3	16	38.1
Father/chaotic	2	1.6	4	9.5	2	4.2	35	30.7	8	19.0
N/ans	5	4.1	4	9.5	3	6.2	7	6.1	3	7.2
24.a. Worship time (mins.)	No.	%	No.	%	No.	%	No.	%	No.	%
0	20	16.4	1	2.4	14	29.2	21	18.4	5	11.9
1-15	32	26.2	6	14.3	24	50.0	40	35.1	--	--
16-30	6	4.9	27	64.2	--	--	44	38.6	2	4.8
Greater than 30	--	--	2	4.8	--	--	--	--	4	9.5
N/ans	64	52.5	6	14.3	10	20.8	9	7.9	31	73.8
24.b. Prayer time (mins.)	No.	%	No.	%	No.	%	No.	%	No.	%
0	3	2.5	11	26.2	6	12.6	18	15.8	--	--
1-15	42	34.4	22	52.4	32	66.6	49	43.0	--	--
16-30	9	7.4	3	7.1	--	--	36	31.6	3	7.2
Greater than 30	4	3.2	--	--	--	--	2	1.8	8	19.0
N/ans	64	52.5	6	14.3	10	20.8	9	7.8	31	73.8
24.c. Bible study (mins.)	No.	%	No.	%	No.	%	No.	%	No.	%
0	--	--	--	--	--	--	5	4.4	--	--
1-15	1	0.8	3	7.1	--	--	4	3.5	--	--
16-30	11	9.0	27	64.3	10	20.9	48	42.1	2	4.8
Greater than 30	46	37.7	6	14.3	28	58.2	47	41.2	9	21.4
N/ans	64	52.5	6	14.3	10	20.9	10	8.8	31	73.8

	Accra		Bombay		Caracas		Chicago		Moscow	
24.d. Sharing time (mins.)	No.	%	No.	%	No.	%	No.	%	No.	%
0	30	24.6	2	4.8	13	27.2	29	25.4	8	19.0
1-15	22	18.0	25	59.5	18	37.4	26	22.8	--	--
16-30	4	3.4	9	21.4	5	10.4	43	37.7	1	2.4
Greater than 30	2	1.6	--	--	2	4.2	6	5.3	2	4.8
N/ans	64	52.4	6	14.3	10	20.8	10	8.8	31	73.8
24.e. Social time (mins.)	No.	%	No.	%	No.	%	No.	%	No.	%
0	55	45.1	25	59.5	33	68.8	75	65.8	2	4.8
1-15	3	2.5	10	23.8	2	4.2	9	7.9	--	--
16-30	--	--	1	2.4	3	6.2	16	14.0	3	7.1
Greater than 30	--	--	--	--	--	--	4	3.5	6	14.3
N/ans	64	52.4	6	14.3	10	20.8	10	8.8	31	73.8
24.f.Other activity time (minutes)	No.	%	No.	%	No.	%	No.	%	No.	%
0	37	30.4	27	64.3	38	79.2	94	82.4	7	16.7
1-15	21	17.2	5	11.9	--	--	9	7.9	--	--
16-30	--	--	4	9.5	--	--	1	0.9	--	--
Greater than 30	--	--	--	--	--	--	--	--	4	9.5
N/ans	64	52.4	6	14.3	10	20.8	10	8.8	31	73.8
25. No. of new people in 6 months	No.	%	No.	%	No.	%	No.	%	No.	%
0	6	4.9	2	4.8	1	2.1	--	--	--	--
1-2	20	16.4	15	35.7	2	4.2	9	7.9	4	9.5
3-4	30	24.6	13	30.9	7	14.6	16	14.0	21	50.1
5-6	23	18.9	4	9.5	5	10.4	12	10.5	9	21.4
7-8	8	6.6	1	2.4	7	14.6	12	10.5	3	7.1
9-10	9	7.4	1	2.4	10	20.8	12	10.5	--	--
11-15	6	4.9	3	7.1	1	2.1	18	15.8	--	--
16-20	4	3.3	1	2.4	--	--	13	11.4	--	--
Greater than 20	1	0.8	1	2.4	4	8.3	5	4.5	--	--
N/ans	15	12.2	1	2.4	11	22.9	17	14.9	5	11.9
26. No. who stayed	No.	%	No.	%	No.	%	No.	%	No.	%
0	16	13.1	5	11.9	1	2.1	7	6.1	--	--
1-2	35	28.7	10	23.8	8	16.6	19	16.7	14	33.3
3-4	30	24.6	10	23.8	9	18.8	19	16.7	12	28.6
5-6	11	9.0	3	7.1	6	12.5	13	11.4	4	9.5
7-8	8	6.6	1	2.4	6	12.5	12	10.5	1	2.4
9-10	3	2.5	1	2.4	1	2.1	14	12.2	--	--
11-15	1	0.8	1	2.4	--	--	13	11.4	--	--
16-20	2	1.6	1	2.4	1	2.1	2	1.8	--	--
Greater than 20	1	0.8	1	2.4	--	--	--	--	1	2.4
N/ans--don't know	15	12.3	9	21.4	16	33.3	15	13.2	10	23.8
27. Confidence factor	No.	%	No.	%	No.	%	No.	%	No.	%
Strongly Agree	69	56.6	18	42.9	25	52.0	46	40.4	17	40.5
Agree	41	33.6	20	47.6	19	39.6	55	48.2	23	54.7
Disagree	6	4.9	3	7.1	3	6.3	8	7.0	1	2.4
Strongly disagree	2	1.6	--	--	--	--	1	0.9	--	--
N/ans	4	3.3	1	2.4	1	2.1	4	3.5	1	2.4

	Accra		Bombay		Caracas		Chicago		Moscow	
28. No. who shared personal problem	No.	%	No.	%	No.	%	No.	%	No.	%
0	9	7.4	1	2.4	3	6.3	7	6.1	--	--
1-5	78	64.0	27	64.3	27	56.2	62	54.5	14	33.3
6-10	12	9.8	7	16.7	--	--	29	25.4	10	23.9
11-15	5	4.1	1	2.4	2	4.2	7	6.1	13	30.9
16-20	2	1.6	1	2.4	--	--	--	--	--	--
Greater than 20	9	7.4	--	--	--	--	--	--	1	2.4
N/ans	7	5.7	5	11.8	16	33.3	9	7.9	4	9.5
29. Leader selection	No.	%	No.	%	No.	%	No.	%	No.	%
Church chooses	48	39.3	40	95.2	36	75.0	79	69.3	22	52.3
Leader volunteers	13	10.7	1	2.4	5	10.4	19	16.7	6	14.3
Starts own group	5	4.1	--	--	2	4.2	3	2.6	--	--
Cell chooses leader	47	38.5	--	--	--	--	1	0.9	1	2.4
Other	7	5.8	1	2.4	--	--	9	7.9	11	26.2
N/ans	2	1.6	--	--	5	10.4	3	2.6	2	4.8
30. How leaders trained	No.	%	No.	%	No.	%	No.	%	No.	%
Pastor/church trains	116	95.2	34	81.0	36	75.0	68	59.6	23	54.8
Self-taught	2	1.6	5	11.9	6	12.5	7	6.1	1	2.4
Learn from models	2	1.6	3	7.1	4	8.3	26	22.8	9	21.4
Other	--	--	--	--	--	--	5	4.4	5	11.9
N/ans	2	1.6	--	--	2	4.2	8	7.1	4	9.5
31. Apprentice	No.	%	No.	%	No.	%	No.	%	No.	%
Yes	64	52.5	27	64.2	30	62.5	91	79.8	32	76.2
No	53	43.4	13	31.0	7	14.6	20	17.5	6	14.3
N/ans	5	4.1	2	4.8	11	22.9	3	2.7	4	9.5
32. Leaders' ongoing relationship	No.	%	No.	%	No.	%	No.	%	No.	%
Little to none	1	0.8	2	4.8	--	--	1	0.9	2	4.8
More organizational	58	47.5	8	19.0	18	37.5	31	27.2	2	4.8
More relational	31	25.4	23	54.8	17	35.4	47	41.2	31	73.7
N/ans	32	26.3	9	21.4	13	27.1	35	30.7	7	16.7
33.a. Leader qualities: Caring, compassionate, sensitive to people	No.	%	No.	%	No.	%	No.	%	No.	%
No	39	32.0	9	21.4	15	31.2	13	11.4	3	7.1
Yes	78	63.9	30	71.5	32	66.7	99	86.8	39	92.9
N/ans	5	4.1	3	7.1	1	2.1	2	1.8	--	--
33.b. Leader qualities: Growing relationship with God	No.	%	No.	%	No.	%	No.	%	No.	%
No	31	25.4	8	19.0	21	43.7	38	33.3	10	23.8
Yes	86	70.5	32	76.2	26	54.2	74	64.9	32	76.2
N/ans	5	4.1	2	4.8	1	2.1	2	1.8	--	--

	Accra		Bombay		Caracas		Chicago		Moscow	
	No.	%	No.	%	No.	%	No.	%	No.	%
33.c. Leader qualities: Bible/Theo. knowledge										
No	90	73.8	15	35.7	22	45.8	90	78.9	34	81.0
Yes	26	21.2	25	59.5	25	52.1	22	19.3	8	19.0
N/ans	6	5.0	2	4.8	1	2.1	2	1.8	--	--
33.d. Leader qualities: Good leadership style	No.	%	No.	%	No.	%	No.	%	No.	%
No	44	36.1	29	69.0	14	29.2	60	52.6	23	54.8
Yes	73	59.8	11	26.2	33	68.7	52	45.6	19	45.2
N/ans	5	4.1	2	4.8	1	2.1	2	1.8	--	--
33.e. Leadership qualities: Other personal qualities	No.	%	No.	%	No.	%	No.	%	No.	%
No	80	65.6	25	59.5	26	54.2	41	36.0	37	88.1
Yes	37	30.3	15	35.7	21	43.7	71	62.2	5	11.9
N/ans	5	4.1	2	4.8	1	2.1	2	1.8	--	--
33.f. Leader qualities: Other	No.	%	No.	%	No.	%	No.	%	No.	%
No	113	92.6	38	90.4	45	93.7	99	86.8	42	100
Yes	4	3.3	2	4.8	2	4.2	13	11.4	--	--
N/ans	5	4.1	2	4.8	1	2.1	2	1.8	--	--
36. How Bible lesson selected	No.	%	No.	%	No.	%	No.	%	No.	%
Cell Leader chooses	17	13.9	29	69.0	12	25.0	70	61.4	14	33.3
Cell chooses/vote/discuss	7	5.8	1	2.4	25	52.1	12	10.5	7	16.7
Church prescribed prog.	94	77.0	1	2.4	1	2.1	14	12.3	--	--
Other	4	3.3	2	4.8	--	--	1	0.9	14	33.3
N/ans	--	--	9	21.4	6	12.5	17	14.9	7	16.7
37. How decision is made if disagreement in cell	No.	%	No.	%	No.	%	No.	%	No.	%
Cell leadership	10	8.2	15	35.7	9	18.8	33	28.9	15	35.7
Cell chooses	25	20.5	3	7.1	18	37.5	12	10.5	10	23.8
Leadership considers cell	14	11.5	6	14.3	7	14.5	27	23.7	--	--
Church prescribed prog.	70	57.3	--	--	--	--	6	5.3	1	2.4
Other	3	2.5	12	28.6	--	--	2	1.8	10	23.8
N/ans	--	--	6	14.3	14	29.2	34	29.8	6	14.3
38. Meet William on way to meeting	No.	%	No.	%	No.	%	No.	%	No.	%
Schedule another time	22	18.0	11	26.2	12	25.0	13	11.4	14	33.3
Talk to him now	7	5.7	8	19.0	14	29.2	34	29.8	9	21.4
Invite him to cell	85	69.8	21	50.0	17	35.4	53	46.5	7	16.7
Talk now but involve grp.	6	4.9	--	--	--	--	11	9.7	4	9.5
Other	2	1.6	2	4.8	--	--	--	--	7	16.7
N/ans	--	--	--	--	5	10.4	3	2.6	1	2.4

	Accra		Bombay		Caracas		Chicago		Moscow	
39. Sarah gives wrong info	No.	%	No.	%	No.	%	No.	%	No.	%
Correct directly	82	67.2	23	54.8	31	64.5	77	67.5	35	83.3
Correct indirectly	26	21.3	5	11.8	9	18.8	23	20.2	--	--
Correct after meeting	13	10.7	11	26.2	3	6.3	6	5.3	1	2.4
Say nothing	--	--	1	2.4	--	--	3	2.6	--	--
Other	--	--	1	2.4	--	--	1	0.9	5	11.9
N/ans	1	0.8	1	2.4	5	10.4	4	3.5	1	2.4
40. Leader unsure of what to do with incorrect ans.	No.	%	No.	%	No.	%	No.	%	No.	%
Correct directly	69	56.6	16	38.1	23	47.9	69	60.5	32	76.2
Correct indirectly	37	30.3	4	9.5	15	31.2	26	22.8	--	--
Correct after meeting	12	9.8	7	16.7	2	4.2	2	1.8	--	--
Say nothing	--	--	7	16.7	1	2.1	7	6.1	--	--
Other	--	--	5	11.9	--	--	1	0.9	6	14.3
N/ans	4	3.3	3	7.1	7	14.6	9	7.9	4	9.5
41. Handling of overbearing person	No.	%	No.	%	No.	%	No.	%	No.	%
Confront in group	52	42.6	19	45.2	20	41.6	41	36.0	20	47.6
Confront outside group	18	14.8	10	23.8	7	14.6	32	28.1	--	--
Work through 3rd person or leader	40	32.8	10	23.8	1	2.1	18	15.8	5	11.9
Say nothing	6	4.9	2	4.8	6	12.5	7	6.1	10	23.8
Other	4	3.3	--	--	3	6.3	4	3.5	6	14.3
N/ans	2	1.6	1	2.4	11	22.9	12	10.5	1	2.4
42. Crisis situation	No.	%	No.	%	No.	%	No.	%	No.	%
Maximum interaction	7	5.7	14	33.3	5	10.4	23	20.2	--	--
Spiritual interaction	37	30.4	14	33.3	16	33.3	46	40.4	36	85.8
Group divides, unsure	1	0.8	--	--	4	8.3	16	14.0	--	--
Leader takes charge	76	62.3	10	23.9	10	20.8	18	15.8	3	7.1
Do not know	--	--	--	--	1	2.1	8	7.0	--	--
N/ans	1	0.8	4	9.5	12	25.1	3	2.6	3	7.1

Appendix C

Contact Quotient Evaluation — Question 11

Accra

(Standard Deviation = 2.3)

Home Group Designation	Total number of contacts within home group [A]	Total number of completed questionnaires [B]	Contact Quotient [A]/[B]
ba1	130	5	26.0
ba2	212	5	42.4
ba3	40	2	20.0
ba4	168	7	24.0
ba5	301	14	21.5
bb0	55	3	18.3
bc1	776	18	43.1
bd0	807	18	44.8
bd1	189	5	37.8
bd2	214	5	42.8
bd3	55	3	18.3
bd4	160	4	40.0
bd5	166	5	33.2
bd6	315	8	39.4
bd7	380	7	54.3
bd8	133	2	66.5
bd9	375	5	75.0
Total	4476	116	38.6

Bombay

(Standard Deviation = 1.7)

Home Group Designation	Total number of contacts within home group [A]	Total number of completed questionnaires [B]	Contact Quotient [A]/[B]
ca0	76	3	25.3
ca1	81	5	16.2
ca2	170	9	18.9
ca3	126	5	25.2
ca4	253	6	42.2
ca5	409	12	34.1
Total	1115	40	27.9

Caracas

(Standard Deviation = 2.7)

Home Group Designation	Total number of contacts within home group [A]	Total number of completed questionnaires [B]	Contact Quotient [A]/[B]
da1	78	4	19.5
da2	221	7	31.6
da3	419	13	32.2
da4	508	10	50.8
da5	196	10	19.6
Total	1422	44	32.3

Chicago

(Standard Deviation = 1.9)

Home Group Designation	Total number of contacts within home group [A]	Total number of completed questionnaires [B]	Contact Quotient [A]/[B]
aa0	861	51	16.9
ab0	120	5	24.0
aa1	77	7	11.0
aa2	122	10	12.2
aa3	94	7	13.4
aa4	59	7	8.4
aa5	124	9	13.8
aa6	164	9	18.2
Total	1621	105	15.4

Moscow

(Standard Deviation = 1.9)

Home Group Designation	Total number of contacts within home group [A]	Total number of completed questionnaires [B]	Contact Quotient [A]/[B]
ea0	138	8	17.3
ea1	136	5	27.2
ea2	176	8	22.0
ea3	126	9	14.0
ea4	229	9	25.4
Total	805	39	20.6

About the Author

Mikel Neumann asked his wife to marry him during the final hymn at a mission conference. When Mike turned to Karen and asked if she would like to go forward with him and present herself for missionary service, she said yes.

Mike and Karen served as missionaries with CB International for 23 years in Madagascar. During that time their focus became church planting in urban areas, developing churches through small-group ministry. Karen also developed biblically-based visual Christian education aids and worked with prayer and Bible study groups among women.

Mikel's goal is to mentor church planters around the globe. The Neumanns have led seminars relevant to Christian leadership in countries such as Brazil, Honduras, Latvia, the Middle East, Kenya, Uganda, and Zambia. They have written more than 200 lessons for small groups and have prepared a training manual for leaders. This manual, originally written in Malagasy, has been translated into French, Spanish, English, and Portuguese.

Mikel Neumann received a bachelor of science degree from the University of Oklahoma, a master of divinity degree from Western Seminary, and a master's and doctor of missiology from Fuller Theological Seminary.

Since 1991, the Neumanns have served as International Resource Consultants with CB International, stationed at Western Seminary in Portland. There Mikel teaches Intercultural Communication, Church Planting and Development, and Contextualization. Mike and Karen have two adult children and two grandchildren.

During 1995-96 Mikel served as the tenth Missionary Scholar in Residence at the Billy Graham Center on the campus of Wheaton College in Wheaton, IL.